A League of Democracies

In the 21st century, as the peoples of the world grow ever more closely tied together, the need for transnational government—and the insufficiency of "network" governance—will become more apparent. But it has now become clear that the UN Security Council will never implement the Responsibility to Protect doctrine that was designed to prevent new mass atrocities.

So the end of the Cold War has not brought the peace, freedom from genocide, and decline of tyranny that we expected. Instead, both older and developing democracies are increasingly under threat from new forms of despotism and cyber-propaganda. Problems such as economic instabilities, tax havens, and environmental degradation arising with global markets are far outstripping the governance capacities of our 20th century system of distinct nation-states and intergovernmental treaty regimes.

This work defends a cosmopolitan approach to global justice by arguing for new ways to combine the strengths of democratic nations in order to resist tyranny and secure global public goods, while protecting cultural pluralism. Davenport draws on the *Federalist Papers* and game theory to argue that a properly designed Democratic League could unite the strength and moral vision of democratic nations to improve international security, end mass atrocities, assist developing nations in overcoming corruption and poverty, and pressure entrenched dictatorships to reform.

This work will be of great interest to students and scholars of international relations, international organizations, political philosophy, human rights and global justice.

John J. Davenport is Professor of Philosophy at Fordham University in New York City, where he directed the Peace & Justice Studies program from 2014 to 2018. In addition to two monographs on topics in moral psychology, and two co-edited collections on Kierkegaard and virtue ethics, John has published several essays on just war theory, the responsibility to protect, and the idea of democratic federation (as well as other topics in democratic theory). He is now preparing books on a Habermasian argument for a universal right to democracy, justice as stewardship of public capital, the errors of political libertarianism, and the need for a new constitutional convention to fix the United States.

Routledge Global Institutions Series

Edited by Thomas G. Weiss
The CUNY Graduate Center, New York, USA
and Rorden Wilkinson
University of Sussex, Brighton, UK

About the series

The "Global Institutions Series" provides cutting-edge books about many aspects of what we know as "global governance." It emerges from our shared frustrations with the state of available knowledge—electronic and print-wise, for research and teaching—in the area. The series is designed as a resource for those interested in exploring issues of international organization and global governance. And since the first volumes appeared in 2005, we have taken significant strides toward filling conceptual gaps.

Global Governance and China (2018)
edited by Scott Kennedy

Global Business Associations (2018)
by Karsten Ronit

A League of Democracies (2018)
Cosmopolitanism, Consolidation Arguments,
and Global Public Goods
by John J. Davenport

Moral Obligations and Sovereignty in International Relations (2018)
A Genealogy of Humanitarianism
by Andrea Paras

A complete list of titles can be viewed online here: https://www.routledge.com/Global-Institutions/book-series/GI.

A League of Democracies

Cosmopolitanism,
Consolidation Arguments,
and Global Public Goods

John J. Davenport

Routledge
Taylor & Francis Group

LONDON AND NEW YORK

First published 2019
by Routledge
2 Park Square, Milton Park, Abingdon, Oxon OX14 4RN

and by Routledge
711 Third Avenue, New York, NY 10017

*Routledge is an imprint of the Taylor & Francis Group,
an Informa business*

British Library Cataloguing-in-Publication Data
A catalogue record for this book is available from the
British Library

Library of Congress Cataloging-in-Publication Data
Names: Davenport, John J., 1966- author.
Title: A league of democracies : cosmopolitanism,
consolidation arguments, and global public goods /
John J. Davenport.
Description: Abingdon, Oxon ; New York, NY : Routledge, [2019] |
Series: Routledge global institutions series | Includes
bibliographical references and index.
Identifiers: LCCN 2018024098 | ISBN 9781138485228 (hbk) |
ISBN 9781351050036 (ebk)
Subjects: LCSH: Cosmopolitanism. | Democracy—
International cooperation. | Public goods—International
cooperation. | Globalization—Political aspects. | World
politics—21st century.
Classification: LCC JZ1308 .D39 2019 | DDC 306.2—dc23
LC record available at https://lccn.loc.gov/2018024098

ISBN: 9781138485228 (hbk)
ISBN: 9781351050036 (ebk)

Typeset in Times NR MT Pro
by Cenveo® Publisher Services

To Robin, for all her indispensable support.

And to Samantha Power, Christiane
Amanpour, Richard Holbrooke,
Eric Reeves, Arwa Damon, Jo Cox,
George Mitchell, John Kerry, and all
the other journalists, diplomats,
and scholars who have worked so tirelessly
to stop mass atrocities since 1989.

Their vision deserves to be fulfilled.

Contents

Lists

Tables

Acknowledgments

This project began back in 2003 with a series of conference presentations and journal articles. I'm indebted to members of the Critical Theory Roundtable, audiences at Central Connecticut State University, Jeremy Waldron, Thomas Magnell, A. Pablo Iannone, and to Jean Elshtain for reactions to this proposal and related arguments (I had a bet with Jean that Václav Havel would have agreed with me rather than with her). Many graduate students and colleagues at Fordham University have given helpful feedback, including the well-put question from my former chairperson, John Drummond: "why do you want all wars to be civil wars?" I hope this work is an adequate answer. A reading group on Humanitarianism at Fordham was also instrumental in educating me about aid agencies, and several cohorts of students in courses on Human Rights and the Federalists to Lincoln also gave insightful responses. At least four Fordham undergraduates wrote papers on the league idea, including Lieutenant John Lee's fine senior thesis (partly disagreeing with the proposal). Eric Reeves has answered despairing inquiries from me, and several other scholars such as Didier Jacobs, Allen Buchanan, and Thomas Weiss have given much-needed encouragement.

I'm grateful to Fordham University for two sabbaticals that have aided in the development of this work, and support from our Research Office as well. I'm also grateful to the *Journal of Religious Ethics, Journal of Value Inquiry, Fordham International Law Journal,* and *Ethics & International Affairs* for permission to redeploy some text and themes from my articles on the "federation of democracies" idea. For a philosopher previously focused on Kierkegaard, free will, autonomy, and narrative identity, it has been a steep road to learn enough about economics, political theory, and global governance to write this work. I have benefitted enormously from Weiss's books, and relied extensively on the many insights and great clarity of Todd

Sandler, Katarina Holzinger, and David Gauthier on game theory and collective action problems. I gratefully acknowledge permission from Sandler to cite his *Global Collective Action* in particular at several junctures. Discovering James Yunker's work was another great boon to this project, and I'm very indebted to him for several valuable points and suggestions. I'm far from the first person to suggest a league of democracies, and certainly will not be the last.

All this said, my interests in international affairs have been nearly constant since teenage years, when I would debate issues raised in the *International Herald Tribune* with my mother, father, and their friends, and with my high school history teacher, Betty Dessants, who ran our Model UN program. My parents, brothers, Uncle Jim, Aunt Nancy, Aunt Shannon, and other relatives have been constant supports.

In getting this manuscript ready for production, I also benefited from copyediting by Nick Humez and Surbhi Mittal, and style advice from Nick Micinski at CUNY. The series editors offered helpful suggestions and prods for revisions throughout several stages, which improved the work. Robert Sorsby at Routledge also kept me on course. At an earlier stage, my graduate assistant Johnny Brennan read the 265,000-word original version of this manuscript. Pat Perrier did most of the work on the index.

My largest debt, as with my previous books, remains to my wife Robin, who so kindly read three different iterations of this manuscript (including the long version with chapters on human rights, democratic rights, and just war theory—all saved for the sequel). She has been my rock and beacon, like Dante's Beatrice. Only she can fully understand why I drove to Akron and suffered through an entire Trump rally to ask Donald Trump not to ally us with Assad (he promised me "we won't"). While our time descends into a new darkness, refugees whom I have met from Syria convinced me that the continuing horrors of mass atrocity must not be the end of the story for human rights. For their children and ours, democracy must have a future. *Utúlie'n aurë.*

Abbreviations

AG	Assurance game
ASEAN	Association of Southeast Asian Nations
AU	African Union
BDR	Bill of Basic Democratic Rights
BF	Battle of friends ("battle of the sexes")
BRICS	Brazil, Russia, India, China, and South Africa
CAPs	Collective action problems
CDem	Community of Democracies
CI	Categorical imperative
CP	Consolidation principle
CPRs	Common pool resources
CWC	Chemical Weapons Convention
DC	Democratic Council [part of the UDL]
DEP	Distributive equity problem
DP	Democratic principle
DRC	Democratic Republic of Congo
ECHR	European Court of Human Rights
ECOWAS	Economic Community of West African States
EU	European Union
FAO	Food and Agriculture Organization (of the UN)
FUDN	Federal Union of Democratic Nations [from Yunker]
G7	Group of Seven nations
G8	Group of Eight nations
G20	Group of 20 forum for political leaders and national bank directors
GPGs	Global public goods
HI	Hypothetical Imperative
IAEA	International Atomic Energy Agency
ICBL	International Campaign to Ban Land Mines

ICC	International Criminal Court
ICISS	International Commission on Intervention and State Sovereignty
ICJ	International Court of Justice (within the UN system)
IDPs	Internally displaced persons
IEDs	Improvised explosive devices
IGOs	Intergovernmental organizations
IMF	International Monetary Fund
ISIS	The Islamic State in Syria (also known as ISIL, the Islamic State in the Levant, or Daesh)
LCR	League Court of Review
MDGs	Millennium Development Goals (of the UN)
NATO	North Atlantic Treaty Organization
NGOs	Non-governmental organizations
NPOs	Non-profit organizations
OAS	Organization of American States
OECD	Organization for Economic Development
P5	Permanent Five members of the UNSC
PD	Prisoner's dilemma game
P-optimality	Pareto-optimality or efficiency
R2P	Responsibility to Protect doctrine
RBS	Rights-based sovereignty
SB	Principle of Subsidiarity
SDGs	Sustainable Development Goals (of the UN)
START	Strategic Arms Reduction Treaty
TPGs	Transnational public goods
UDHR	Universal Declaration of Human Rights
UDL	United Democratic League—the proposed new organization
UN	United Nations
UNAMID	African Union - United Nations Mission in Darfur
UNDP	United Nations Development Programme
UNHCR	United Nations High Commission for Refugees
UNSC	United Nations Security Council
USSR	Union of Soviet Socialist Republics (pre-1991)
WMDs	Weapons of mass destruction
WTO	World Trade Organization

Introduction: Our opportunity to secure a democratic future

- Libya and Syria: The argument in a nutshell
- The solution in brief
- The fleeting chance afforded by this unique historical moment
- Conclusion: Two possible futures

Libya and Syria: The argument in a nutshell

The triple-horned problem that this book is meant to solve can be illustrated concisely by popular responses to the continuing mass slaughter in Syria from 2012 on, along with similar reactions to the disorder in Libya following the overthrow of Muammar al-Qaddafi's regime in 2011.

Horn (1): Many Americans and Europeans have taken the view, articulated by Senator Ted Cruz (R-Texas), that we should stop trying to topple brutal dictators like Qaddafi, even though they have committed serious atrocities, because their fall leads to extremist groups taking power. The response to this simplistic notion is two-fold. (1a) Chaos has often followed revolutionary overthrows of tyrants when no reconstruction is undertaken to secure a just peace, as happened in Libya; (1b) but the opposite holds when serious reconstruction and peace-building efforts follow the conflict, as in Bosnia after 1994, and Germany and Japan after 1945. So Cruz's statements on this issue were grossly misleading and reprehensible.[1]

Horn (2): But suppose we had followed Cruz's policy and stayed out of Libya. Qaddafi's forces would then have slaughtered tens of thousands of innocent people in Benghazi, and driven as many more into exile. This scenario has played out at a higher order of magnitude in Syria: because no group of nations organized a coalition to intervene, Assad's Shia-dominated regime (supported by some members of other minority groups) has succeeded in killing at least 400,000 Syrians from the Sunni majority and driving millions more into exile.

Horn (3): Some western nations might have intervened to stop Assad's unremitting slaughter with chemical weapons and daily air-strikes aimed at burying enemies both dead and alive in rubble. (3a) In mid-2013, the United States, Britain, and France seriously considered strikes to knock out Assad's air force and perhaps enforce a no-fly zone protecting his opponents. In Britain, Edward Miliband launched a last-minute lobby against this idea, narrowly swinging the vote in parliament against limited military intervention; he argued that nego-tiation would be better, while knowing that only military threat could pressure Assad to compromise.[2]

However, if these three allies had acted together in 2013, they would have required help from a much larger set of nations to invest sufficient money and troops to "win the peace" after Assad's fall, without which we return to horn (1a). In particular, if western nations had stopped Assad's barrel bombs, artillery, and air strikes, they would have needed robust support by Turkey, Jordan, Saudi Arabia, Egypt, and other Gulf partners for reconstruction. Without such an inclusive coalition (option 3b), many citizens in western nations would naturally have resented these Islamic-majority nations in the region as free riders.

So instead we have ended up on horn (2), with over half a million people dead, the greatest refugee crisis since World War II, dictators everywhere emboldened, and the Islamic State in Syria (ISIS) caus-ing massive devastation everywhere between Raqqa and Mosul. ISIS propaganda has become a major threat to western nations, inspiring numerous deadly terrorist attacks. The United Nations (UN), para-lyzed by repeated Russian vetoes, again appears impotent, encour-aging future mass murder. Turkey is at war with Kurdish groups that fought ISIS for western nations, thus dividing NATO. All of this shows that the Cruz-style isolationist response can also open the door to chaos that is easily exploited by terror groups.

Are we then stuck choosing between inaction that permits evil regimes to carry out genocide and mass ethnic cleansing before the eyes of the world, making a mockery of all our moral principles and promises to victims of past atrocities (horn 2), or half-hearted inter-ventions that may topple the tyrannical regime but fail to follow through with reconstruction and cultural change (horn 1a)? Or should western nations exhaust our citizens and our budgets with deeper mil-itary interventions to address the post-conflict phase more adequately, while nations in the immediate region of the crisis sit on the sidelines and cheer us on (horn 3a)?

None of these options looks either morally or strategically viable. To sit by and allow mass atrocities and scorched-earth campaigns is an anathema that erodes the moral foundation on which democracies rest. The abused and slaughtered people rightly see idle nations who could have helped them as traitors to humanity. Mass refugee movements also destabilize whole regions, leading to endless spillover effects.[3] Yet unilateral intervention by a few nations has proven too expensive for them to do properly with reconstruction; the free riders rob us of the resources needed to win a just peace, and create a sense that military risks are not fairly shared. But we have no way to assure support from a wide enough group of nations when the crisis is raging (option 3b).

Thus we desperately need a way of overcoming this free rider problem. We must create an institution that can pool the resources of many nations to stop such mass atrocities and remove tyrannical regimes that attempt them. This new institution must follow up humanitarian interventions with adequate disarmament and rehabilitation of the nation affected, and broker partition plans when absolutely necessary. Following the UN's 2005 Responsibility to Protect doctrine (R2P), this institution should act to prevent genocidal campaigns, bend back corruption, and foster pluralistic concord in weak states that are sliding toward civil war.[4] If we did this reliably enough, eventually there would be no more mass atrocities requiring intervention to stop them. To achieve this, a transnational institution would have to ensure that all able nations do their fair share, including nations in the region most affected. These would be significant powers, but nothing short of them can solve the trilemma that led to grossly inadequate responses to mass murder in Bosnia, Rwanda, Darfur, Libya, Syria, and Myanmar in quick succession—a parade of scenes from hell that should motivate any decent person to demand a permanent, sustainable solution.

Such nation-making powers should never be given to any governing institution without democratic answerability and limits set by basic human rights that the powers exist to protect. This new alliance of many nations, with consolidated decision-making powers sufficient to ensure action backed by the whole, must, then, be a league of *democratic* nations—or at least of nations willing to democratize their domestic political systems sufficiently to cooperate within an elected transnational body.

The trilemma of mass atrocities is part of a larger story; a democratic league is also needed to counter growing threats from Russia and China, as I argue later in this chapter. My proposal should also be compared to several related ideas offered since the 1940s. These political proposals all respond to problems arising from globalized interdependencies, but I base my version on central themes in the much older cosmopolitan philosophical tradition (chapter one), which support both democratic legitimacy conditions and recognition of shared transnational interests.

These themes provide the basis for a contribution to cosmopolitan political theory: this book develops a conceptual framework with general parameters for justification of different levels of government. This framework clarifies all of the components involved in a compelling argument for a league of democracies, but its import is more general. The paradigm of a "consolidation argument" for a new level of government is found in the *Federalist Papers*, from which we can reconstruct the principles that license such an inference (chapter two). My proposal is that cosmopolitans adopt this framework in analyzing the need for actual government, in addition to "governance" networks, beyond the national level. The consolidation argument paradigm shows how findings in basic game theory and economic accounts of market failures plug into cosmopolitan arguments through evidence for transnational public goods (TPGs; see chapter three). Readers who are skeptical about my league proposal may still find this modular analysis of consolidation arguments helpful: it clarifies how seemingly disparate pieces of a cosmopolitan theory, such as a conception of universal human rights, problems created by tax havens, and overreliance on nongovernmental organizations (NGOs) to solve environmental problems, function as parts of the case for stronger transnational government.

I apply the consolidation argument paradigm by constructing a global consolidation argument for a league of democracies. This argument begins with crucial public goods that can only be secured by transnational cooperation—according to empirical evidence for their public features, such as nonexcludability and nonrivalry, as well as normative arguments for the importance of some goods (chapter three). The collective action problems (CAPs) that must be overcome to secure these transnational goods require more than the current world order can provide (chapter four). Lastly, we need to know that the proposed remedy is not worse than the disease—i.e., that a democratic league is workable and can avoid causing excessively harmful side effects. That is the task for the last two chapters, which explain how a league could get started and operate (see chapter five), respond to common objections, and consider other familiar alternatives (such as reforming the UN) (chapter six). However, readers who remain skeptical about a democratic league may still be convinced by this application of the consolidation argument that we need to consider game theory in evaluating centralization of currently distributed governance powers.

Given space constraints, I focus most on arguing that global public goods (GPGs) concerning security and atrocity prevention cannot be secured either by the current UN system or by alternative intergovernmental or "network" solutions (chapters three and four). The global consolidation argument would be strengthened by analogous arguments for other categories of GPGs, such as global financial security, fair immigration and asylum protection systems, stable world climate and wetlands, and so on. I offer examples suggesting that such public goods are also beyond the reach of the UN system and transnational networks, but a systematic case for this would require more empirical evidence and institutional experiences around each of these putative GPGs. Still, the range of likely GPGs found in recent analyses (see chapter three) suggests several tasks beyond common security that may also require a league of democratic nations.

The remainder of this chapter outlines my institutional proposal, distinguishes it from a full world government, and explains the bargain that could make it politically possible. I argue that democracies made serious mistakes after 1989 that squandered vital opportunities, especially with Russia. This analysis supports the global consolidation argument with evidence that democratic ideals and norms are in serious danger from the rise of a new kind of despotism. Public goods that are increasingly under threat include the stability of democratic nations, the integrity of their democratic processes, and their capacities to cooperate effectively. This analysis makes a case for urgency: while it is still feasible now, it may become impossible to form a league of democracies if we do not act decisively within roughly 20 years.

The solution in brief

This book is about a single idea: for the sake of humanity and our common future, people in democratic nations around the world need to unite their collective strength by forming a worldwide league of democracies to uphold the moral ideals and hopes embodied in our national constitutions. I argue that we *ought to* do this because there are vital public goods that cannot otherwise be secured—including fundamental liberties, protection from systemic atrocities, and other human rights that are essential for any government to count as legitimate. We should not hesitate to press this ethical demand, which has arisen in response to past horrors and oppressions, to the bold conclusion that it implies: a world order led by democratic nations that finally makes it impossible to carry out genocides, ethnic cleansing, sustained persecutions, and other crimes against humanity. The murderous dictators, warlords,

terrorists and other ideological fanatics who impose these horrors on
the world are destroying our collective future, and our divided, passive
responses are weakening prospects for democratic societies.

It is time for us all to stand up for a world in which tyranny of this
kind is impossible, backing this ultimatum with military force as a
last resort. The R2P doctrine, born in response to the rivers of dead in
Rwanda, must become the heart of a new global order on Earth. There
is no other adequate way to keep faith with the millions of victims of
genocides during the last 120 years, along with all those who gave their
lives in trying to stop these ultimate wrongs. A system that could fulfill the R2P ideal would also be strong enough to secure other global
goods on which a decent future depends—from food security, stable
management of the global economy, and fair immigration patterns,
to sustained biodiversity and protection from pandemics. If we can
found a league of democracies in our lifetime, we may bring about a
humanly feasible age of peace and prosperity. But if we do not rally
to pool our strength and moral will in time, then the horrors of the
twentieth century may pale in comparison to those our grandchildren
will live through by this century's end.

I also argue that we *can* do this: it is not an impossible utopian
dream. If democratic leaders educate their peoples about atrocities,
transnational interactions, and basic economic facts, they can understand the need for a global new deal. And if democratic peoples work
together for their common benefit, their collective powers would be
more than sufficient to establish a new world order based on universal human rights. Others have already reached this conclusion. Garry
Kasparov, the Russian chess master, calls on us to remember how the
Cold War was won, instead of trying in vain to appease brutal dictators such as Vladimir Putin:

> The world needs a new alliance based on a global Magna Carta,
> a declaration of fundamental rights that all members must recog-
> nize. Nations that value individual liberty now control the greater
> part of the world's resources as well as its military power. If they
> band together and refuse to coddle the rogue regimes and sponsors
> of terror, their integrity and their influence will be irresistible.[5]

This is a feasible goal: as Kasparov argues, forming "a strong united
front against Putin," including military support for Ukraine and alternatives to Russian energy for Europe, could "provide a foundation for a new
alliance of the world's democracies."[6] Nor would the United Democratic
League (UDL) envisioned here promote "western hegemony," despite

understandable suspicions deriving from injustices committed during the Cold War. We cannot let past grievances hold back the cooperation we desperately need among democratic nations today. While critics stuck in a Cold War mentality debate about "American imperialism," Russia and China are building new empires tailor-made to block all progress toward protection of human rights. Rather than seek to impose a "liberal capitalist" ideology, the UDL would promote peace and stability by preventing mass atrocities and providing the needed bulwark against rising military dictatorships.

To secure this moral minimum, we should begin a treaty process in stages like the one that developed the European Union (EU) from an economic trade partnership into something closer to a federal union. Like the North Atlantic Treaty Organization (NATO), the proposed democratic league would begin as primarily a security union charged with collective defense of its members against external threats and aggressions, with these additional mandates:

- The United Democratic League would take over the United Nations Security Council's (UNSC) responsibility to authorize and organize the use of sanctions and military means to stop aggressive wars and protect national boundaries against forcible change. In particular, the league would assert its authority to take such actions even if the UNSC fails to act, or continues to operate in parallel.
- The UDL would claim a final authority to approve various forms of force, including military intervention as a last resort, to prevent or punish attacks by terrorist groups, deprive such groups of safe havens, capture and prosecute leaders of such groups, and hold convicts. Member nations would retain unilateral discretion only over direct defense of their own territories.
- The UDL would uphold human rights by fulfilling the responsibility to protect civilians from the war crimes and crimes against humanity listed in the Statute of the International Criminal Court (ICC). This includes the power to levy sanctions, to compel assistance from able nations in the region, and to use all necessary military means as a last resort to prevent systematic and protracted attacks on civilian groups.
- The UDL would organize reconstruction of nations wracked by civil war or mass atrocities after the end of major hostilities, calling on the resources of all interested nations, coordinating with peacekeepers, protecting humanitarian aid workers, and adjudicating new national boundaries when needed.

- Eventually, the democratic league could take on authority over international courts that prosecute war crimes and crimes against humanity. It could appoint their judges and prosecutors, determine their functions, enforce their subpoenas and indictments, and impeach them in cases of high crimes or gross negligence.

We will consider the UDL's enumerated powers and responsibilities in more detail later (see chapter five), but these functions are the core of my proposal. The league of democracies should replace the UNSC system with one that can actually provide global security and make the R2P doctrine into a cornerstone of international law: no more Syrias, no more Darfurs, no more Rwandas, no more genocides or mass persecution of ethnic and religious groups. The purported rights of national governments have zero weight when it comes to such mass atrocities, and misplaced concerns about respect for cultures have even less relevance when thousands are being systematically bombed, tortured, raped, and exiled by force for no crime other than their identity and location. These are not expressions of culture; they are signs of its disintegration.

Yet this democratic league is emphatically *not* a proposal for a single world government. As James Yunker has argued in several works, our goal should be a transnational government with "significant ... but not excessive power and authority," i.e., an institution that can rectify the UN's weakness while avoiding the dangers of an "omnipotent world state."[7] The new global order envisaged here would preserve national governments and multicultural diversity; democracy and full respect for other basic human rights will require robust nation-states for the foreseeable future, and democratic values and practices can flourish in many different cultural contexts. The trajectory toward human rights standards is also compatible with nondemocratic regimes in some places, including moderate religious theocracies. Moreover, the right to emigrate to nations with other styles of government is an important part of individual autonomy. To keep this option available, the proposed democratic league would *not* aim to persuade every nation to join, so that families could leave the UDL if they wish.

Thus the UDL proposal aims to overcome *a false trichotomy* that has hobbled much recent work on global governance. Too often, commentators assume that our options are limited to (i) today's system of nation-states loosely coordinated under the UN umbrella; (ii) networks of stronger inter-state agencies and transnational civil society groups that try to limit actions by national governments (like a thousand tiny Lilliputians putting strings on giant Gullivers); or a (iii) a federal world state encompassing all nations. Because the current system is so dysfunctional, while a world state seems both impossible and dangerous, the dichotomy drives cosmopolitans toward the network solution. But there is a fourth option: a government that is "global" in the sense of including several nations in every region, while leaving many others free to go their own way within limits set by the most basic human rights. Moreover, within such a global league, a wide variety of constitutional systems could all meet the same fundamental conditions of government answerable to collective practical reasoning. A wide range of different life-ways and economic arrangements would be possible and encouraged in a world led by an effective league of democracies.

To avoid any taint of American dominance, the envisioned democratic league should include at least thirty founding member nations drawn from all inhabited continents (see chapter five). As with the UN and EU, the initial nations would set the criteria defining democratic ideals and conditions for new members, and provide aid for developing nations seeking transition to full democracy, with the goal of growing to at least fifty member nations within two decades. In fact, a successful UDL could do so much good that it would attract many more prospective members and build friendly relations with many others.

The design of the UDL should aim to make it democratic in all the ways that the UN is not. This moral desideratum ensures that the UDL would not be merely another "concert of great powers" or a strategic interest group; as Ivo Daalder and James Lindsay argue, such an approach risks stalemate between powerful nations on key issues and lacks legitimacy.[8] Indeed the UN has failed largely because "the Security Council institutionalizes the deficiencies of a great-power concert more readily than its benefits."[9] The UDL's authority must rest on the legitimacy of its member nations and the justice of its goals and methods, rather than simply on clout. However, its importance would also rest on being far more effective than the UNSC (chapter four).

The UDL's democratic desideratum makes this proposal fairly demanding: the league's legislators should be *directly elected* by citizens of each member-nation, and the weight of each nation in the league's lower house should be largely proportional to its population. Its upper chamber, the Democratic Council (DC), should have the final authority to authorize several types of force, including military action, to prevent crimes against peace and to stop massive atrocities in civil wars and similar contexts. While there are several possible ways of structuring the DC, in contrast to the UNSC, *no member state would have a veto*. The DC might require three-fifths supermajority votes for the gravest kinds of decisions, such as military deployments (see chapter five).

Finally, the UDL must have a strong executive authority, ideally a chancellor or president, and *standing* armed forces constituted by volunteers from the member nations—including rapidly deployable units that are directly at the disposal of the league's executive. In sum, as Yunker proposes, this union of democracies should be a "permanent and continuous governmental structure comprised of legislative, executive, and judicial branches," with powers to enforce "binding legislation" and military forces under its direct command.[10]

These proposals combine, in a more feasible package, the most important reforms proposed by critics of the UN. They are feasible precisely because three distinct groups of stakeholder nations would all reap enormous gains from the proposed UDL, even though they would also have to make significant concessions to the other groups, as follows:

- European nations that have objected to unilateral American action (such as the 2003 invasion of Iraq) would finally gain binding US agreement to abide by a collective decision-making process—the multilateralist norm for the sake of which they have supported the UN system—while also achieving a way to fulfill the R2P ideal without shouldering undue military burdens.
- In turn, the United States would gain the binding promise of European nations and other powerful democracies around the world to *do their fair part* through sanctions and necessary military actions to stop aggressive wars, war crimes, terrorist threats, mass atrocities, and other humanitarian catastrophes.
  - Long-standing American objections to a UN system that empowers undemocratic regimes, European passivity in the face of growing threats, and the willingness of some leaders in other democratic nations to be bound by Russian and Chinese vetoes in the Security Council, would all be resolved in the new structure of the UDL.
  - Thus the United States would no longer have to take the lead in almost all interventions to stop the spread of terrorist organizations, or to stop systemic atrocities against civilians.
  - Americans would also avoid the high costs of being perceived as trying to rule the world, which helps to make us a lightning rod of hatred.
- Europeans and Americans together would gain the support of democracies in Asia and across the global South, which would

join in supporting crisis prevention, supplying military forces needed for humanitarian rescue operations, and in funding post-conflict reconstruction

- Finally, non-western democracies would at last be guaranteed a truly equal place in a new multilateral process that would assure them of global cooperation for peace and stability in their regions, and greater control over global systems that affect their future prospects.

  - For example, Brazil and Argentina are home to over 250 million people; together with other Latin American democracies, South America would have more representatives than the United States in the league's legislature.
  - The same holds for Indonesia, South Korea, and the Philippines as a regional group.
  - India would be the largest single delegation at the UDL, with more representatives in the lower house than the United States, Canada, and Europe together.

- This in turn would provide a robust incentive for more developing nations to democratize. This is especially important in the cases of Russia and China, whose partnership are needed to make the UDL a full success in the long run.

These are strong reasons for democracies in North America, Europe, Asia, Latin America, and Africa to cooperate in founding an effective league of democracies. They would gain a united front against growing threats from China's military dictatorship, from its vassal state North Korea, and from counter-democratic forces emanating from Russia. That a UDL could eventually stand a much better chance of securing a just two-state solution to the Israel-Palestine problem and perhaps even global climate protections are only two among its many further potential benefits.

Of course, the different advantages to the three groups involve a grand compromise in which each group makes significant concessions. The United States would have to give up its alleged license to intervene unilaterally in other nations whenever the US administration sees fit; this concession is absolutely essential for the league proposal to gain support among democracies in Europe and around the world. But the benefits to the United States far outweigh this concession, which only a minority of Americans today will even see as a cost.

On their side, Europeans will have to give up misplaced faith in the Security Council and revise qualms about using hard power to secure even minimum human rights, as several French leaders have done in responding to the crises in Rwanda, Mali, and the Central African Republic. Europeans who opposed forceful action against Assad will have to recognize that negotiation with a genocidal tyrant is worse than useless without first establishing a meaningful threat to his regime. Non-western democracies will have to recognize that blaming all global ills on the legacies of colonialism does nothing to help collectively secure our shared future. But they would gain enormously from the proposed UDL, becoming full partners in the new order that protects the free trade on which their growth depends, while doing their share to help implement R2P, defend democratic values, and promote global security.

I do not pretend that such a grand compromise would be easy to forge, but the world's democracies have no other option that is *even close* to being this good for their interests—considered collectively or separately. As a result, democratic nations should pursue such a league treaty without delay. The grand compromise sketched here could lead to a renewal of faith in democracy within many nations where people feeling alienated by the effects of "globalization" are reverting to insular, nationalist, or antiliberal ideologies (see chapter one). Rather than heed skeptical counsels of despair, we must teach our publics to understand the urgency of the league issue, given the severe perils that democracies face if we stay on our present trajectory. The next section explains these transnational harms to democratic nations *in particular*, which only a league of democracies can avert.[11]

The fleeting chance afforded by this unique historical moment

The current historical window

We live in a special time in world history: despite numerous terrible setbacks caused by war, disease, and racism, over the previous three centuries, freedoms have spread to the point that democratic peoples could now finally unite to make fulfillment of their ideals secure for the foreseeable future. This opportunity should be recognized for the near-miracle that it is. No chance so precious has existed since the Roman Republic flourished over 2,000 years ago before collapsing into dictatorship. For at least six millennia since the beginning of kingdoms and cities, almost all people have lived under some form of autocratic rule. It was not until the mid-twentieth century that the oldest democracies achieved universal suffrage. And even after the Allied victory in World War II, these nations still did not have the upper hand: the swift rise of the Soviet Union and Mao's totalitarian regime in China caused millions more deaths and largely stopped the spread of democracy that had taken place since the revolutions of 1840s.

Only since 1989 have the countries devoted to democracy held the greater share of the world's military and economic power—something completely unimaginable throughout all prior human history. If our ancestors had witnessed this golden opportunity, they would surely have urged us in one great voice to take this invaluable chance to make democratic rights permanent by uniting the world's democratic nations to overcome the remaining tyrannies and stand up to other dictatorships. They would surely be aghast to see us instead squabble over trade and how to deal with civil wars in other nations, while settling into comfortable lifestyles premised on the assumption that there is no big danger. They would have been shocked to witness democratic nations fail to aid Russia in the aftermath of the Cold War, fail to address the weakness and corruption that have held back many nations in Africa and Southeast Asia following decolonization, leave a billion people in absolute poverty living on less than $1.15 a day, fumble in response to the rise of pseudo-Islamic terrorism, and succumb to Putin's many stratagems. How could we possibly be so cavalier, so quick to assume that the expansion of democratic values would just continue of its own accord?

Unlike the Roman senators, we stand on the threshold of changes to our planet's biosphere that may last for many millennia or, in the case of mass extinctions, never be undone. We are also immersed in a globalization of commerce and communication for which there is no foreseeable reversal. So the stakes now are much higher; but without adequate historical knowledge, most of our citizens do not perceive the *fragility* of our present way of life in free nations. This is partly because few of us in wealthy nations experience firsthand what people suffer in many developing nations. We do not see the total destruction they experience in natural disasters; we do not feel directly the boot of tyranny on our families, the terror of war, or the existential insecurity occasioned by political chaos and full economic collapse, e.g. in Venezuela today. The "great recession" of 2009–2011 was not that deep in comparison. We have forgotten the enormous threats that democratic nations overcame, often just barely, in the twentieth century.

We lowered our guard: A lost quarter-century

Our present opportunity was opened by the fall of the Iron Curtain during 1989–1991—one of the great turning points in modern history. Within a few months, some of the most oppressive dictatorships ever

seen collapsed one after another because of the courage of the
Solidarity movement in Poland and the reasoned determination of
the Soviet leader Mikhail Gorbachev to restructure Russia. That
moment was not an "end of history" or ultimate triumph of market
capitalism, as some hoped at the time, although free markets have
since spread. As Garry Kasparov rightly said, "Communism did not
disappear when the Wall came down. Nearly 1.5 billion human beings
still live in Communist dictatorships today," with another 1.5 billion
in "unfree states of different stripes—including, of course, much of
the former Soviet Union," such as Kazakhstan and Uzbekistan.[12] But
the end of the Union of Soviet Socialist Republics (USSR) did bring
freedom to most eastern European nations. With dictatorships ending in Latin America as well, democracy began to spread again after
44 years of hiatus and regression. The hope we still have today for
a realistic utopia was born from the picks and bare hands that tore
apart the Berlin Wall.

After eastern Europe was freed, and just months before the formal
end of the USSR, President George H.W. Bush spoke hopefully of a
"new world order....A world where the United Nations, freed from
cold war stalemate, is poised to fulfill the historic vision of its founders. A world in which freedom and respect for human rights find a
home among all nations."[13] Tragically, his hope has not been fulfilled.
Instead, democratic nations treated the end of dictatorship in Europe
as a "mission accomplished" moment after which we could focus on
tending our own gardens. Thus western nations failed to help the
Russian people in their currency crisis during the early 1990s, after
which the Russian economy lost *almost 40 percent* of its value (similar to US depression of the 1930s). Democracies are generally at their
weakest when newly established, and Russia in 1990-1996 needed a
new Marshall Plan to secure its democratic future. Instead we left it to
the wolves: it was plunged into deep mafia-style corruption.

This predictably opened the door to strongman rule by a dem-
agogue like Vladimir Putin, who rose to fame by crushing rebel-
lions in Chechnya and Dagestan with massacres that helped foster
a generation of terrorists. As with Napoleon following the French
Revolution, Russian dictatorship was reestablished early in the new
century. Kasparov explains how western leaders tried to appease
and mollify Putin while he eliminated any serious opposition at
home, took over major media outlets, began enriching himself and
his circle of robber barons by seizing major industries, and started
whipping up nationalist fervor by demonizing western democracies:
"Every newborn democratic institution in Russia" was destroyed by

Putin "while the [Condoleezza] Rices and Kissingers of the world looked on."[14] Joe Biden and Michael Carpenter agree: Putin had opposition politicians harassed or murdered; "Basic freedoms of assembly and expression have been restricted, and Russian elections have become choreographed performances that are neither free nor fair."[15] Putin's ambitions to reestablish a "greater Russia" were ignored until they became a global problem, just as Kasparov had warned. At this point, some analysts also believe Putin is the richest single person on Earth.

Thus the failure to aid the newly democratized Russia proved to be almost as significant as 1989 itself. As former Canadian ambassador Jeremy Kinsman says, their slow recovery left "Russians with genuinely private lives and growing prosperity, but in the messy process, 'democracy' became code for convulsive change, market failures, deep social inequity and violence."[16] This enabled Putin to restore crony control of industries and invoke absolute sovereignty to justify the brutal suppression of opposition around the edges of the Russian Federation—e.g. in Dagestan, Georgia, Moldova, and Belarus. Following Boris Yeltsin's vetoes blocking UN action in Bosnia and Kosovo, Putin joined with China to prevent the UN from realizing its potential to stop mass atrocities. This is clearest in his expanding support of the Assad regime, which tried to stop a peaceful, home-grown democratic reform movement by sending parents back the tortured and mutilated bodies of their children—the atrocities that turned unarmed Syrian protesters toward armed resistance in 2011.[17] From late 2015, Putin's air force joined Assad's in bombing rebel-held civilian areas of Syrian cities such as Aleppo, killing thousands of civilians and creating hundreds of thousands more refugees.[18] Russian foreign policy today is "realism" and total war unencumbered by any moral limits.

Emboldened by NATO's failure to form a coalition with Middle Eastern partners to stop the Assad-Iran-Hezbollah alliance from ravaging Syria, Putin also seized Crimea and fomented civil war in eastern Ukraine without any western military response. As Larry Diamond says, he has "used violence and intimidation and has funneled money to support separatist movements and to prop up pro-Russian, antireform political forces in Georgia and Ukraine," while supplying Ethiopia, Iran, Tajikistan, Turkmenistan, and Uzbekistan with "internet and telecommunications surveillance technology" to help suppress their democratic dissent movements.[19] Western nations have met this existential challenge with pinprick sanctions and useless scoldings.

But despite Putin's potent efforts, democracy has spread to many nations since the eastern European revolution of 1989. Beyond those in the former Warsaw Pact, democracy has come to western Ukraine and to the former Yugoslav republics; to Mongolia and new parts of southeast Asia such as Indonesia; to almost all of Central and South America; and slowly, haltingly, to parts of the Middle East and Africa. The Arab Spring and the revolution against Qaddafi in Libya are only the latest steps in a massive transformation that Putin seems desperate to halt. If democracy can be strengthened in eastern Europe and on Russia's eastern borders, e.g. in Kazakhstan and Kyrgyzstan, it will be harder for the Russian regime to promote autocratic nationalism against democratic principles.

At the same time, democratic norms have been written into international law, and the very idea of transnational standards has taken firmer root as international tribunals tried military leaders for war crimes in Yugoslavia, Rwanda, and (very belatedly) even in Cambodia. This trajectory culminated with the Rome Statute of the ICC, which remains the most comprehensive statement of humanitarian law. Despite cynical efforts to reject such standards as "cultural imperialism," human rights norms are more widely accepted today than in 1989.

Thus we still have a real chance to make the recent historical trajectory toward rights-respecting democracy permanent on Earth. For better or worse, the world will be very different in 30 to 50 years. With cooperation among democracies, we may reach the peak of human population size on Earth with democracies on the upswing, economic inequality declining, and social justice standards improving throughout most of the developing world. Or we may enter a new dark age of massive environmental destruction, dictatorships ruling more of the world, and small elites that own ever more of the world's wealth supporting the dictatorships and controlling public opinion in weak democracies through heavily biased medias.

Seizing the brief chance we still have to build a world secure for democratic ideals by the century's end requires democratic peoples everywhere to understand our interdependence and to recognize that if we do not start working together, our children and grandchildren may inherit the wind. It requires leaders who work to educate their people rather than feed them propaganda or follow polls, leaders who are willing to declare "that evil still exists in this world and that it must be fought on absolute terms, not negotiated with" or appeased.[20] Examples such as ISIS rising to power within the chaos of Syria and Iraq show again that when massive wrongs are left unchallenged, their moral and social cancers spread, metastasizing into cultural forms that are much harder to root out.

Soft despotism: The new challenge to democracies

Among contemporary challenges to democratic nations, none is greater than the new forms taken by despotic rule in the internet age. This is not immediately apparent on a long view: according to Freedom House, "the number of democratic governments increased from 44 in 1977 to 86 in 2015."[21] But now that trend has reversed, driven by longer-term challenges that our news cycles fail to clarify while focusing on Presidential tweets or more immediate threats from terrorism. The Democracy Index published by the *Economist* reported in 2013 that on its broad series of measures, progress toward democracy has stalled. Roughly "half of the world lives under a democracy of some form. However, only 15 percent of countries enjoy full democracy and nearly a third of the world's nations are ruled by authoritarian regimes."[22]

In May 2015, Freedom House cited "Russia's invasion of Ukraine, a rollback of democratic gains by Egyptian president ... al-Sisi, Turkish president ... Erdogan's intensified campaign against press freedom and civil society, and further centralization of authority in China" as major setbacks.[23] Then, after a failed military coup in the summer of 2016, the Turkish government "fired or suspended about 130,000 [persons] suspected of being dissidents from the public and private sector," seeking out any possible opponent of Erdogan.[24] In 2017, he pushed through constitutional amendments that give the President excessive powers to rule by decree,[25] and reduced references to Atatürk and objective science in the nation's curriculum. These developments are a full-scale disaster for NATO, which could have wooed Erdogan by answering his call for a coalition against Assad. Instead, he is now working with Moscow on Syria issues.

By 2018, Freedom House reported 12 straight years of net declines in democratic freedoms.[26] Even established democracies have suffered losses of civil rights and voting rights as populist anger rises. In eastern Europe, things are worse. In Poland, for example, Russians bugged pro-democratic politicians to swing an election to a far right, pro-Putin administration. Anti-immigrant populism has also led to an openly racist regime in Hungary. In both nations, as in Turkey, the right-wing governments have been rewriting constitutional rules to favor their bloc and to reduce checks and balances.[27] In short, "democracy is in crisis. The values it embodies—particularly the right to choose leaders in free and fair elections, freedom of the press, and the rule of law—are under assault and in retreat globally."[28]

Diamond summarizes the trend in his analysis of "Democracy in Decline:" "Between 2000 and 2015, democracy broke down in 27 countries," including some large ones such as Kenya, Russia, and Turkey.[29] The causes are numerous, but the global nonresponse to atrocities in the Darfur region of Sudan in 2004 helped to start the reversal (see chapter six). The spread of militancy across the African Sahel and massive refugee flows have destabilized newer and older democracies from Kenya to Europe. And autocrats are learning: following Putin's example, "many existing authoritarian regimes have become even less open, transparent, and responsive to their citizens. They are silencing dissent by censoring, regulating, and arresting" critics, swamping them with cyberattacks, and requiring foreign companies to store data on their citizens within their nation,[30] so their governments can weaponize this data.

As a result, policy journals are full of articles sounding alarm bells. Robin Niblett warns that dreams of a liberal world order are slipping away because leaders of democratic nations have allowed economic inequality and financial bubbles to increase while failing to coordinate their efforts to counter new tactics by dictatorial regimes.[31] Joseph Nye worries that progress in democratization depended too much on US leadership, for all its faults. The success of the liberal order in "helping secure and stabilize the world over the past seven decades led to a strong consensus that defending, deepening, and extending that system … [is] the central task of U.S. foreign policy." But now, misinformed by their political leaders, Americans have become more isolationist, removing the main support that has sustained the liberal world order.[32] Surveying such problems, Richard Haass, the President of the Council on Foreign Relations, rightly concludes that our neo-Westphalian world order "built along the protections and prerogatives of states" is no longer working for the protection and advancement of democratic ideals.[33] Securing and promoting democracy will now require a more transnational approach that shares the burden among democratic nations.

The situation looks better if we consider that the well-established democracies now comprise over 80 percent of the world's economic wealth and productivity and over 90 percent of its military power.[34] By that measure, we might wonder why progress toward democracy has not been even swifter since 1989, and why democratic nations have not pressed for the advantage they would gain from pooling their weight in international affairs. If the world had looked like *this* in 1945, we would have created a United Democratic Nations rather than the present UN (see chapter four). There would have been no good reason to do anything less. So why have savvy political leaders not moved in this direction? The answer involves four developments that make the threats to democratic nations more precise, and help explain why only a league of democracies can cure their root causes.

(a) First, our leaders irenically expected economic liberalization in former communist nations to facilitate democratic reforms organically without much pressure from us. China plays a special role in this part of the story. While few people in dictatorial nations suffer under the sort of absolute tyranny that we see in Syria or North Korea today, or that the Taliban hope to reimpose on Afghanistan, more than a third of all people without democratic rights live in China. For China resisted the tide of democratic revolutions by crushing the Beijing uprising in 1989; since then, one Chinese leader after another has rejected any democratic reforms at the national level. They and their enormous party apparatus have grown an amoeba of state intelligence networks more powerful than Orwell's "Big Brother:" these agencies control internet sites, try to manage foreign coverage of China, deploy facial recognition systems to hunt opponents, and prevent reformers from organizing in China or even more widely in the Chinese diaspora.

Democracy advocates are severely repressed: for example, the Chinese regime kept their Nobel Prize winner Liu Xiaobo under house arrest until his death on 13 July 2017. Chinese human rights lawyers and other reformers feel ever more abandoned by western governments, and say that the pro-democracy movement "is now at its lowest point since the Tiananmen Square crackdown in 1989."[35] Even Chinese human rights advocates living abroad are not safe: there are hundreds of examples of their relatives in China being assailed or threatened in reprisal. China's central planners work tirelessly to move farmers to the cities,[36] expand private ownership of land and wealth, and grow market power; but they swiftly stamp out any critique and or effort to start reform movements—even when reformers only target local corruption. Instead, the central leadership selectively uses corruption charges when convenient to weed out potential opponents within the party.

No serious diplomatic efforts have been made since 1989 to nudge China closer to democratizing in any meaningful way. Internally, the material benefits of being part of the ruling elite are too enticing to give up; this elite is addicted to the one-party rule that made it so rich. While the USSR faced daunting and very costly American challenges, China has been given a largely unhindered path to growth. As Niblett comments, "Western policymakers were confident that transitions to open markets would inevitably lead to the spread of democracy."[37] That strategy, adopted by Clinton and both Bush administrations, has absolutely failed, except as a rationalization for filling Walmart with cheap products. It has only reduced our leverage; now, for example, we let western media companies and tech giants like Google bow to pressure from the Chinese regime in order to retain access to China's markets. The result is a new form of dictatorship, which I term *soft despotism*, given that it uses economic growth derived from trade and limited market freedoms to stay in power.

This grim reality for over 1.4 billion residents of China is the largest challenge to democracy in our time. It is an even bigger danger than Putin's rule, because China is growing in economic wealth at a staggering rate and no internal challenges to its one-party rule seem to be on the horizon: thus Xi Jinping felt confident enough to make himself ruler for life. Although China faces ecological and demographic challenges in coming decades, its ruling party knows how to sell sophistical rationalizations for soft despotism. The core of its narrative is that economic progress to bring people out of poverty requires that hundreds of millions be managed by a small elite with nearly absolute police powers, and that people with little education cannot be trusted to vote.[38]

The regime also offers Chinese people the pride of economic strength and the premise (also at work in Russia) that blind communal solidarity is more important than free speech, free media, free elections, impartial courts, rights of redress, and accountability for political leaders and their families. Its paradigm bets that nationalist pride and economist desire will inspire loyalty to an elite that deprives people of their basic liberties. It teaches would-be dictators that a large public may tacitly accept economic progress *as an alternative* to popular sovereignty if they are also sufficiently scared by the government and brainwashed by state control of popular medias.

Thus the challenge of soft despotism in China is much different than that posed by Mao's or Khrushchev's belligerence during the Cold War: while the USSR threatened nuclear war, the main threat today is *more psychological*. It lies in the possibility that masses of people in advanced industrial societies around the world might one day accept material wealth and the pleasures of a consumerist culture as their opiate, in return ceding to their ruling elite any remaining pretensions to democratic control and civil liberties.

Some might say that we are already traveling this path, as civic knowledge and political participation erode in the United States, and state education requirements do nothing to counter this slide.[39] While people in China have not yet won democracy, we are on the verge of losing ours to cyber trolls, fundamentalists, media demagogues, and corporate lobbyists, who all influence too many legislators.[40] These and other structural problems in our federal system should be addressed by a new convention to pass a set of amendments to the US constitution.[41] Otherwise our reputation with other peoples around the world will continue to erode.

China, by contrast, looks strong; it is not an artificial composite of peoples forced together, like Yugoslavia or the old USSR. It is an ancient and great nation, largely unified in culture (despite some oppressed minorities in its outlying regions), with tremendous economic, scientific, and social prospects. Unlike India, China has not benefitted from a transformative leader like Mahatma Gandhi who believed in democratic ideals. In China, no one with the courage of Mikhail Gorbachev or F.W. de Klerk has been able to secure the position of Chairman and gain military support for democratic reforms. Instead, China's leaders are taking ever-more belligerent stances in their region to promote more Chinese nationalism, while keeping North Korea in a buffer state status.

Yet if China did become democratic within the next 20 years, the realistic utopia of a *Pax Democratica* would be quite probable—even though we would still face large global environmental, security, and economic challenges. There is no higher priority for the future of the human race than real democracy in China, but this problem gets almost no attention from our political leaders. Beyond occasional media reports about repression of dissidents and religious minorities, there is no large-scale global advocacy for free media and free multiparty elections for China's national government—nothing like the global movements against greenhouse gases or Apartheid in South Africa, for example. Because the Chinese regime is not seen as overly threatening to western nations (yet), and its injustices are not mainly about one racial or religious group persecuting others, we ignore all that is at stake in China.

This great omission shows how passive democratic nations have become. In China, *one sixth* of all humanity continues to live in fear of an oligarchic, military regime that increasingly threatens its whole region, and yet hardly anyone in the free world seems to care: there are no mass protest marches, no sleep-in camps or boycotts of China-made goods, or calls for divestment from Chinese businesses around the democratic world. Perhaps we are still deluded into thinking that capitalism makes transition to democracy is inevitable in China. On the contrary, China has proven that autocracies can secure economic growth if rich democ-racies trade with them—especially when they embed meritocratic procedures into their bureaucracies.⁴² The soft despotist model is not unstable in the way that the Soviet model was; instead, the Chinese politburo could succeed in spreading it.

(b) Our leaders were also overconfident because the world's democ-racies held the lion's share of economic and military power after the USSR's end. They saw no rush to act after 1991. But now it will take a united effort by many democratic nations to encourage democratic reforms in China. The founding of a UDL would occasion fundamen-tal soul-searching among the ruling elite in Beijing, and it would offer potent possibilities. For example, democratic nations could enforce a wide reduction in trade with China until China adopted reforms to bring about multiparty democracy with media freedoms and an inde-pendent judiciary.

Yet the window for such an effective kind of pressure short of war is rapidly closing as China's power and influence waxes. Within 25–30 years, if current trends continue, China will be the greatest eco-nomic power on the planet, and eventually draw many other nations into its orbit. Hence, if China does not democratize by 2040–2050, the world will enter a massive confrontation of civilizations simulta-neous with a bottleneck of environmental crises. Democracies have not faced such a combination of great economic strength and mili-tary dictatorship in a single regime since Nazi Germany. Clearly we should not wait for that point to act. We have tried to cooperate with Russia and China for three decades since 1989 to make the UN system work, while they instead fought for the view—mislabeled as "national self-determination"—that any government may do whatever it likes to its own people.⁴³ At this point, democratic nations need a fundamen-tally different strategy.

(c) Our leaders also failed to foresee new Chinese and Russian strategies to pit old and emerging democratic nations against each other, thus blocking the natural tendency for these countries to ally. The massive transitions to democracy in India, parts of Southeast Asia, and Latin America are among the greatest triumphs of human-ity after World War II. If western governments had been friendlier to them, these developing democracies could joined us in an alliance that clearly rejected old colonial attitudes and Cold War strategies involving anti-socialist manipulations. But suspicions built up from decades of abuse by Britain, France, and the United States, when we supported too many right-wing military strongmen in develop-ing nations, made it easy for Russia to organize the "BRICS" block, which includes Brazil, Russia, India, China, and South Africa. Supposedly acting as a counterweight to NATO nations and their allies in other western style democracies, the BRICS idea implies that Brazil, India, and South Africa have more interests in common with the world's leading dictatorships than they do with other democratic nations.

Western leaders should have fought harder against this "divide and conquer" stratagem, by which Russia and China lulled some politicians in developing democracies. While ANC party leader Jacob Zuma in South Africa supported Mugabe's tyrannical regime in Zimbabwe, some Indian and Brazilian leaders put trade and economic ties with dictatorships ahead of standing up for the human rights so flagrantly violated by their new friends. Thus the spectacle of Brazil's Dilma Rousseff backing Russia's opposition to any military action to stop Assad's mass murder in Syria. The BRICS coalition is designed to undermine R2P by talking up imagined "western aggressions" rather than defending innocent lives from ethnic cleansing, chemical warfare, and genocidal mayhem.[44] Nations that have survived oppression by fascist death squads and brutal colonial rule should not be tricked into overlooking the obvious similarities between Putin and Marshal Branco, or between the Communist party elite in China and the British Raj.

A league of democracies would fundamentally alter this new alignment, encouraging nations like Brazil, India, Argentina, South Africa, and Indonesia to cooperate more closely with peoples who share their fundamental ideals and principles, and with democratic governments that would give them a "most-favored" status in trade relations. New leadership in South Africa, Brazil, and other developing democracies may open up such possibilities, if we had a better model to offer them. A UDL would also contradict the narrative that Putin has been spreading since 2007 that "Washington aimed at nothing less than world domination," as Daalder put it.[45] If Russia's new belligerency was partly motivated by the 2003 Iraq invasion, as Daalder argues, a democratic league could also assure Russians that the United States would never again invade other nations without approval by a diverse group of other democratic nations.

We will not have this opportunity for long if fast-growing democratic nations such as Brazil and India abandon the principles for which they resisted military dictatorships at home and instead move closer to China and Russia. China is also expanding its influence in several African nations by buying up vast tracts of land and other natural resources.[46] And Putin's regime is successfully making economic and political threats to keep former Soviet nations like Moldova and Belarus from democratizing or moving toward the EU. He is also manipulating social media across former Warsaw Pact nations to weaken the NATO alliance, among other goals.

(d) In the 1990s, western leaders also imagined only positive developments from the internet and the expansion of NATO and the EU. We were caught off guard by Putin's all-out crusade to roll back the tide of democratization; we have not faced a Russian leader with this level of resourcefulness and cunning since Stalin. In addition to targeted assassinations, Putin has often used energy supplies as both threats and enticements in eastern Europe; he even cut off natural gas to Ukraine for periods during the winters of 2006 and 2009.[47] Tensions there ramped up when Putin imposed an almost-total blockage on trade in August 2013 in order to force Ukraine to abandon its deal to join the EU.[48] As in 1956, western nations made no serious response, even though Ukrainian reformers were attacked by forces loyal to Putin's puppet, Viktor Yanukovych, and by Russian snipers sent into Kiev. These brave reformers were left entirely on their own through the winter of 2014 until Yanukovych gave up and fled into Russia.

In response, recognizing western apathy, Putin was emboldened to annex Crimea, seize the Ukrainian navy, and then arm, train, and fund pro-Russian militias in eastern Ukraine, encouraging them to declare unilateral secession. "For the first time in postwar European history, one country had annexed territory from another by force."[49] These offensives were so brazen that NATO should probably have launched a military counteroffensive; instead, western democracies did not even supply Ukraine with the money or weapons needed to fight back. Even when Ukrainian separatists backed by Moscow used a Russian missile to shoot down a commercial airplane full of civilians, nothing more than puny financial sanctions resulted. A functioning league of democracies would have made such Russian war crimes impossible.

Putin was also emboldened by western inaction in Syria to such an extreme that he even launched a major air offensive in support of Assad, as noted earlier. For comparison, imagine how leading democracies would have responded if Russia had bombed Tutsi villages in support of the Hutu genocidaires in Rwanda. Our nonresponse to this enormous outrage in Syria encouraged Putin to extend the covert tactics he uses against internal opponents to other nations by cyber-sabotage. As Biden and Carpenter argue, Putin exported financial corruption, laundered money through western banks, and used business ties to gain leverage over many western companies and politicians they advise.[50] Putin's regime also employed an extensive array of hackers to seek dirt on political candidates, and set up legions of cybertrolls to create false rumors on social media sites in order to shape social opinion to his liking, e.g. by promoting anti-immigrant bigotries and attack mainstream western medias. By spreading fabricated stories, they aim to erode the confidence of average citizens in western democracies, and make them doubt reliable fact-checked information sources so they can be manipulated by propaganda, just as citizens are in Russia.[51] Putin's agents have also hacked the internal communications of political organizations that he dislikes—Watergate-style theft done electronically. Our collective response to these shocking acts has been insufficient to deter even worse cyber-attacks in the future (see chapter four).[52]

In sum, there are dotted lines extending from Miliband's fateful act of parliamentary sabotage in mid-2013 through the rise of ISIS, Assad's successful genocide, and resulting refugee flows, to the Russian seizure of Crimea, the UK Brexit vote, and Putin's manipulations of the French and American presidential elections. When these dots are connected, an extraordinary new combination of threats to democracies comes into focus.

Conclusion: Two possible futures

In sum, democracies are now in serious peril from the rising economic and political power of China's soft despotism, Putin's military aggressions and cyber-invasions, and the many transnational consequences of mass atrocities. While people are focused on terrorism, these larger existential threats to democracy are much less noticed. These developments since 1989 support my larger argument for a new transnational institution in three ways. First, they suggest that existing institutions such as NATO are not sufficient to secure TPGs shared by democratic nations; western democracies need more support from younger democracies around the world. Rather than try to make the UN system work, China and Russia have largely used it as a cloak to hide their intensions while they perfected new strategies to undermine democracy.

Second, my analysis suggests that a much better approach to cooperation among democracies is still feasible. Asian and South American democracies would probably stand with older western democracies if a democratic league were organized in a way that was fair to them. Emerging African democracies and nations still deciding their

direction in central Asia would be encouraged by the opportunities
that such a league would provide. A UDL would offer them a viable
alternative to the emerging Russia-China axis of corrupt power.

Moreover, within a UDL, would-be democratic nations struggling
against ultrafundamentalist religious movements, such as Pakistan
and Iraq, would have massive support from a broad group of democracies without risk of unilateral control by Washington. Then the anti-
democratic forces in China would be weakened, and Russians might
be enabled to save their nation. The great courage of the Ukrainians
at the Kiev Maidan should be a wake-up call: if these ordinary
Ukrainians could stand alone against Putin's despotism, imagine
what a broad league of democracies could do.

The time we have left to turn things around is shortened by other
factors such as fast-rising US federal debt (and interest on the debt),
rising tensions within Europe, and environmental challenges—not
only climate change but also loss of fisheries, loss of topsoil and farm-
land, the destruction of coastal wetlands, and the ongoing erasure of
tropical rainforests and the biodiversity they contain. By 2050 there
may be little of these priceless ecosystems left to save, whereas a UDL
formed during the next ten years could coordinate strong preservation
initiatives.

Third, the history since 1989 will shed light on several recent versions of the democratic league idea discussed in the next chapter,
and explain why they have remained on the sidelines. For example, consider the sentiments expressed by Senator Tim Kaine in an
insightful recent article. He calls for the United States to renew
Harry Truman's policy of supporting "free peoples who are resisting attempted subjugation by armed minorities or outside pressures,"[53] such as Syrian Sunnis. He rightly cites the Marshall
Plan for rebuilding Europe into a continent of stable, friendly
democracies—the precedent that led to our decades-long efforts
to support weak nations through foreign aid. A democratic league
might extend that idea to parts of Africa. Kaine recognizes the mistakes that the United States made in following Truman's doctrine,
including intervening in Vietnam. But he adds that *non*intervention can also be disastrous: "I believe that the Obama administration's unwillingness to forcefully intervene early in the Syrian
civil war will come to haunt the United States in the future, much
as the Clinton administration's failure to help avert the horror in
Rwanda haunts the United States today."[54]

My analysis supports this conclusion. The shattered remnants
of Mosul and Raqqa after ISIS,[55] and the thousands of crazed ISIS

admirers we must now try to monitor, are partly due to Assad. But the trouble is, such problems are *not only* (or even mainly) America's responsibility. Kains graspe only one horn of the atrocity trilemma that we considered at the outset. He recommends "looking for cooperative, not coercive, ways to shore up the world's existing democracies" and working together in meeting global challenges like Syria.[56] But he offers no clear institutional mechanism for doing that. A sustainable, legitimate, and sufficiently powerful institution must share both decision-making powers and the burdens of nation-building among many democratic nations—which means that it must be a broad league of democracies. In a case like Syria, it would have had to compel significant assistance from other nations in the region too.

∞

The next chapter reviews other recent proposals for cooperation among democracies in order to defend my version by comparison. It then explains the need for a deeper theoretical foundation in the cosmopolitan tradition of political thought to clarify the challenges of globalization. The insights of this tradition lead to a general framework for analyzing arguments in defense of higher levels of government. This form of argument, which is implicit in the recent league proposals, should be rigorously set out so that we can see exactly how needs arising from global interdependencies and basic requirements for legitimacy entail something like a democratic league. The components of such "consolidation arguments" are explained in chapter two through the American case and other historical examples. By analogy, a contemporary argument for a new governing authority spanning all continents must begin from TPGs affecting its potential member nations (as set out in this Introduction) and from several crucial GPGs.

Chapter three offers an inventory of GPGs based on recent scholarship in order to indicate how wide a set of issues potentially call for coordination via a global league of democracies. Game-theoretic analysis also suggests that the network approach will not be adequate for several GPGs. Chapter four then considers the GPGs bearing on security in more detail, arguing that the UN system has proven unable to provide these GPGs. Treaties and transnational networks have done better, but their limits are all too apparent in the face of new arms races. Chapters five and six then explain in more detail how a democratic league could be designed to protect peoples from new military technologies, terrorism, and mass atrocities. Unified action made possible by such a league would eventually help with other crucial GPGs in the environmental and economic categories as well.

Notes

1. Cruz was hardly alone, Senator Tulsi Gabbard (D Hawaii) and Senator Rand Paul (R-Kentucky) made similar egregious errors in extended statements on Syria, sometimes even repeating lines from Assad's propaganda.
2. See, for example, Matthew D'Ancona, "Ed Miliband's Shameful Role in Assad's Aleppo Victory," *GQ Magazine,* 13 December 2016, www.gq-magazine.co.uk/article/aleppo-syria-news.
3. Elizabeth Ferris and Kemal Kirişçi, *The Consequences of Chaos* (Washington, DC: Brookings Institution Press, 2016), ch. 2.
4. On *jus post bellum* duties implied in R2P, see the International Commission on Intervention and State Sovereignty (ICISS), *The Responsibility to Protect* (Ottawa, ON: International Development Research Centre, 2001), ch. 5. Central elements of this report were adopted in Security Council resolution 1674, 28 April 2006.
5. Garry Kasparov, *Winter Is Coming* (Philadelphia, Penn: Perseus Group, 2015), xii; compare 261.
6. Ibid., 27.
7. James A. Yunker, *The Idea of World Government* (New York: Routledge, 2011), 105–6.
8. Ivo Daalder and James Lindsay, "Democracies of the World Unite," *The American Interest* 3 no. 1 (2007), 2. This article was reprinted in *Public Policy Research* (March–May 2007): 47–58.
9. Ibid., 3.
10. Yunker, *The Idea of World Government*, 106. Compare James A. Yunker, *Political Globalization: A New Vision of Federal World Government* (Lanham, MD: University Press of America, 2007), 45.
11. In other words, these considerations are partly *additional* to the global public harms listed in chapter three.
12. Kasparov, *Winter Is Coming*, xxii.
13. George H.W. Bush, Address Before the Special Joint Session of Congress, 6 March 1991, www.presidency.ucsb.edu/ws/?pid=19364.
14. Kasparov, *Winter Is Coming*, xiv-xix; compare 9-12. Putin has also tried to turn Orthodox religion into a support network for Slavic nationalism by demonizing gays and portraying western resistance to Serb fascism in the 1990s as an attack on Slavic and Orthodox cultural identity.
15. Joseph Biden, Jr., and Michael Carpenter, "How to Stand Up to the Kremlin," *Foreign Affairs* 97, no. 1 (2018): 44–57, 46.
16. Jeremy Kinsman, "Democracies of the World Unite," *International Herald Tribune* and *New York Times*, 15 September 2010, www.nytimes.com/2010/09/15/opinion/15iht-edkinsman.html.
17. A representative story from May 2011 concerns the torture and murder of 13 year-old Hamza Al-Khateeb. See www.aljazeera.com/indepth/features/2011/05/201153185927813389.html. See my political history of the Syrian Civil War at faculty.fordham.edu/davenport/Syria/Syria-History.html.
18. See Robert S. Ford, "Keeping Out of Syria: The Least-Bad Option," *Foreign Affairs* 96 (November/December 2017): 16–22. Ford had been one of the strongest advocates for military action against Assad.

19. Larry Diamond, "Democracy in Decline," *Foreign Affairs* 95 (July/August 2016): 151–159, 153.
20. Kasparov, *Winter Is Coming*, xix.
21. Robin Niblett, "Liberalism in Retreat: The Demise of a Dream," *Foreign Affairs* 96, no. 1 (2017): 17–22, 18.
22. See the Democracy Index report of 2013, www.huffingtonpost.com/2013/03/21/democracyindex2013economistintelligenceunit_n_2909619.html.
23. See Arch Puddington, "Discarding Democracy," *Freedom in the World 2015*, https://freedomhouse.org/report/freedom-world/freedom-world-2015#.WrCum8szWpq.
24. Patrick Kingsley, "With Thousands Purged, Chaotic Turkey Struggles to Fill the Void," *New York Times*, 13 April 2017, A1.
25. Steven Cook, "RIP Turkey, 1921–2017," *Foreign Policy*, 16 April 2017, foreignpolicy.com/2017/04/16/ripturkey19212017/.
26. Michael Abramowitz, "Democracy in Crisis," *Freedom in the World 2018*, https://freedomhouse.org/report/freedom-world/freedom-world-2018WrCum8szWpq.
27. Ivan Krastev, "Eastern Europe's Illiberal Revolution," *Foreign Affairs* 97 (May/June 2018): 49–56. He notes the impact of "brain drain" in eastern Europe since 1989 as well.
28. Abramowitz, "Democracy in Crisis."
29. Diamond, "Democracy in Decline," 151.
30. Ibid.
31. Niblett, "Liberalism in Retreat."
32. Joseph Nye, Jr., "Will the Liberal Order Survive? "*Foreign Affairs* 96, no. 1 (2017): 10–16, esp. 12.
33. Richard Haass, "World Order 2.0. The Case for Sovereign Obligation," *Foreign Affairs* 96, no. 1 (2017): 2–9.
34. See the statistics in Sarah Jansesen, ed., *The World Almanac and Book of Facts 2017* (New York: World Almanac Books, 2017), 165, 732.
35. See Javier Hernández, "Some in China Despair for Democracy After Nobel Laureate's Death: Sense That the West Refuses to Help," *New York Times*, 21 July 2017, A7.
36. China's government forces farmers off their land when it wishes: "New China Cities: Shoddy Homes, Broken Hope," *New York Times*, 10 November 2013, A1–A3.
37. Niblett, "Liberalism in Retreat," 18.
38. This argument, which should remind us of literacy tests in pre-civil rights America, was made explicitly by General Secretary Jiang Zemin in his CNN interview with Andrea Koppel, 9 May 1997, www.cnn.com/WORLD/9705/09/china.jiang/transcript1.html.
39. See Timothy Snyder, *On Tyranny* (New York: Duggan Books/Penguin Random House, 2017); and Steven Levitsky and Daniel Ziblatt, *How Democracies Die* (New York: Crown Publishing/Penguin Random House, 2018).
40. On the rise of lobby powers, see Lawrence Lessig, *Republic, Lost* (New York: Twelve Publishing, 2012).
41. See Davenport, "Constitutional Amendments and the Convention Idea," http://philosophy.nyc/?author=7.

42. Yuen Yuen Ang, "Autocracy with Chinese Characteristics," *Foreign Affairs* 97 (May/June 2018): 39–46.
43. Compare the analysis in Daalder and Lindsay, "Democracies of the World, Unite," 3.
44. The major BRICS Declaration of New Delhi on 29 March 2012 is mostly about economics. It supports "recognized norms of international law and multilateral decision-making," and mentions human rights only once, i.e. in urging that "peaceful means" be used to stop violence in Syria. See www.brics.utoronto.ca/docs/120329-delhi-declaration.html.
45. Ivo Daalder, "Responding to Russia's Resurgence," *Foreign Affairs* 96 (November/December 2017): 30–38, 32.
46. See Michael Kugelman and Susan Levenstein, eds., *The Global Farms Race* (London: Island Press, 2013).
47. Biden and Carpenter, "How to Stand Up to the Kremlin," 51.
48. See Leonid Bershidsky, "Putin's Low Blows Drive Ukraine Away from Europe," Bloomberg.com, 22 November 2013.
49. Daalder, "Responding to Russia's Resurgence," 33. Daalder notes how Moscow used "cyber-operations and relentless disinformation" to hide their deployment of unmarked special forces throughout Crimea.
50. Biden and Carpenter, "How to Stand Up to the Kremlin," 52.
51. Massimo Calabresi, "Hacking Democracy: Inside Russia's Social Media War on America," *Time*, 29 May 2017, 30–35.
52. These military, economic, and cyber strategies of manipulation have been ably described by Douglas Schoen in his insightful book, *Putin's Master Plan* (New York: Encounter Books, 2016).
53. Tim Kaine, "A New Truman Doctrine," *Foreign Affairs* 96 (July/August 2017): 36–53, 38, citing Truman's March 1947 speech to Congress.
54. Ibid., 41.
55. See James Verini, "Life After ISIS," *National Geographic* 231 (April 2017): 96–123.
56. Kaine, "A New Truman Doctrine," 44. He suggests that the United States and its allies "should establish a global pro-democracy initiative—one separate from military alliances like NATO—that will highlight and advance the virtues and viability of democracy world-wide" (48). I agree that a massive public relations campaign is needed, but we clearly need a new military alliance as well.

1   The United Democratic League as a cosmopolitan Idea

- Six recent precedents for the league proposal
- Economic versus political globalization: Inarticulate debates
- Maritain versus Hobbes: An introduction to cosmopolitanism
- Cosmopolitanism, governance networks, and transnational government
- Grounds for the cosmopolitan framework
- Conclusion

The Introduction argued that democratic nations face several rising threats that may best be countered through a United Democratic League (UDL). These are urgent issues for democracies; we have to choose now between two global futures:

- A world in which most of humanity lives under peaceful democratic governments that do a better job of respecting basic human rights with each passing decade, working with their citizen groups and cooperating across national borders to solve endemic problems of violence, poverty, and overuse of ecological resources; *or*
- A world divided between older democratic nations in the west joined by a few elsewhere (e.g., Japan and Australia) that find their influence fading as their relative wealth and military advantage declines versus growing nations run by elites on the soft despotist model, collaborating for economic gain at the expense of political rights and regional environmental stability.

In the second scenario, the world will continue to lurch from crisis to crisis, with billions at risk under tyranny and military oppression, and millions more potentially starving when there is any significant shock to local water supplies or to world food production. In this dystopia, civil wars will rage unchecked, destabilizing whole regions; famine and pandemics will be more likely; and the pressures caused by peak human population later this century may cause extreme conflicts.

By contrast, in the first scenario, we have a chance to make the trajectory toward democracy permanent and strengthen the mechanisms available to head off the greatest environmental catastrophes. In the second, we can expect ruinous inequality, devastating cyberwars and terrorism, ecosystem collapses that leave many areas looking like scenes from *Blade Runner*, and a Universal Declaration of Human Rights (UDHR) that is regarded as a quaint memento of forgotten hopes. This is no exaggeration; it is the hard truth. A UDL is the only feasible way at present to ensure a future closer to the first scenario.

This chapter begins with an overview of several recent proposals for a league or concert of democracies. Comparing and contrasting them with my proposal helps clarify crucial issues that must be resolved. The later sections introduce Cosmopolitanism as a foundation for political globalization, as distinguished from economic and cultural globalization. When rightly understood, cosmopolitan principles provide a better framework for evaluating the advantages of the league proposal over other contemporary solutions, such as the network approach to global governance.

Six recent precedents for the league proposal

Although it is not widely known, ideas for associations of democratic nations have been around under various titles for a long time. As James Yunker describes, although 'world federalist' proposals peaked immediately following World War II and tapered off during the Cold War, proposals for uniting democracies continued. In 1940, the American journalist, Clarence Streit, suggested an alliance of Atlantic nations, which helped inspire NATO. In his 1961 book, Streit then proposed that NATO nations found a new confederation aimed at becoming a tighter union over time.[1]

Following Streit and John Ikenberry, James Huntley proposed an "Intercontinental Community of Democracies" based on a treaty for mutual defense, a free trade zone modelled on the EU, and a central council initially composed of democracies with advanced economies, significant militaries, and "a demonstrated willingness to share burdens fairly."[2] By contrast, my proposal would include more non-western and developing democracies as equal partners and add mass atrocity prevention to the organization's purposes. Huntley also suggested a broader Democratic Caucus at the UN and a "Parliamentary Assembly of Democracies," including up to 70 nations made up initially of delegates appointed by their governments (and eventually, elected directly by their peoples).[3] This looks like a smaller version of the UN limited to democracies, with a central council larger than the UNSC's but still much smaller than the Assembly. My proposal is structured differently (see chapter six), but I will develop Huntley's proposals for global arms controls and measures to resist "democide" by coup.

In recent policy circles, a concert of democracies has been a bipartisan idea in the United States, and it has European proponents as well. Perhaps inspired by Huntley, Secretary of State Madeleine Albright and her Polish counterpart, Bronislaw Geremek, organized the Community of Democracies (CDem)[4] beginning with a 2000 conference in Warsaw attended by 106 nations. The resulting Warsaw Declaration is a bold statement that lays out a demanding set of principles defining democracy, which a future UDL could use as criteria for membership. CDem's "Governing Council" is made up of 27 well-established and solidly democratic nations that could become future founders of a UDL.

Yet most people have never heard of CDem because it has operated only as a meeting of ministers taking little concrete action. CDem's function is mainly symbolic, and it has no aspirations to step into the breach when the Security Council fails to act. But it is a promising first step that led Kinsman, as representative for Canada, to call for CDem to play a stronger role. Against rising isolationist sentiments, he affirms Franklin Roosevelt's sentiment that "other people's lives do matter, because people 'everywhere in the world, including Russia, aspire to human rights we take for granted and [they] *look to democrats beyond their borders for solidarity*' with their struggles."[5] To provide that solidarity would be a main function of a democratic league.

More recently, in a 2004 editorial, James Lindsay and Ivo Daalder (who later served as President Barack Obama's ambassador to NATO), proposed an "alliance of democracies" in response to the tensions occasioned by the American invasion of Iraq.[6] Around the same time, I outlined a "federation of democracies" in a debate on just war theory with Jean Elshtain.[7] In 2006, the Princeton Project on National Security finished its "bipartisan initiative" to develop a national security strategy for America. Anne-Marie Slaughter, dean of the Wilson School, and John Ikenberry published the final report advocating for a "Concert of Democracies" to act as a backup to the UN and regional institutions, rather than as a replacement for the Security Council.[8] They envisioned this concert as a new treaty organization devoted primarily to strengthening "security cooperation among the world's liberal democracies" by operating whenever possible through "existing regional and global institutions," but also acting directly when the UN fails. Its membership would be "selective, but self-selected," meaning that member nations would abide by key norms. In particular, they would

> commit to holding multiparty, free-and-fair elections at regular intervals; guarantee civil and political rights for their citizens enforceable by an independent judiciary; and accept that states have a "responsibility to protect" their citizens from avoidable catastrophe and that the international community has a right to act if they fail to uphold it.[9]

Clearly this early endorsement of R2P, and their proposed institution to fulfill it goes in the direction that I advocate, especially if the R2P principle is considered binding on all nations. Yet Ikenberry and Slaughter weaken this proposal by suggesting that the democratic concert would not initially be founded as "a new alliance system" to supersede NATO or the UN "as long as those institutions can be successfully reformed." They clarify, however, that if the UNSC cannot be reformed within a few years, then "the Concert could become an alternative forum for the approval of the use of force" when UNSC vetoes prevented "free nations from keeping faith with the aims of the U.N. Charter" and R2P. This could require the concert to add agreements on "approving the use of force by a supermajority of member states, with no veto power" when needed to defend peace or to stop mass atrocities.[10]

These very promising provisions are incorporated within the UDL proposal. However, I maintain that a league of democracies should be founded from the beginning as a democracy-only organization with a vetoless version of the Security Council that is directly elected by individual citizens of member nations and authorized to act even before attempting to get UNSC approval. As I argued in the Introduction, it is too late to adopt a more incremental approach, and the main arguments for a democratic league depend on giving it binding power to make collective decisions about security and humanitarian crises like Syria. In other words, one of the main reasons to create it would be to *replace* the Security Council and thereby express the free world's determination to end cynical manipulation by antidemocratic regimes. It was never realistic to hope for UNSC implementation of R2P, given R2P's tensions with the principles on which the UN was built, as I will argue (chapter four). A league of democracies is needed to proclaim a more adequate basis for both R2P and the entire system of international law, which must finally be aligned with democratic ideals.

I will also argue that such a league should immediately supersede NATO because mutually assured security and determination to end mass atrocities should wed together *all* of the world's liberal or sufficiently rights-respecting democracies (see chapter four). Ikenberry and Slaughter propose that NATO should be revived and updated with new bargains to strengthen its purpose, and to give the EU a clearer role within its framework. By contrast, while an improved NATO might continue for some time alongside a fledgling UDL, the democratic league would need to have primacy to give developing nations enough reason to join it (see chapter five). Moreover, replacing NATO would bring crucial advantages, because NATO is associated with the Cold War and thus widely misunderstood as an institution that exists only to promote western interests. Even significant expansion of NATO's mission could not easily shake this image, whereas replacing NATO with a new UDL would offer invaluable leverage with Russia.

These points bear directly on Didier Jacobs's 2007 argument for expanding NATO into something like a global concert of democracies.[11] Jacobs also suggests that political scientists focusing on transnational governance have been too reluctant to embrace direct democratic control of global institutions by individual citizens,[12] when in fact there is no adequate substitute for democratic answerability at any level of law and policy. He makes good points: NATO is an alliance of democratic nations that, unlike the Security Council, has proven itself by using the huge military power at its disposal effectively. It thus has the credibility to attract new members, and its expansion would make it more legitimate as a global authority: "The bet of global democracy is thus that the incremental expansion of an organization like NATO could increase its legitimacy, as well as its military might, without decreasing its credibility."[13]

Jacobs is right that a more inclusive NATO would be more legitimate—especially if its council were directly elected—and that an effective global democratic institution would have to wield serious enforcement power, giving its decisions real teeth. However, directly electing NATO's Atlantic Council and allowing it to operate by majority rule (rather than current consensus requirements) are changes too radical to achieve through the existing NATO amendment process; they would require a whole new treaty. In that case, why retain an identity associated with western Cold War policy? In a later editorial, Jacobs acknowledges that "an open League of Democracies would be less threatening than a closed club like NATO," and he supports this proposal[14] (although in another article, he still entertains the expansion of NATO as the way to create such a league).[15]

I believe that a fresh start without any direct association with NATO stands a better chance of buy-in from democracies in Asia and the global South, including such nations as founding members of the UDL is crucial to its legitimacy, and to solving a range of global problems, from mutual security to a stable global financial system and fair global immigration processes. If most NATO nations (including the largest powers) were founding members of a new democratic league, it would inherit some of the credibility that NATO has built up, while billing it as a new organization would express willingness to lay aside Cold War mind-sets and any associated hegemonic ambitions. For NATO nations would be pledging themselves to live by the decisions of a global democratic league that gave non-western democracies a strong voice and voting weight (see chapter five).

However, Jacobs is correct that in NATO we already have an effective institution for limited forms of cooperation among a historically linked set of democratic nations: there is a real basis here for mutual trust. The option of growing a wider league out of NATO should be kept in mind as a fallback if other options fail. But obviously the name would have to be changed in order to encourage Russia to reform sufficiently to join it. Any pragmatic route towards forming a UDL must take into account Putin's 20-year strategy of building nationalist fervor by flooding his people with constant lies that NATO is trying to encircle and destroy Russia. A democratic league must be designed to break through this web of demagoguery and other conspiracy theories that cause fear of NATO elsewhere in the world too.

In the same year as Jacobs's book, Lindsay and Daalder published an influential call for democracies around the world to unite.[16] Like Ikenberry and Slaughter, they use the language of a "Concert of Democracies, with a full-time secretariat, a budget, ministerial meetings and regular summits." In other words, they envision a council of ambassadors with "some five dozen countries" eligible for membership under reasonable basic standards similar to those outlined in Ikenberry and Slaughter's report.[17] They envision this concert tackling a wider range of global problems beyond security, from preventing atrocities and promoting democracy and human rights more broadly, to economic development, stability in energy supplies, and tackling threats of pandemic disease[18]—a danger since underlined by the 2014 Ebola crisis in West Africa. I include meeting these needs among the functions of the UDL.

Yet they also envision this concert as a "D-60" coalition working within the UN framework, rather than making a decisive break with the UNSC. Daalder and Lindsay are correct that a wider coalition of democracies would give the United States an ideal way to "regain the trust" of allies and to reach out to other nations who should be our allies, namely democracies in Asia, Africa, and Latin America,"[19] But for the reasons Jacobs rehearses, a concert with a secretariat is not enough to meet today's global needs: only a treaty organization that is granted real *governing powers* can be a credible enforcer of the most vital international laws. And only an institution with directly elected representatives, not mere ambassadors, will be sufficiently legitimate to wield such powers as the globalization process progresses (see chapter two).

The theoretical framework developed in this chapter will enable a detailed defense of each of these claims. In particular, the cosmopolitan framework will clarify why consolidated sovereignty is needed, given what we know about the nature of global problems today. The recent versions of the league proposal were motivated by a narrower set of issues, and in particular by awareness that new answers were needed after the US-led 2003 invasion of Iraq. Following this fiasco, as Ikenberry and Slaughter put it, cooperation between America and Europe will require America to "bind our nation to and share decision-making with our European partners,"[20] which a working UDL would achieve on a wider scale. The problems made glaring in 2003 were not just unilateral action by powerful nations such as the United States and Britain, but also the prior failure of the UN to enforce weapons inspections in Iraq (which would have revealed the errors in US intelligence about Saddam Hussein's weapons programs).[21] In the background were the UN's deeper failures to punish Hussein's repeated use of chemical weapons on enemy soldiers and civilians, and to pressure totalitarian dictatorships to give way to better regimes. Discussions of a democratic concert were also informed by the widespread sense among Americans that the UN would be largely useless in halting terrorism.

These concerns were also uppermost for Senator John McCain, who made a "league of democracies" central to his foreign policy during the 2008 presidential campaign.[22] But discussion of these crucial ideas from both Democratic and Republican authors took a back seat to the enormous financial crisis of 2008–2009, even though the subsequent global recession was another indication of the need for quick decision-making that can effectively coordinate many nations to prevent cascading financial collapse. McCain conceived his league primarily as a security apparatus like NATO, which is too narrow a focus. Subsequent developments from the Arab Spring to the current multi-layered catastrophes of Syria and Yemen today underline the critical importance of developing a global institution that could have helped Egypt, supported reconstruction of Libya in the post-Qaddafi period, stopped civil war in Yemen, and prevented Assad's regime from burying hundreds of thousands of its own people in blasted rubble. Yet while he is rightly passionate about Syrian issue, McCain has unfortunately not continued to push the league proposal since the 2008 election.

In response, my broader argument for a democratic league will reframe these issues that drove the post-2003 proposals for a democratic concert. In the context of the consolidation argument, the pitfalls of American unilateralism and UN weakness are recognized as symptoms of more fundamental problems: for terror threats are related to other global problems, such as humanitarian crises and mass atrocities, that democratic nations are not yet sufficiently coordinated to solve.

The five versions of the league idea outlined above were all political proposals by policy experts who had no reason to engage the longer tradition of world federalist ideas in writing for policy-makers. By contrast, deep engagement with that tradition informs James Yunker's detailed proposal for a "Federal Union of Democratic Nations" (FUDN). This would be a permanent government with "clearly defined geographical boundaries," three distinct branches, and genuine enforcement powers. Its unicameral legislature would represent peoples of its member nations with dual votes weighted by their nation's population and by budgetary contributions to the FUDN.[23]

Our proposals are remarkably similar in several respects, with two key differences. First, Yunker's proposal is tailored to reassure skeptics that the federation cannot impose massive taxes to redistribute wealth to poorer nations, given how decisively this would alienate wealthier democracies. At the same time, he suggests a ministry for protection of natural resources and infrastructure, a World Development Authority for physical and human capital, and a global Marshall Plan to speed capital accumulation in the least-developed nations.[24] Although I agree with these ambitions, I focus less on these topics given my assumption that a democratic league would initially prioritize security, prevention of mass atrocities, and control of global banking for stability and resistance to kleptocracy (see chapter five). Given the rapid pace of global economic growth, developing democracies should not demand massive transfers of wealth as a price for joining the UDL.

Second, despite requiring freedoms of speech, press, and political organization, Yunker suggests a latitudinarian approach to membership requirements when beginning a FUDN: in particular, he optimistically hopes not to "exclude a nation as large and important as China," noting that membership would provide China's leaders an incentive for democratic reform."[5] I wholeheartedly agree with this aspiration, as indicated in the Introduction. Yet, unfortunately, China's strategy since 1989 makes this impossible. As I argued, China's initial exclusion from a democratic league would be a more potent incentive for Chinese democratization. In light of recent history, a league of democracies must be designed to confront China and Russia before it can include them.

In sum, these six recent accounts from Streit to Yunker show that a new institution for cooperation among democracies makes sense to experts from across the political spectrum. This is hardly surprising. As Churchill observed, this would be a natural extension of a historical trajectory developing from full parliamentary rule in Britain, through the birth of American and French democracies, to the UDHR in 1948. But without a more wholistic framework, we cannot determine whether the recent policy proposals by Daalder and Lindsay, Slaughter and Ikenberry, Jacobs, or Yunker address the problems that only a democratic league could solve, or articulate the best feasible institutional solution. The philosophical framework needed for such a systematic evaluation also clears up common confusions about how the functions of political institutions relate to economic, technological, and cultural changes involved in globalization, which we turn to next.

Economic versus political globalization: Inarticulate debates

Political philosophy in the modern period has largely assumed a world system centered around nation-states, whereas the problems unique to our era virtually all trace to *globalization*—a series of rapid changes in markets, communication, travel, education, family connections, and culture that have transformed ways of life almost everywhere since the 1960s. These changes have caused much confusion, not only because people do not understand the market forces that are altering the jobs that are available to them and the sectors in which their home nation has or could gain a comparative advantage in world trade, but also because their leaders have not given people the concepts they need to distinguish different aspects of globalization. Thus democratic citizens have not been able to make informed choices about how to respond to the realistic contemporary options.

When this terminology became popular, people in industrialized nations mainly understood "globalization" as shorthand for threats to domestic jobs by cheaper foreign competition, or the expansion of capital markets and ever-larger multinational corporations with growing power over the lives of people everywhere. The lingo glossed over crucial distinctions between alterations in facts and controversial normative claims. For example, John Saul used "globalism" for the thesis that "global economic forces, if left unfettered by willful man," will lead to a better life for all, with its corollary "that the public good should be treated as a secondary outcome of trade and competition and self-interest."[26] Saul recognized this as the libertarian ideology developed from neoclassical economic theory and discredited by monopolies, the Great Depression, and the findings of welfare economics. It is simply a global version of the fallacy that markets will spontaneously produce all the goods we need for decent and happy human lives, when in fact the ones we call "public goods" can only be realized by collective action through law and government policy, or through other kinds of relationships and nonprofit entities (e.g., families, clubs, and other networks) that coordinate the relevant parties.[27]

There is a key difference between globalized free markets as an economic phenomenon and globalized libertarian ideology, which is correctly described as "Friedman's Folly" on a planetary scale.[28] For the latter is a *political* doctrine suggesting, in effect, that we do not need to globalize governing powers to keep up with globalized trade, finance, and multinational corporations. This conflation leads citizens who are disturbed by various economic and cultural results of globalized markets and movements of people to assume that the solution must lie in an isolationist retrenchment rather than in multinational political controls—as if the facts of global trade, finance, travel, and international mixing of peoples and ideas were evils in themselves.

The whole cosmopolitan tradition asserts the opposite, citing massive verifiable benefits of such developments, while arguing that the significant problems created by economic, epistemic, and cultural globalization are much better addressed by *global law* and stronger global civil society, rather than by an inevitably futile attempt at isolationist retreat. As Ulrich Beck argues, we should distinguish economic globalization from growing cross-border social connections, issue campaigns, and transnational NGOs.[29] We should also distinguish multinational social or cultural ties, charities, and professional organizations from direct political powers to coordinate policies among nations. Until popular parlance incorporates these distinctions, many people will misunderstand any talk of transnational governance as simply opening us to more of the same problems they perceive in worldwide trade, global communication, excessive immigration, or cultural osmosis—a conflation now promoted by Fox News propagandists like Laura Ingraham. It is an ironic error, because transnational governance is the only viable way to shape globalizing economic and cultural forces for the common good.

More generally, everyone needs to understand why there are public goods, i.e., why the spontaneous order produced by markets is not always optimal, and learn about the range of goods with public features (see chapters three and four). Such an understanding is *itself* a crucial epistemic good for functioning democracies, which has to be provided by educational and media systems aiming at truth and insight rather than (only) at economic gain.[30] Unfortunately, seven decades of libertarian ideology, along with for-profit media systems, have eroded this understanding of public goods in the United States.

As a result, people are especially confused about the factors that obstruct public goods in transnational contexts and how these obstructions can be overcome, as we see in populist reactions across the political spectrum. For decades, some progressive protesters at World Trade Organization (WTO) and Group of Eight (G8) meetings have lumped together reduced legal restrictions on capital flows between nations, and the consequent mobility of industrial production, with the powers of the International Monetary Fund (IMF), the World Bank, and regional authorities like the European Central Bank. While these organizations are crucial for economic stability, as shown during the Greek financial crisis of 2009–2010, historically they have tended to use loans to developing nations in crises as incentives to adopt austerity in domestic spending, increase free trade, and open their lands and markets—especially to investment by multinational corporations. Although these are contingent policy stances rather than essential features of the IMF and World Bank, they have given the false impression that political globalization necessarily gives economic growth and transnational investment priority over social values that may conflict with likely free-market outcomes. For example, as Joseph Stiglitz notes, present forms of economic globalization force nations to compete in lowering their tax rates (mainly benefiting the richest 1 percent). Similarly,

> the Financial Services Agreement of the World Trade Organization (WTO) ... has tried to force financial market liberalization, requiring governments to allow foreign banks into their countries and restraining their ability to impose regulations to ensure that the financial system is stable and actually serves the economy and society in the way that it should.[31]

Peter Singer has voiced similar worries about the excessive weight of developed nations in the WTO, and its tendency to treat environmental laws as merely protective tariffs. Of course, developing nations have also gained much comparative advantage in lower-technology production: thus average income in developing nations almost doubled from 1975 to 1999, though not in sub-Saharan Africa.[32] From 1990 to 2015, the percentage of people living in extreme poverty fell from 37 percent to under 10 percent; and the bottom third saw their incomes rise between 40 percent and 70 percent.[33] These are good signs, although rapid changes in developed nations have caused dislocation.

An articulate evaluation, then, requires a framework clarifying the relevant public goods, along with the distinction between the expansion of *free market forces* beyond national boundaries and globalized *political powers* that try to steer or control economic forces in various ways. The latter also come in two basic varieties, with many subtypes: international treaty bodies and other intergovernmental organizations (IGOs) that influence the background conditions in which markets operate, and enforceable transnational regulation and global law (e.g., the global ban on slavery). All three manifestations of "globalization" are often criticized simultaneously, as if they were identical. For example, the Occupy Wall Street movement (prominent during 2011 and 2012) construed global corporate power as a kind of oppression supported by technocrats in international organizations like the World Bank, IMF, and WTO. On the contrary, the mostly underpaid professionals staffing these IGOs are not "bought" or controlled by global megacorporations like legislators who have to raise large funds for paid advertising in elections.

Yet IGOs lack democratic legitimacy: they answer only to sitting administrations in the national governments of their member states, which have often appointed officials who believe in reducing regulatory limits on markets in commodities, capital, and labor. Their primary aim has been GDP growth rather than setting legal bounds on acceptable market outcomes in the name of basic human rights, worker safety, environment preservation, maintaining local communities, minimum standards of living, and other social goods necessary for human flourishing. But, as noted, that is a complaint about (a) the particular policies of these IGOs and (b) the fact that they are not democratically answerable to people affected across the world—something that only *stronger* transnational government could solve (see chapter three). So what is expressed as a generic critique of all "globalization" is actually a complaint about problems that only *more political globalization* could fix.

Thus the insightful trilemma that Stiglitz attributes to Dani Rodnik: "one cannot simultaneously have democracy, national

self-determination, and full and unfettered [economic] globalization."[34] The nationalist solution of rejecting most economic and cultural globalization is an unfeasible dead end. So we must either reduce
national control over some issues to enable transnational collective
self-determination, or let unsteered global economic forces determine
our destinies. Contrary to the hopes of nationalist populism, problems
arising from globalized markets, movements of people, and flows of
ideas increasingly transcend the power of individual national governments to control—even if they are as big as the United States.[35] Trade
imbalances and the "offshoring" of low-tech manufacturing furnish
easy examples. Trying to keep manufacturing jobs in the United States
via large hikes in tariffs on Chinese or Mexican goods has simply led
them to slap reciprocal tariffs on US farm produce and factory goods.
Similarly, the recent massive reduction in the US corporate tax rate
may temporarily help American companies, but it will eventually be
undercut by other nations in a race to the regulatory bottom.

Consider asymmetries between global capital and labor. As Francis
Fukuyama notes, capital already had the advantage of concentra-
tion, which makes collective action among capital owners easier than
among labor organizers.[36] Now it has also become easier for big companies to move production to places with lower wages (and costs of
living), while it has become harder for would-be *employees* to move
between nations, most of which have strict immigration policies.
Ironically then, barriers on immigration help keep wages much lower
in developing nations, making it attractive to relocate labor costs
there. This asymmetry greatly favors corporations over workers; productivity gains and resulting wage increases would actually be greater
if more people moved.[37] Thus inequalities in wealth have been rising
in many developed nations.

At the same time, competition between nations creates an incentive for developing nations not to adopt adequate worker safety
and environmental laws. Thus we get disasters like the collapse of
the Rana Plana garment factory in Bangladesh in April 2013 due
to shoddy construction and extra floors later added to the building.
In this case, global safety laws enforced by a transnational institution like a democratic league would benefit both Bangladeshi and
American workers as costs of Bangladeshi labor rose modestly
with better occupational safety standards. With the same minimum
standards everywhere in the league, Bangladesh could protect workers without being undercut. Yet without globalized political power
to enforce such regulations, we will never have adequate checks on
multinational corporations.

Maritain versus Hobbes: An introduction to cosmopolitanism

We have seen that political globalization is the vesting of sovereign powers either in (a) new treaty agencies and technical IGOs, or (b) in new
levels of government above traditional nation-states. Both are intended
to secure public goods that cannot be realized without collective political
action on the global level to correct many of the bad side effects of globalization in markets, communication, culture, and movement of people,
while retaining their enormous benefits. The two kinds of transnational
political authorities are distinct from (c) NGOs and other transnational
civil society groups that are usually considered "nonpolitical," although
these nonprofit entities also respond to market failures and thus arguably
substitute for government in action in many cases.

Many ills of economic and media globalization, such as expanding trade in dangerous weapons, the spread of terrorist ideologies,
monopolies in multinational industries, dilution of safety and environmental standards, violent global market swings, and small nations
specializing in tax-haven services, are due (at least partly) to insufficient transnational regulation. Only stronger transnational institutions can adequately control the global market forces behind these
trends.[38] Weak treaty regimes have not been able to regulate economic
interactions sufficiently to stop such harms arising from them.

Transnational political institutions must also respond to ethical
imperatives, because some limits on market forces are justified by basic
human interests, environmental values, and other goods with objective
merits that markets, by their nature, cannot sufficiently register (see
chapter three). For example, to prevent a genetic arms race, we might
want global limits on genetic engineering to enhance certain human
capabilities well beyond their normal ranges. As Kasparov says,

> [w]e cannot resolve the problems of globalization with the same legal
> and economic tools that created it. We need new, morality-based
> frameworks to confront the dictatorships in Russia and China now
> that they have so thoroughly become a part of our globalized world
> [markets]. We need new alliances to combat the stateless terror net-
> works that use our technology against us [e.g., online recruiting].
> These frameworks and alliances must be based on moral principles,
> the only weapon the enemies of democracy cannot match.[39]

The deeper philosophical framework we need, then, starts with fundamental moral principles and the human rights that these imply, and

makes room for other objective goods as well. These are the grounds that can guide policy choices made by IGOs, transnational governments, and independent NGOs, and determine how their power should be legitimated. To assess what types of governing power are needed, the framework must also include a detailed account of the public goods that free markets cannot provide by themselves—drawing on economic theory, ethics, and experience in a globalizing world.

This has been recognized explicitly in philosophical works at least since the period of the UN's founding. For example, the eminent Catholic philosopher Jacques Maritain anticipated Rodnik's trilemma when he wrote in 1950 that

> an essentially economic interdependence, without any corresponding fundamental recasting of the moral and political structures of human existence, can but impose by material necessity a partial and fragmentary ... political interdependence which is reluctantly and hatefully accepted ... as long as nations live on the assumption of their full political autonomy.[40]

Maritain saw clearly that, despite the formation of the UN to replace the failed League of Nations, modern states still mistakenly demanded a "right of absolute sovereignty."[41] As a result, even democratic states that respond to their own citizens' views would still operate in relation to other states like agents unchecked by any "organized international public opinion."[42] In other words, the world still lacked a formalized institutional way for sentiments and concerns in many nations to be expressed in global collective action that would limit what national regimes can do to each other. *Maritain's thesis*, as I will call it, is that an institutional power vacuum at the global level leaves nations no sure ways to coordinate via enforceable common policy or joint actions that can be democratically approved by a transnational public. He hoped that, in time, people would develop enough sense of the global common good for nations to give up some of their independence to a world government.[43]

Maritain's thesis is easily confused with Thomas Hobbes's view that national governments stand in the "natural condition of mankind," a state of nature amounting to anarchy in which their actions are determined primarily by their desire to secure their economic and military interests (or advance priorities of their ruling administrations).[44] As Timothy Sinclair explains in his useful review of variant positions on global governance, this Hobbesian "realist" view returned to prominence in reaction to the more "idealist vision" in President Woodrow

Wilson's famous "Fourteen Points" speech and his policies after World War I: "Realists thought the Liberal-Idealist views championed by ... Woodrow Wilson and the League of Nations had been proven wrong by the renewal of great-power war" in the late 1930s.[45] This is ironic, given that Nazi-led nationalism might have been averted by a stronger League of Nations. The US Senate's rejection of Wilson's League shows how badly national interests can be misjudged when moral considerations and the need for collective assurance are ignored.

To deduce a Hobbesian realist doctrine from Maritain's thesis about global anarchy, we would need to add the premise that national governments *can* only care about their national strategic interests or about the material advantage of the groups in power. This premise is one of two logically distinct claims that are rolled together in the old adage from Thrasymachus, the Sophist in Plato's *Republic*, that "justice is the advantage of the stronger." Thrasymachus meant both that (a) sovereigns, who could be a king or an oligarchy, simply act for their own gain; and (b) that there is no other objective measure of justice or right/wrong to check the sovereign's will. Claim (a) is an empirical assertion of psychological egoism, whereas (b) is normative, telling us that *might makes right*, i.e., there is no valid moral standard prior to an imposed settlement or negotiation among parties motivated solely by (material) self-interest.[46]

Following Plato and Aristotle, virtually every theory of just government in western history rejects (b), and most theories of international relations now reject (a) on empirical grounds. The collective rejection of (b) is summed up in the ultimate norm that raw force justifies nothing: government powers ought instead to be justified to the governed in terms of reasons that they can rationally accept—rational persuasion being fundamentally distinct from sheer coercion. Given its centrality to modern European political thought, I call this the *Enlightenment principle* (EP), although it dates at least to Socrates. EP is consistent with Maritain's thesis but not with the Hobbesian claims (a) or (b).

As the world has evolved since 1945, acceptance of EP has given many governments motives to attend to ethical concerns, both because they see that effectiveness depends partly on reasons for their policies being accepted by their own people and other states, and because they desire to cooperate for mutual advantage with other nations that are wary of dealing with "tainted" agents. As Sinclair notes, so-called transnationalist theory that stresses the potential of IGOs, NGOs, and other nonstate actors to persuade political leaders is based on recognizing that "[s]tates are worried about their reputations ... and are eager to adopt international norms."[47] Few leaders are willing to partner with rogue regimes that reject all moral limits on their conduct, and thus become international pariahs. Yet this moderation of the realist view is compatible with recognizing that nations often compete with each other, or pursue national interests, in ways that are harmful to the larger common good of the human race. Even well-meaning leaders are driven to this result by the anarchy that Maritain feared. Thus Stan van Hooft, for example, is incorrect in claiming that "[a]dvocacy of global government with the power to enforce international law depends on a Hobbesian theory of political realism."[48] On the contrary, it depends only on Maritain's thesis concerning the existence of collective action problems (CAPs) between nations that only a global government can adequately overcome.

While EP opens up the possibility of transnational cooperation, Maritain's thesis clarifies why such cooperation is needed. Contemporary cosmopolitan conceptions of a just global order combine Maritain's point with universal moral bases for international relations founded on EP. In this way, Cosmopolitanism is heir to both the classical liberal and civic republican traditions, each of which flowed from EP combined with varying theories of social relations.[49] Cosmopolitanism extends to the global level the Enlightenment idea that government is just only when it protects basic liberties and upholds universal human rights, including democratic rights. Given Maritain's thesis, these moral goods, along with several other social goods, can now be adequately secured only with the help of stronger governance institutions above the national level. Cosmopolitanism thus provides a basis for political globalization, and for transnational consolidation of government powers in particular.

Cosmopolitanism, governance networks, and transnational government

There is no single consensus definition of Cosmopolitanism among other theories of political justice today. But it may be described as a theory uniting ideas from classical liberal and republican traditions that emphasizes universal moral principles and public goods with transnational scope, including some that require global coordination. Sinclair focuses on implications of these two features: Cosmopolitanism is a theory distinguished by holding both that "democratic choice is legitimate and should be available increasingly to all," and that "it is only through global governance that the human population can effectively tackle these global forces [of markets and information], which are increasingly too big for national governments."[50]

According to cosmopolitans, then, we need powers with global reach to secure some common goods, and such powers ought to be democratically controlled. As we will see in chapter two, this is a global analog of the position on national government defended by the American Federalists. I argue in this section that Cosmopolitanism, so understood, offers the theoretical framework that we need to determine the best case for a league of democracies. More generally, when clarified and developed, this framework allows us to explain how the different parts of a sound argument for any transnational governance system fit together.

In western history, David Held identifies "three broad accounts" of the cosmopolitan kind. The first was developed by Greek and Roman Cynics and Stoics of the Hellenistic age, who tended to reject claims of priority for one's own local community or nation: "Allegiance is owed, first and foremost, to the moral realm of all humanity, not to contingent groupings or nations"—an idea also promoted by prophetic Judaism, Christianity, and arguably other axial religions as well. The Stoics stressed universal standards of reasoning and interests common to all peoples as bases for collective problem solving.[51]

The second account emerged from Immanuel Kant's defense of the "public use of reason" and free speech, and related Enlightenment emphases on "a sphere of reason free from 'dictatorial authority'" that in principle extends globally through discourse across borders. The Kantian idea of "cosmopolitan right" refers not only to a right to visit and communicate across state boundaries, but more deeply to a requirement that nations should be willing "to enter into dialogue and interaction [including trade] constrained only by elementary principles of reason, impartiality, and the possibility of intersubjective agreement"[52]—the bases of the universal *jus gentium* or customary law of peoples.

Held identifies a third, contemporary strand introduced by Charles Beitz, Brian Barry, and Thomas Pogge, among others, which starts from the thesis that "the ultimate units of moral concern are individual human beings, not states," groups, or other collectives (pace consocial or corporatist theories such as Hegel's). Contemporary cosmopolitan theories also affirm a basic equality in the status of all persons—at least at the constitutional level of personhood, prior to individuals' varying merits. This strand helps explain cosmopolitan claims that people deserve an equal voice in democratic control over the institutions that shape their life-prospects,[53] as Sinclair noted.

Generalizing, we can recognize four central features of cosmopolitan thought in these strands. First, such conceptions of political justice defend objective, universal moral norms based in part on the inherent value of each person's potential to reason and make informed decisions about her or his life-direction. Thus, like older liberal and republican theorists of natural rights, cosmopolitans typically affirm personal autonomy as a basis for moral principles with universal scope binding *all* persons and requiring fairness to *each* person as a distinct individual, whatever their more particular group memberships and contingent social relations. Hence Cosmopolitanism is at least partly *deontological*: it recognizes a distributive aspect of justice involving fairness to each individual, in addition to collective concerns, both of which are supported by theories of public goods (see chapters two and three).

Second, for cosmopolitans, the moral importance of each individual conflicts with associationist conceptions of justice that give priority to obligations involved in non-universal social roles or communal relations and group memberships. There are weaker and stronger versions of this anti-associationism; their shared minimum is Richard Vernon's "cosmopolitan regard," which acknowledges that "the interests of all human beings" deserve individual consideration, even if obligations to our co-nationals occupy most of the available moral space.[54] If instead we have some robust moral obligations to every person, including to help ensure real opportunities to develop capacities necessary for a minimally decent life, we get stronger cosmopolitan theories, such as Marthan Nussbaum's or Brian Orend's. But all the versions share a commitment to EP: interpersonal power-relations require universally intelligible justification because, by themselves, brute preferences and the raw power of groups justify nothing. Thus cosmopolitans support the contractualist thesis that basic institutions constituting our society and shaping our opportunities, which now have a global scale, should be justifiable to each of us.

This justificatory individualism leads to the third feature, namely the belief in universal canons of rational inquiry and argument aiming to discern a shared reality—an idea defended in western traditions stretching from Socrates, Plato, Aristotle, the Stoics, and Augustine through medieval natural lawyers to Enlightenment rationalists and empiricists. This is the guiding idea today in the discourse ethics of Jürgen Habermas, on which he based arguments that democratic procedures can operate above the level of nation-states.[55] Cosmopolitan theories deny that rational debate and its implicit presuppositions are limited to people sharing certain cultures, worldviews, or "conceptual schemes," even though they usually recognize fallibilist limitations.

This universal phenomenon of reason ultimately underpins EP itself, which in turn entails standards of impartiality in rational decision:

people should not be silenced by force, persuaded by deception, or manipulated to consent; instead we should support their freedom to participate in enquiry and decide on bases that can be made intelligible to them and others (even when disagreement persists). Such bases for rational consent include avoiding serious harms and developing the capabilities involved in full human agency, even if interpretation of these goods varies to some extent between cultures.[56] Ulrich Beck calls this "cosmopolitan empathy:" we are able, within limits, to take the perspective of people anywhere in the world who are suffering, and thus "the spaces of our emotional imagination have expanded in a transnational sense."[57] This feature is also connected to a sociocultural cosmopolitanism—a partial blending of identities that breaks down ethnic and national divisions, as people's sense of their group affiliations responds to intersections of multiple cultural sources.[58]

Fourth, cosmopolitans affirm the factual theses outlined earlier: "interdependence" among nations is growing[59] because there are numerous goods with vital importance to all persons that can only be adequately secured by collective action involving many nations across all continents. As Robert Fine summarizes, connections among societies lead to a "proliferation of global risks ... that have no respect for national boundaries."[60] Because wars, movement of weapons, economic crises, disease, ecological disaster, money laundering, and people trafficking in one nation will generally affect several others, nations must work together to fix these problems. Cosmopolitanism is distinctive in arguing that such "cosmopolitan realities" require more centralized transnational authorities—including powers to enforce uniform policies across nations.

This support for global authorities comes in degrees depending on the version of cosmopolitan theory. For example, like Held, Slaughter, and Thomas Weiss, Sinclair asks what system of global governance can recognize the continuing primacy of nation-states in the organization of our world, yet call on other agents—including for-profit multinational businesses, IGOs, and "civil society actors" such as aid charities and issue campaigns—to solve problems that are beyond the power of national governments to solve by themselves.[61] Like many analysts, Sinclair focuses on IGOs and NGOs on the assumption that our best international political institutions can only be servants of nation-states, such as treaty organizations with only derivative authority.

This is what I have called the "network" approach to global *governance*—a term now widely used to suggest some measure of "political union in a place of political division" at the global level, yet without the full powers of "government."[62] "Governance" is weaker because it implies voluntary (and revocable) national cooperation with agencies that are allowed to make international policies because of their effectiveness or expertise: a governance network lacks sovereign authority or final power to make decisions that other agencies cannot override (see chapter two).[63]

In short, today's global governance institutions lack the monopoly on legal powers that would enable them to directly enforce their decisions without the consent of national governments. Mere "governance" is an ongoingly consensual affair, a *modus vivendi,* in which various kinds of pressure (e.g., by diplomacy or shaming in the media) may make collective decisions hold for a time. Thus in terms of the traditional branches of power, "governance" tends to concentrate in the legislative and judicial areas, e.g. in international courts and arbitration panels; it is only weakly executive. Global governance agencies operate between markets and sovereign governments, trying to sustain global goods through voluntary coordination of nations, interest groups, and firms.

As James Yunker notes, this network approach is widely favored because it is assumed that stronger global government would be either unfeasible or despotic.[64] However, transnational networks are also problematic: in many cases, they lack either the power or legitimacy to sustain permanent solutions that get to the roots of global problems (see chapter three). This will be clearer once we strengthen the cosmopolitan framework with insights from the federalist tradition and contemporary game theory—the tasks of the next chapter. As Sinclair says, conditions concerning the legitimacy of global governance institutions and powers needed to remedy global harms are linked in practice:

> Cosmopolitans assume that normative concerns such as justice and fairness are central to global governance, and that the point of making change [in our global order] is to make the world a better, fairer, more just place. Not only is the normative element desirable – it is also essential to the effectiveness of global governance.[65]

In other words, some level of perceived moral legitimacy has become necessary to sustain sufficient coordinative power, and both are necessary for overall political legitimacy. More deeply, these two conditions are connected by the EP requirement that coordinative powers be justifiable not only to groups but ultimately to individual persons: authority temporarily delegated to IGOs by national governments is not enough. As Held states, even at the transnational level, "single persons are recognized as subjects of international law and, in principle, the ultimate source of political authority."[66]

According to the first and second features of cosmopolitan theory, then, legitimacy conditions follow from universal respect for each person's basic status as an agent capable of reasoning with others about how institutions and practices should meet human needs and enable pursuit of other valuable goods. Traditions, shared histories, and group identities may play secondary roles. The legitimacy of government understood this way is a second-order public good that is widely shareable and sustainable over time. The result will be a cosmopolitan theory that unites federalist ideas on effective governing power and deontological conditions for moral legitimacy.

Grounds for the cosmopolitan framework

Defending the cosmopolitan framework summarized above is a large task for another work,[67] but it will help readers to know what this defense would involve. As indicated, all cosmopolitan accounts will start with universal canons of reasoning and dialogue. These include some substantive, albeit abstract, conditions that follow from the ideal of seeking the best-warranted conclusions for their own sake. Such requirements are not difficult to defend: they are implicit in worldwide recognition of their violation in informal fallacies and dialectical errors in reasoning, in addition to formal fallacies of inference. Moreover, *pace* much recent communitarian and postmodern theory, the hermeneutic tradition supports the cosmopolitan claim that there are universally acceptable bases of evidence and shared standards of relevance, even when their content varies to some extent by context. These are grounds for optimism about the possibility of transnational deliberation and decision-making. Ultimately, those who flatly reject standards of evidence and claims regarding interests and needs can only do so coherently by appealing to deeper shared standards, which they allege are being violated or ignored.[68]

Cosmopolitans must also identify moral sources that can ground universal human rights, including a right to popular sovereignty. Despite the prevalent challenge of cultural relativism, it is not difficult to defend EP itself: this principle is implicitly or explicitly accepted by every culture that rejects caste systems, rule by aristocratic lineage or mere charisma, and similar ways of determining power by fortune alone. To reject EP requires one to deny the most basic meritocratic practices that hold people criminally responsible for wanton harms to others, and that award some jobs or social roles on the basis of objective qualifications that people can work to acquire. Few defenders of relativism are willing to go this far, given nearly endless empirical evidence that people from all backgrounds can develop qualifications for good job performance, or commit crimes that no stable community can accept. In conceiving accountability for actions, the distinction between reasons and arbitrary chance is recognized in all human cultures, even when there are debates about its application in particular cases. Moreover, EP is also implicit in the entire tradition of just war theory, which has deeply influenced the development of international law. In their western, Asian, and Islamic forms, customary norms defining just war begin from the presumption that the use of military means—like all force—must be justified.[69]

Furthermore, empirical evidence for universal features of human biology and psychology supports certain universal requirements of basic autonomy: the conceptual distinctions between informed choice and deception, like voluntary action versus coercion, are recognized everywhere. Similarly, the basic conditions of human well-being are "not defined by geographical or cultural location." As Held says, such arguments help assure doubters that cosmopolitan universal rights are not a product of "Western yearning for a form of ideological dominance or imperial control;"[70] on the contrary, human rights follow precisely from *the rejection of imperialism* implicit in EP.

Held argues that we should distinguish (a) well-intended criticisms of cases where rights-rhetoric is abused for strategic purposes from (b) insincere critiques of human rights that really aim to "obscure or underpin particular interests and power systems" that give advantage to select groups.[71] In the latter cases, the critics are hardly high-minded theorists; they are sophists who know their privileges cannot withstand moral scrutiny. They preach cultural authenticity and loyalty to communities only to provide a thin rationalization for the hegemony of elites (such as male members of a particular ethnic or religious group).

Universal moral principles are not unique to Cosmopolitanism, but all distinctively cosmopolitan theories recognize the moral importance of each person's potential (in principle) for rational choice and socially effective agency.[72] In a plenary address on global justice, Charles Beitz calls this "moral cosmopolitanism," which rejects "any view that limits the scope of justification to the members of particular types of groups," whether racial, religious, or national. This requires us to jettison the "morality of states" paradigm according to which states rather than persons are "the principal bearers of rights and duties," and thus to reject associationist conceptions of political obligation that support statist accounts of global justice.[73] Yet moral cosmopolitanism is not excessively individualistic: as Allan Buchanan argues, individual rights protect collective as much as individual interests, and are compatible with giving great weight to some common goods or group interests. Moreover, oppressed groups may often be better protected by individual rights than via group rights.[74]

Beitz worries that moral cosmopolitanism is indeterminate concerning whether "there should be a sovereign global authority" or whether a progressive version of the Westphalian states-rights view might be sufficient.[75] In other words, is a system of sovereign nations limited only by transnational network governance sufficient, or do we also need a global government of some kind? But this is to expect the moral principles in the cosmopolitan framework to do the work that properly belongs to an account of public goods, along with analysis of CAPs that must be overcome to secure such goods. Only clarifying these grounds for the fourth distinctive aspect of Cosmopolitanism can resolve Beitz's question: cosmopolitans should not simply opt for network solutions before examining what the global needs imply (see chapters three and four).

On the normative side, cosmopolitan moral principles need not include a complete moral theory ranking all relevant kinds of moral considerations; and they may allow us to give some range of priority to our local community or nation (an analog of legitimate partiality in individual decisions). Yet such moral principles, together with general facts about political and social relationships, will provide grounds for a fairly determinate conception of the human rights that are required of all legitimate governments—the basic rights that are elucidated in adequate arrays of legal rights within national constitutions.

At this point, cosmopolitans have a number of options. The approach I favor argues that basic human rights are moral rights to certain goods *as realized* by social institutions and practices that coordinate people at local, national, and ultimately global levels. The secure access to these goods provided by basic institutions at any level has global implications, because systemic obstacles to these goods anywhere threaten support for them elsewhere and erode trust in common standards (see chapter three). On this "linkage" approach, basic human rights are linked in their content to what Rawls called the "basic structure" of society—the fundamental expectations, along with institutions and practices securing them, that most deeply shape people's life-prospects and opportunities. In other words, human rights are rights *to collective goods* secured by the basic structure.

Cosmopolitan theories of human rights are distinctive in recognizing that this basic structure is ultimately global: social systems operating at regional, national, and local levels are nested within and deeply affected by global dynamics. Basic rights may be rights to negative or positive goods, but they include socially and legally secured access to these goods, as Thomas Pogge has proposed.[76] Thus the schedule of human rights is a function of both (a) their moral grounds in the conditions of meaningful personal agency and requirements of human well-being, and (b) the need to articulate them in the positive laws and social practices of different societies, as well as in the policies of transnational agencies and institutions.

Conclusion

According to this linkage conception, basic human rights point toward legal and social mediums of human interaction. They are not "pre-social" rights of isolated individuals—the view often dubiously ascribed to older theories of natural rights. Instead, human rights are linked to the global order and to the subsidiary orders of basic institutions at regional, national, and local levels. As Habermas argues, the form of modern legal orders inescapably shapes social life across the world today, and brings normative demands of equal treatment with it.[77] The linkage approach extends this point to civil society agents, social networks, and informal expectations and traditions that also regulate interactions throughout human communities of all kinds. It thus develops Pogge's insightful suggestion, following Paragraph 28 of the UDHR, that we conceive human rights as rights to an "international order" in which people are positively enabled to resist domination, or to avoid standard threats to the objects of their rights.[78]

This overview provides most of the cosmopolitan framework needed to evaluate arguments for global government, but it leaves one crucial issue for next chapter. In his helpful summary, Fine suggests that the greatest strength of contemporary cosmopolitanism is its aspiration to "*reconcile* the idea of universal species-wide solidarity with more particular" loyalties to regions, nation(s), or identity groups, and to "integrate" individual rights with "the common good" of collectives at multiple levels.[79] But what principles should guide this balancing or division of labor? To answer this question, the next chapter argues that insights from the federalist tradition and basic game theory must be added to complete the cosmopolitan framework outlined above. Cosmopolitans can then develop distinctions between global, regional, national, and local public goods to fulfill Fine's aspiration (chapter three).

Notes

1. Clarence Streit, *Freedom's Frontier: Atlantic Union Now*, Book 1 (New York: Freedom & Union Press, 1961). Streit notes that Nelson Rockefeller and (for a time) Richard Nixon favored a confederation of democracies to succeed NATO (ch. 3).
2. James R. Huntley, *Pax Democratica: A Strategy for the 21st Century* (New York: Macmillan and St. Martin's Press, 1998), ch. 6, esp. 98–99.
3. Ibid., ch. 8
4. See the Warsaw Declaration at www.community-democracies.org/values/warsaw-declaration/.
5. Kinsman, "Democracies of the World Unite," *International Herald Tribune and New York Times*, 15 September 2010 (my italics).
6. See Ivo Daalder and James Lindsay, "An Alliance of Democracies," *Brookings*, 6 November 2004, www.brookings.edu/opinions/an-alliance-of-democracies-our-way-or-the-highway/.
7. Davenport, "Just War Theory Requires a New Federation of Democratic Nations," *Fordham International Law Journal* 28, no. 3 (2005): 763–85.
8. G. John Ikenberry and Anne-Marie Slaughter, *Forging a World of Liberty Under Law* (Princeton, NJ: Woodrow Wilson School of Public and International Affairs, September 2006), 25.
9. Ibid., 25–26.
10. Ibid., 26.
11. Didier Jacobs, *Global Democracy* (Nashville, TN: Vanderbilt University Press, 2007), ch. 13.
12. Ibid., 31.
13. Ibid., 120.
14. Didier Jacobs, "A League of Democracies," *Policy Innovations* (Carnegie Council, March 2008), www.policyinnovations.org/ideas/innovations/data/000035.
15. Didier Jacobs, "From a League of Democracies to Cosmopolitan Democracy," in the *Global Democracy* Symposium, ed. Daniele Archibugi, *New Political Science* 32, no. 1 (2010): 116–21.
16. Ivo Daalder and James Lindsay, "Democracies of the World, Unite," *The American Interest* 3, no. 1 (2007). Also see James Lindsay, "The Case for a Concert of Democracies," *Ethics and International Affairs* 23, no. 1 (spring 2009): Roundtable section, www.carnegiecouncil.org/publications/journal/23_1/roundtable/002.
17. Daalder and Lindsay, "Democracies of the World, Unite," 6–7.
18. Ibid., 8.
19. Ibid., 10.
20. Ikenberry and Slaughter, *Forging a World of Liberty Under Law*, 26–27.
21. See Michael Walzer's editorials in the lead-up to the Iraq war, reprinted as "Five on Iraq" in Walzer, *Arguing About War* (New Haven, Conn: Yale University Press, 2004): 143–68.
22. John McCain, "An Enduring Peace Built on Freedom," *Foreign Affairs* 86 (November/December 2007), www.foreignaffairs.com/articles/2007-11-01/enduring-peace-built-freedom. Also see McCain's editorial, "Why We Must Be Firm with Moscow," *Financial Times*, 12 June 2007.

23. James A. Yunker, *Political Globalization* (Lanham, MD: University of America Press, 2007), 45–56. Similar ideas have been proposed via UN reform (see ch. 6). Among proponents of world federalism, Yunker cites Louis Pojman, Daniel Deudney, Richard Falk, and Philip Isely. See the history in Yunker, *Rethinking World Government* (University Press of America, 2005), ch. 1. For Pojman's "moderate cosmopolitan" argument for a worldwide federation with central powers mainly limited to security and protecting rights, see Pojman, *Terrorism, Human Rights, and the Case for World Government* (Lanham, MD: Rowman & Littlefield, 2008).
24. Ibid., 56, 59, and ch. 6.
25. Ibid., 46.
26. John R. Saul, "The Collapse of Globalism," *Harper's* Magazine (March 2004): 34–35.
27. Ibid., 37.
28. Jeff Madrick, *Seven Bad Ideas* (New York: Vintage/Penguin, 2014), ch. 6.
29. Ulrich Beck, *Cosmopolitan Vision,* tr. Ciaran Cronin (Malden, Mass: Polity Press, 2006), 9.
30. See my webpage on the need for a required civics course in high school; also see Al Gore, *The Assault on Reason* (New York: Penguin, 2007).
31. Joseph Stiglitz, *The Price of Inequality* (New York: W. W. Norton, 2013), 140.
32. Peter Singer acknowledges this complexity in *One World: The Ethics of Globalization*, 2nd ed. (New Haven, Conn: Yale University Press, 2004), 77–85.
33. Peter Singer, *One World Now* (New Haven, Conn: Yale University Press, 2017): 98–101.
34. Stiglitz, *The Price of Inequality*, 140.
35. On this loss of national "steering power" there is wide agreement in cosmopolitan scholarship; e.g. see Singer, *One World Now*, ch. 3, and Jürgen Habermas, "The Postnational Constellation and the Future of Democracy," in *The Postnational Constellation*, tr. Max Pensky (Cambridge, Mass: MIT Press, 2001), ch. 4.
36. Francis Fukuyama, "American Political Decay or Renewal?" *Foreign Affairs* 95 (July/August 2016): 58–69, 65.
37. Stiglitz, *The Price of Inequality*, 59–63.
38. Stiglitz suggests further banking reforms, closing offshore regulation havens, and "regulations on cross-border capital flows" (*The Price of Inequality*, 269–70 and 277–80).
39. Kasparov, *Winter Is Coming*, xxiv.
40. Jacques Maritain, *Man and the State* (Chicago: University of Chicago Press, 1951), 190.
41. Ibid., 191.
42. Ibid., 193.
43. Ibid., 206–11.
44. See Thomas Hobbes, *Leviathan* [1651], ed. C.B. Macpherson (New York: Penguin Books, 1985), Part I, ch. 13, 183–86.
45. Timothy Sinclair, *Global Governance* (Malden, Mass: Polity Press, 2012), 13–14.

46. The logical relations among these claims are as follows. Maritain's thesis about weak global anarchy [MT] & the empirical claim of psychological egoism [PE] ↔ the Realist view [R]. And, PE & the might-makes-right doctrine [-EP] ↔ Thrasymachus's claim T. So MT shares nothing with T.

47. Sinclair, *Global Governance*, 62. He cites in particular the work of Robert Keohane on this point.

48. Stan van Hooft, *Cosmopolitanism* (Montreal, QB: McGill-Queens University Press, 2009), 121.

49. For example, EP is implied in the theories analyzed in J.G.A. Pocock's landmark study of the Atlantic republican tradition, *The Machiavellian Moment* (Princeton, NJ: Princeton University Press, 1975). Philip Pettit's conception of freedom as non-domination furnishes a contemporary example: see *Republicanism* (New York: Oxford University Press, 1997, 2010 repr.). On the possibility of "republican liberalism," also see Richard Dagger, *Civic Virtues* (New York: Oxford University Press, 1997).

50. Sinclair, *Global Governance*, 84.

51. David Held, *Cosmopolitanism: Ideals and Realities* (Malden, Mass: Polity Press, 2010), ch. 1, esp. 40.

52. Ibid., 42–43.

53. Ibid., 44–45.

54. Richard Vernon: *Cosmopolitan Regard* (New York: Cambridge University Press, 2010). David Estlund uses "associationism" in a weaker sense that need not conflict with Cosmopolitanism: it merely maintains that groups have some "nonderivative moral standing:" see Estlund, "Liberal Associationism and the Rights of States," *Social Philosophy and Policy* 30 (2013): 425–49, 429.

55. Jürgen Habermas, "Citizenship and National Identity," in *Between Facts and Norms*, tr. William Rehg (Cambridge, Mass: MIT Press, 1996): 491-515. Also see Habermas, *The Inclusion of the Other*, ed. Ciaran Cronin and Pablo De Greiff (Cambridge, Mass: MIT Press, 1998), Part III.

56. See Held, *Cosmopolitanism*, 47–49.

57. Beck, *Cosmopolitan Vision*, 6–7.

58. Ibid., 3.

59. Ibid., 7.

60. Robert Fine, *Cosmopolitanism* (New York: Routledge, 2007), 5.

61. Sinclair, *Global Governance*, 85–87.

62. Ibid., 21.

63. Ibid., 28.

64. See Yunker, *Rethinking World Government*, ch. 6; and Yunker, "Beyond Global Governance," *International Journal on World Peace*, 26 (June 2009): 7–30. For example, Richard Falk assumes that the only feasible cosmopolitan alternatives are networked global governance or "a world state," which could easily become a "world tyranny": see Falk, *Achieving Human Rights* (New York: Routledge, 2009), 62.

65. Sinclair, *Global Governance*, 89.

66. Held, *Cosmopolitanism*, 54.

67. My manuscript on this topic is tentatively titled *The Universal Human Right to Democracy*.

68. For one version of this Habermasian argument, see Davenport, "In Defense of the Responsibility to Protect: A Response to Weissman," *Criminal Justice Ethics* 35 no. 2 (2016): 1–20.
69. James Turner Johnson, *Morality and Contemporary Warfare* (New Haven, Conn: Yale University Press, 1999), 35.
70. Held, *Cosmopolitanism*, 55 and 19. Held also notes Kant's own "striking rejection of colonialism" (43), even though he harbored some of assumptions of European superiority that were so common in his day.
71. Ibid., 64.
72. Ibid., 69–72. Compare Martha Nussbaum, *Creating Capabilities* (Cambridge, Mass: Harvard University Press, 2011), ch. 2; James Griffin, *On Human Rights* (Oxford, UK: Oxford University Press, 2009), 33–36 and 44–48; and Thomas Pogge, *World Poverty and Human Rights*, 2nd ed. (Malden, Mass: Polity Press, 2008, 2009), ch. 2.
73. Charles Beitz, "Cosmopolitanism and Global Justice," *The Journal of Ethics* 9 (2005): 11–17.
74. Allan Buchanan, *The Heart of Human Rights* (New York: Oxford University Press, 2013), 259–67. Cosmopolitanism may also accept some group rights: see note 54 above.
75. Beitz, "Cosmopolitanism and Global Justice," 18.
76. Pogge, *World Poverty and Human Rights*, ch. 2.
77. See Habermas, "Remarks on Legitimation through Human Rights," reprinted in Habermas, *The Postnational Constellation*, 113–29.
78. See Pogge, "The International Significance of Human Rights," *Journal of Ethics* 4 (2000): 45–69; also see Pogge's closely related essay, "Human Rights and Human Responsibilities," in *Global Justice and Transnational Politics*, ed. Pablo de Grieff and Ciaran Cronin (Cambridge, Mass: MIT Press 2002), ch. 5: 151–96. Also see Beitz on standard threats in *The Idea of Human Rights* (New York: Oxford University Press, 2009), ch. 5: 17.
79. Fine, *Cosmopolitanism*, 15–16.

2 From the Federalists to a global consolidation argument

- Vattel and Kant: Cosmopolitan federalists
- Collective action problems in the early American republic
- Federalism, subsidiarity, and the consolidation argument
- Conclusion

The previous chapter introduced central parts of a cosmopolitan framework for analyzing global governance needs. That framework, which is further developed in this chapter, is based on Maritain's prescient point that when national governments insist on their "full political autonomy" or reject any collectively binding transnational decision-making processes, they will be at the mercy of international market forces that make them worse off. Similarly, UN Secretary-General Kofi Annan and Peter Singer argue that to stop the worst kinds of large-scale human rights violations, we need to abandon "the absolute idea of state sovereignty that has prevailed ... since the Treaty of Westphalia in 1648."[1] The humanitarian intervention trilemma described at the book's outset confirms this assessment. The present chapter explains how such points fit into a rigorous argument for a league of democracies.

Yet many cosmopolitan writers today do not conclude that we need a global government when they address what Thomas G. Weiss calls the "gaps" between "global governance" mechanisms that we currently have and those that we need to solve problems arising from global interdependencies—for example, gaps in knowledge-sharing between nations, in policy coordination, in normative consensus, and in institutional powers.[2] Instead, as we saw with Sinclair, many theorists focus on filling these gaps with more robust networks of IGOs, NGOs, trade associations, and panels of experts sharing best practices—partly due to skepticism about all idealistic proposals for "world government,"[3] which is conflated with government that coordinates multiple nations in all regions, as I explained. Perhaps network solutions also feel more compatible with respect for national differences or fears that universalism can inspire hegemonic ambitions. In this spirit, while combining cosmopolitan and postmodern ideas, Ulrich Beck insists that "there is no direct, linear, proof of the cosmopolitan project," or demonstration of its functional superiority.[4]

This chapter will show that Beck is incorrect: I present such a proof showing that, in addition to global governance networks, we need a transnational government with global reach. The valid form of this practical argument can be reconstructed from federalist debates among classical liberal and republican thinkers in the revolutionary period, as well as contemporary developments in game theory that help explain the federalists' main points. Their examples can shed light on our current predicaments, and their argument for strong central government provides the template for an argument for a league of democracies today. The cosmopolitan framework is strengthened by incorporating these insights, which clarify how the pieces of a good argument for any level of government fit together.

Vattel and Kant: Cosmopolitan federalists

My focus will be on American Federalist arguments, but seventeenth- and eighteenth-century Europeans thinkers were already drawing analogies between the individual, national, and international levels of interaction in discussing the laws of war. For example, building on Hugo Grotius's *Laws of War and Peace* (1625), Emir de Vattal argued in 1758 that nations have the "right to form a coalition" or temporary alliance to "suppress and chastise" any belligerent nation that launches aggressive wars or grossly violates national rights.[5] His proposal was effectively for *confederal* cooperation among nations maintaining their sovereignty, a temporary bargain that they could leave when it suited them.

Immanuel Kant wanted something stronger in his famous essay on "Universal History with a Cosmopolitan Intent," which, three years before the constitutional convention in Philadelphia, declared that the ultimate problem for humanity "is to achieve a universal civil society administered in accord with the right."[6] To order freedom according to a "universally valid will" (an idea Kant adapts from Rousseau's *The Social Contract*), we need a constitution to coordinate free wills.[7] Like the American Federalists, Kant saw that discoordination among individuals is partly replicated among states. To overcome the endless threat of war, nations must then

> leave the lawless state of savagery [between sovereigns] and enter into a federation of peoples. In such a league, every nation, even the smallest, can expect to have security and rights, not by virtue of its own might or its own declarations regarding what is right, but from this great federation of peoples alone, from a united might, and from decisions made by a united will in accord with laws.[8]

In other words, Kant thought that only a league with power to make unified decisions to protect each member state could spare nations from war and thus enable human education and the full development of talents. Such a "cosmopolitan state in which the security of all nations is publicly acknowledged" could stop most threats of war because it would treat all members as equals and thus establish a kind of equilibrium between them. Otherwise nations would remain in a state of perpetual "readiness for war," which is a kind of social dilemma.[9]

Kant extended this argument in his essay on "Perpetual Peace," recognizing that we cannot expect a spontaneous convergence of individual wills to bring about a peaceful world order. Only collective action—"the will of all together (the collective unity of combined wills)"—can achieve this.[10] That kind of coordination requires wise leaders who will give up absolute national sovereignty in order to form a "federative state of nations whose...purpose is to prevent war" and to uphold a just international order with freedom for each nation.[11] In short, Kant argues that the instrumentally necessary *coordinative power* can also be *morally legitimate*, and thus available to morally motivated leaders smart enough to discern the indispensability of a transnational constitution. This is almost an exact analog of the argument that Alexander Hamilton was developing during the same period for the relation among American states, as we will see next.

Collective action problems in the early American republic

CAPs in brief

To reconstruct Hamilton's paradigm-making argument, we first need to distinguish three factors that cause spontaneous interactions among different groups, persons, or institutions motivated by simple (non-comparative) self-interest to produce results that are *worse than*

necessary for some or all of them. This is an informal way of defining collective action problems (CAPs). More technically, CAPs are
dynamics in which the parties acting on separate motives (not referring to each other's satisfactions[12]) can spontaneously arrive at an *equilibrium* outcome that is not *Pareto-optimal* (P-optimal): with planning
to coordinate their actions, at least some of them could have ended up
better off without making any of the others worse off. P-optimality is
thus a minimal kind of efficiency condition.

The central economic argument for free markets invokes this
concept. When all the conditions for a perfect market are met,
competition in a free market moves toward a P-optimal equilibrium outcome involving no waste. As David Gauthier puts it, "the
perfect market ... guarantees the coincidence of equilibrium and
optimality" in the aggregate outcome of people's choices.[13] In contexts where markets work well, no CAPs arise.

However, several factors involved in many goods and services, or
in attitudes toward them, will cause CAPs that turn them into public goods, i.e., things desired or valued but not optimally produced
by free market interactions among the parties. Sometimes such a
mutually self-defeating dynamic is due to a struggle between parties
with contrary priorities: the *combination* of individual choices needed
to achieve "an efficient outcome conflicts with the incentives of the
individual members" in the interaction.[14] For example, "prisoner's
dilemmas" (abbreviated PD) are cases of conflicting interest in which
cooperation could still produce a better outcome—unlike "zero-sum
games" in which one party's gain always causes the other's loss.

To illustrate, Ken Binmore offers a case in which Alice and Bob
can each give the other $20 from a pot of money, or take $10 for themselves. If they try to gain directly, they will each take $10 for them-
selves, although they both could have gained twice as much if they had
cooperated.[15] Similarly, two political opponents in an election would
each fare better if they agree to avoid negative advertising. But because
they have no way to make this agreement binding, and their matchup
happens only once, they each have incentives to cheat or renege on this
deal (especially as election day nears). Arms races between nations
are often PDs with a similar incentive structure: each nation reasons
that it will be better off adding new weapons, *whether or not* its rivals
adhere to past arms-control limitations or cheat by adding new weapons as well.

However, not all CAPs are social dilemmas;[16] there are also cases
involving potential cooperators whose interests can align if they coordinate their moves, usually by communicating a willingness to contribute

to a joint effort. But they can miss the optimal outcome if they lack mutual trust, assurance that the other believes their promises, or knowledge of what the other is planning. For example, in Arthur Miller's famous play, *The Crucible*, to avoid conviction, John Proctor and his wife Elizabeth have to give the same testimony about his relation with Abigail (his accuser). John tells the truth about his affair with Abigail because he knows Elizabeth is honest and so he expects her to say the same. But this one time, unfortunately, she lies in effort to protect John's reputation, denying the affair. Scenarios of this kind are called "coordination" problems: while they have at least one equilibrium outcome that is P-optimal, they also have at least one equilibrium that is sub-optimal.

The best-known kind of coordination CAP is called an "assurance game" (AG): in these scenarios, the parties can all benefit from cooperation; but they will only cooperate if assured that others will also contribute enough to reach the needed threshold of aggregate contribution. For instance, if it takes three people to move Lars' grand piano on Saturday morning, and Bill knows that Harry is unreliable and probably will not show up, then Bill has insufficient reason to get up early for this team effort: his sacrifice will be wasted if Harry sleeps in.

The classic illustration of an AG is Rousseau's famous "stag hunt," in which two hunters can each hunt separately for a hare (a small dinner) or work together to catch a stag. A single hunter is certain to catch a hare, while if he chases the stag but is abandoned by his partner, he will catch nothing. The coordination problem is to get from the suboptimal equilibrium (one rabbit for each) to the optimal outcome that they both prefer (half a large deer for each). Going after the stag is riskier, because it pays off only if the other party reciprocates. Thus if either has doubts about the other, he will take the safer bet on the hare.

An AG is easier to solve than a PD, in which the optimal outcome is not among the equilibrium outcome(s) at all. In an AG, each party has reason to cooperate *if* (but only if) they believe the other will cooperate, whereas in a PD each party stands to gain *most* by defecting when they think the others will cooperate. Thus to overcome a PD may require conditions such as enforcement of promises by an overarching authority, or by other parties in repeated encounters, to change incentives. By contrast, parties can overcome an AG if they have sufficient bases to *believe* that the others will do their parts. This can be secured by trust rooted in a personal relationship, an authority constraining them, or other customary expectations among them.

Third, there are cases in which the parties can only coordinate if they settle on *one among several* possible P-optimal outcomes that could be reached through their cooperation. This will raise questions about which of the options is fairest when each P-optimal result includes a different division of the costs and benefits of cooperation. Insistence on an unfair division of costs and benefits, or disagreement about standards for a fair split, may prevent the cooperation needed for *any* of the feasible P-optimal results. If the proposed division is too unequal, some parties may prefer the sub-optimal status quo on principle—giving up all potential gains involved in the proposed split—rather than accept a P-optimal outcome that is unfair in *comparative* terms.

This dimension of CAPs has become more familiar in recent years in the example of an ultimatum game. For example, suppose two businesses P and Q would increase their profits by a joint total of $40 million if they collaborated on an upcoming project. But the owner of P, being in better financial shape, figures that he needs the deal less than the owner of Q: so he demands $28 million of the prospective gain, leaving $12 million for Q. If the owner of Q is offended by this proposed split and rejects the deal entirely, or if they have insufficient time to find an acceptable compromise, both P and Q lose their opportunity. The minimal criterion of P-optimality cannot help them decide between a 20-20 split, a 17-23 split, an 11-29 split, etc. because all these splits are P-optimal (in every case, each party gains something and there is no waste). So some other set of norms is needed to help them reach a fair bargain.

This *distributive equity* aspect of CAPs is often overlooked because it is usually found in combination with the other two aspects. Consider the coordination game that is traditionally named "battle of the sexes" because it is illustrated by a stereotypical situation where a couple wants to go on a date, but the man wants to go to a football game, while the woman prefers an opera. For a less sexist variant, imagine that two friends have to decide between a reunion at a bowling alley or a casino. This "battle of friends" (BF) structure includes any dynamic in which interacting parties lose out if they do not coordinate to select the same something X—such as the location for a date, genre of movie, vacation, house, business plan, location for tunnel linking two states, etc.—but each prefers their convergence on a *different* instance of X. This last element is not present in AGs or PDs, which have only one P-optimal outcome. In a two-party BF, there is a conflict of interest over *relative* benefits because there are two P-optimal outcomes with unequal payoffs.[17] This is also the case in "chicken" games, where usually one party does all the work while the benefits go to both: in either of the P-optimal outcomes, one party free rides on the other.

This gives us the three main aspects of CAPs, or three distinct causes of sub-optimal results for parties who could have done better with coordination or cooperation.

i   *Social dilemmas:* individual agents directly pursue noncomparative interests that happen to conflict in ways that make them worse off unless they cooperate;

ii *Coordination failures:* agents fail to communicate or are prevented from coordinating to achieve mutual fulfillment of interests that are potentially aligned; and

iii *Distribution tensions:* individuals agree on the superiority of outcomes attainable by cooperation, but disagree on which distribution of the costs and benefits of cooperation is fairest.

Some scenarios (like chicken) involve more than one of these problems, but they can also be found in isolation. Thus they are different dimensions of the CAP space.[18] Of course, this short summary leaves out many important variations (e.g., repeated games, asymmetric moves, and larger numbers of parties); but it will be sufficient for analyzing key arguments in the *Federalist Papers*.

Early American CAPs

The early American republic was an unstable place. To understand how discoordinated the thirteen American colonies were when war broke out with Britain in 1775, imagine that there was no central government in the United States today, and so 50 supreme state government shared a continent-wide economy. They would have 50 different law codes to regulate commerce and industry and make ever-shifting treaties for mutual defense without unified taxes or spending on their shared needs. Despite their efforts to craft aligned priorities, given the lack of any supra-state authority to make their agreements truly binding, each state would often have economic incentives to undercut and free ride on other states—even in crises threatening the interests of several states. Knowing that every state would have similar incentives, their efforts to set common policies would be unstable without a credible enforcement mechanism. In short, they would be caught in a series of CAPs, competing with one another in mutually self-defeating ways. In this bureaucratic nightmare scenario, our national GDP would not be even one-tenth of its present level.

Even in a crisis, the governor of one state might not be willing to send forces or material to help another state repel a foreign attack unless he were sure that enough other states would do likewise so that his sacrifice would not be wasted—an AG. Or he might argue that his state provided the protective forces during the last crisis and so others should bear the costs this time—a chicken game. Thus enemies would benefit by sowing distrust among the states, or exploiting their tendency to be worried more about their own domestic defense than about the national cause.

This was the situation among the original thirteen American states during and immediately after the Revolutionary War. The First Continental Congress was a group of delegates from twelve states convened in September 1774 to pass a common trade embargo against Great Britain. These "Articles of Association" attempted to overcome a PD: almost all the thirteen colonies wanted the embargo to punish the British king for his mistreatment of them; but each state still preferred to continue reaping the benefits of trade with Britain while other states paid the economic costs of maintaining the boycott. In fact, the gains to any state from cheating would increase with the number of other states holding to the embargo. Thus such an embargo requires near-unanimous compliance (the standard remedy for a PD) that can often be secured only through strong enforcement.

Similarly, when the Second Continental Congress gathered in May 1775 to address new grievances, it remained "little more than a conference of ambassadors from the thirteen states. ... In all respects, the states were sovereign."[19] Its members had to send home requests for instructions when anything significant was to be decided. Through incredible machinations, they managed to overcome a PD by passing the Declaration of Independence, an agreement on which no state could easily cheat.[20] Yet, during the ensuing war with Britain, the Congress's Board of War found it very difficult to coordinate the states to support the Continental army: they could not get local leaders to send supplies and men wherever they were needed most, as opposed to defending their own states. General Washington was furious that this useless central authority left his soldiers without adequate clothes, ammunition, food,[21] and new recruits to replace those returning home after short enlistments. When John Hancock sent the Continental troop quotas approved by congress to the states in October 1776, *none complied*; they all preferred to keep their militias at home to protect their own people.[22]

This might be diagnosed as a game of chicken,[23] in which each state expected some other states to supply Washington with enough men and material for the job. In chicken scenarios, each party would prefer others to pay the cost of providing the collective benefit, even though (unlike in a PD), each party would prefer to pay toward the cost themselves rather than forfeit the collective benefit entirely—i.e. lose the whole war, which could easily happen with miscalculation about what other states would do. In other words, each state preferred to free ride on the contributions of other states to Washington's army, although none of the major states wanted to see him fail: when facing that prospect, some of the larger states did send troops and supplies.

Congress approved the Articles of Confederation in November 1777 as a set of procedural laws and began to operate under them even before they were ratified by eleven states at the end of 1778. But Maryland and Delaware acted as spoilers, refusing to make it official for two more years. That was largely because, even with the war still raging, they demanded that states such as Virginia cede their claims to lands west of the Appalachian mountains.[24] But even when this dispute was settled, the Congress of Confederation remained ineffective: bickering over Vermont's petition to become a new state, for example, proved intractable under the Articles.[25] Insufficient power in the congress prolonged the war and embarrassed American officials trying to negotiate alliances and credit abroad. When a messenger from Virginia brought news of the final American victory at Yorktown to the congress at Philadelphia, "there was not sufficient hard money in the treasury for the man's expenses; each member paid a dollar from his pocket."[26]

The Articles were supposed to provide for a single currency, payment of war debts, a unified foreign policy, and a common defense. But, although they made laws of the Confederation supreme, the Articles required approval from two-thirds of the states to enact legislation on most significant matters.[27] Even worse, since the officers of the Confederation had no real executive powers of their own, they depended almost entirely on state officials to enforce national laws. Thus in practice it required near unanimity in congress and help from the states to get anything important done. Although Abraham Lincoln would later call the Articles our first national constitution, Joseph Ellis contends that they were "less a constitution than a ... treaty among sovereign powers."[28] During the two years between Yorktown and the final peace treaty, while the Continental army had to be kept standing, most states did not pay nearly their shares of the cost. In 1781, congress requisitioned "$3 million from the states and received $39,139 in return,"[29] i.e., about *1.5 percent*. In this case, resentment at free riders probably made for a distributive equity problem (DEP): willingness to pay one's share declined due to anger that too many other states were not paying theirs. A similar trend is seen in many "public goods games" where individual contributions to the collective pot (which benefits all parties) decline on each new round because of previous free riders.

As a result, the US Congress had serious problems honoring the obligations made to Continental soldiers, such as back pay, pensions to disabled veterans, and officer pensions.[30] Enlisted men feared that when the army disbanded, they would never collect on the large monetary debts owed to them by the "union." Such resentments almost resulted in a military revolt and sapped loyalty to the central government on which common security clearly still depended.

The problems worsened after the peace: the Confederation Congress pleaded for the power to levy a direct duty of 5 percent on all imports, which would have given it a revenue stream not dependent on state officials. But this required the consent of all the states,[31] and two rejected it. Thus the federal debt crisis worsened. Likewise, because the congress could not make a common tariff policy, states competed with each other by lowering tariffs on foreign nations[32]—a textbook PD. They also imposed mutually harmful tariffs on each other, and nine states kept their own navies (in violation of the Articles), in part to police shipping from other states.[33] Beyond such extra transaction costs, states' rival interests concerning the entry of new states stalled Jefferson's 1784 plan for western territories. It was only through herculean negotiations and bribes that the congress was finally able, in July 1787, to pass and enforce the Northwest Ordinance—one of its only major achievements. This crucial act probably passed only because the situation had become an AG in which all the states gained some net benefit from the plan, although they did not perceive the benefits as equal to all states (which caused tensions over fairness).

In sum, the weak confederal government found it almost impossible to get the states to abide by policies that would benefit the whole if every state made the sacrifices necessary for collective success. Without centralized power to assure compliance from all states, the needed sacrifices appeared to each state as too risky, costly, or unfairly distributed to motivate cooperation. The confederation of southern states during the American Civil War had similar problems in acting for their common strategic interests. Their ideological devotion to the supremacy of state governments, which they learned from antifederalists and relied on to justify secession at will, made it hard for officials in Richmond to enforce sacrifices needed for their victory—fortunately, in this case.

Alexander Hamilton diagnosed such problems earlier and more clearly than anyone else. By the fall of 1780, he wrote to James Duane that "the fundamental defect is a want of power in Congress," i.e, the central government. This in turn resulted from "an excess of the spirit of liberty" that made states jealous of their individual discretion, along with congressmen who refused to interpret their powers broadly as including whatever is necessary "to preserve the republic from harm."[34] The confederation, he concluded, would have to be altered: for "the idea of an uncontrollable sovereignty in each state" would defeat the intended functions of the federal government. State powers were simply too large, making it "too difficult to bend them to the persuit of a common interest, too easy to oppose whatever they do not like and to form partial combinations subversive of the general one."[35] In other words, it was impossible to coordinate states to share the costs and benefits of cooperation—or, equivalently, to overcome the CAPs defeating national public goods. Fixing this would require a new government with its own taxing powers, executive departments under strong individual leaders (rather than boards), and "complete [national] sovereignty in all that relates to war, peace, trade, finance, and to the management of foreign affairs."[36] Thus Hamilton called for a new constitutional convention, and began to persuade James Madison, who in turn persuaded Washington to chair the convention. This helped assure potential delegates that enough states would come.[37] Yet when the convention finally met, the distributive inequities demanded by small states (e.g., state equality in the proposed senate) almost torched the deal.

The resulting new constitution of 1787 then had to be ratified by at least nine states. To reach this threshold, Hamilton, Madison, and John Jay anonymously defended the constitution in *The Federalist Papers*. In these famous pamphlets, they recognize the CAPs experienced under the Articles as grounds for a *higher level of government*, developing a central insight in social contract theory. This ancient form of argument had been modernized by Hobbes in his *Leviathan* and related works: he said that to avoid the "calamities" ensuing from the lack of law and reliable property rights, we should all consent to be governed by an authority sufficient to establish order.[38] But Hobbes cited CAPs in the original "state of nature" only as grounds for moving from anarchy among individuals (or families and small clans) to some first level of government.[39] Two centuries later, the American Federalists explained how an analogous argument applied to state governments that need to cooperate for their peoples to survive and flourish.

For example, in *Federalist* number 2, Jay argues that not only common security but also individual liberties depend on a strong federal union.[40] Jay adds in *Federalist* 3 that individual states are tempted to inconsistencies and injustices to one another that a strong federal government can prevent.[41] He notes in *Federalist* 4 that a federal government can harmonize the interests of the parts in a common foreign policy and "apply the resources and power of the whole to the defense of any particular part."[42] By contrast, three or four American confederacies would be played off against one another by rival European powers, and contribute less than their necessary share to any collective continental defense.[43] In general, Hamilton adds *in Federalist* 6, independent sovereign powers in the same region are liable to "violent contests" with each other.[44]

Hamilton argues that the weakness of the confederation led to conflict and decline in credit.[45] He also predicts that disputes about new western territories could lead to war between the states or multiple confederacies formed among them.[46] Under the Articles, execution of confederal law depended on the local interests of each state, which could often benefit from free riding on others. As we saw, funding for congress and its measures was routinely blocked by distributive inequities and inadequate assurance that enough total contributions would come in: "The greater deficiencies of some States furnished the pretext of example and the temptation of interest to the [initially] complying, or ... least delinquent States."[47] For example, a prominent Virginian complained in 1787 that New Hampshire had paid nothing into the common pot since the peace, and never intended to.[48] Such situations combine partial conflicts of interest and coordination problems arising from uncertainties (a BF structure): some states wanted all the states to cooperate in supporting more confederal initiatives, while other states wanted a more minimal central authority, and neither group was willing to concede.

Yet the congress could not itself provide the needed guarantee that confederal functions would benefit all states proportionately with equitable cost sharing. Hamilton saw to the heart of the matter in *Federalist* 15, in the most important passage in the *Papers*:

> The great and radical vice in the construction of the existing Confederation is in the principle of LEGISLATION for STATES OR GOVERNMENTS, in their CORPORATE OR COLLECTIVE CAPACITIES, and as contradistinguished from the INDIVIDUALS of whom they consist. ... [T]he United States have an indefinite discretion to make requisitions for men and money; but they have no authority to raise either by regulations extending to the individual citizens of America. The consequence of this is that [their laws] ... are mere recommendations which the States observe or disregard at their option.[49]

In other words, a confederal government that can only operate indirectly through state governments, rather than directly enforcing laws on individual people who vote for the legislators, is too *derivative*: it has no final sovereign authority, flowing directly from *the people* of all the states, that can override particular state governments. A federal government with such a direct relation to the people is the solution because it is the only legitimate way to get the authority over all the states that is needed to overcome CAPs between them.

There are two sides to Hamilton's point here. First, there is a principle concerning power: the failures of the confederation can only be overcome by a consolidation of authority. The "characteristic difference between a league and a government" lies in directly addressing individual citizens;[50] to be effective, the federal government must "carry its agency to the persons of the citizens. It must stand in need of no intermediate legislation" or executive action by the states.[51] Second, for such power to be legitimate, the government must "address itself immediately [directly] to the hopes and fears of individuals" and attract their direct support.[52] Together these features clarify how a federal government differs from a mere confederation: it enjoys *primary sovereignty* over subordinate units, which is a right to rule that is unmediated in both directions—coordinating people directly by law rather than through intermediate collectives, and deriving authorization to do this directly from them. Formally stated, the two conditions of primary sovereignty are:

1. DIRECT RELATION: (a) authority to make law that, in its ultimate basis, is derived directly from the actual or implied consent of the people at large (b) who will be directly ruled by the acts and laws of the government, (c) which can therefore be seen as synthesizing their collective will and serving as a conduit for their collective action.

2. SUPREMACY: (a) authority to enforce laws, judicial decisions, and executive acts through police powers that are reserved (in their primary forms) to the government, (b) and which do not depend for their execution on other governing agencies with an authority to contravene them.

Condition 2a says that the sovereign claims a final monopoly on legitimate use of coercive force within the governed territory (compare the Roman concept of *imperium*); 2b is the related idea that a government is sovereign only when it needs permission from no other, i.e., "there is no formal level of authority (in the legal sense) able to override its decisions in its own domestic sphere."[53] Madison and his allies made sure that this principle was embodied in the Supremacy Clause of the 1787 constitution. As a result, the original thirteen states continued to have a direct relation to their citizens, but no longer had supremacy—as the Civil War amendments confirmed. Of course, a federal system will also include indirect relations, but the primary covenant with the people must give it final control over the boundaries between federal and state powers.

By contrast, like the UN today, the League of Nations met none of these conditions. As Yunker says, it possessed "no military force under its direct control" and "no authority to levy taxes;" its member states remained supreme. Similarly, "it was separated from any direct connection" with the peoples represented within it, much like the US confederation.[54]

Hamilton's directness condition is democratic: a government that has de facto supremacy over its nation's territories but no direct rational support from its people is a sovereign, but not a democratic one—and therefore not legitimate according to the republican principles of both the federalists and their critics in 1787–1788. An absolute monarchy, like the Roman empire, would both be supreme in sense 2a and 2b, although an empire usually rules outlying territories less directly (in sense 1b); and both lack the bottom-up democratic directness of 1a and 1c.

Madison says that, at the very least, a government has a "republican" character (i.e., a democracy with representatives free to exercise rational discretion) only if it "derives all its powers directly or indirectly from the great body of the people" and elects its chief officers for limited periods.[55] Hamilton insists that magistrates with the greatest powers, such as taxation and war, must be directly answerable to individual voters.

Hamilton and Madison thus reach the conclusion that the federal government needs primary sovereignty by appealing to *two principles*—often implicitly. The first, which supports the direct relation condition, is a deontological requirement that political power be justified in a way that is fair to each individual. As Madison puts it, "the ultimate authority ... resides in the people alone."[56] As we saw, the cosmopolitan tradition supports this requirement that all legitimation of power must trace back to individual rational approval rather than only to group affirmation (the associative ideal). Thus the federalist and cosmopolitan traditions agree on a Democratic principle (DP) that follows ultimately from the Enlightenment principle.

Yet federalists have been clearer than cosmopolitans on the necessity of supremacy to enable some types of cooperation. This is evident in the second principle underlying their conception of sovereignty, which is so important that it needs a name: I call it the Consolidation principle (CP) because it concerns the unification of powers needed to enable a group of agents to coordinate or cooperate for their mutual benefit. CP tells us how such governing power is justified: it says, roughly, that individuals, groups, and institutions *ought* to coordinate their activities through enforceable results of decision-making processes when this is necessary for their common good—and when necessary to uphold individual rights, if we view these as distinct from common goods.

In past work, I called CP the "coordination principle." But that label may risk confusion because "coordination problems" refers to one dimension of CAPs, as we saw, whereas CP says that government power is prima facie justified when it is needed to overcome any kind of CAP that blocks crucial public goods. In this abstract form, CP does not spell out what kinds of enforcement capacities make for a "government." Robert Keohane and Joseph Nye suggest that, among "governance" processes and institutions that "guide and restrain the collective activities of a group. ... [g]overnment is the subset that acts with authority and creates formal obligations."[57]

More precisely, Hamilton's supremacy condition for sovereignty suggests that *government enforcement* is distinguished by powers to sanction offending parties that do *not* depend on the voluntary decisions of the parties being coordinated to incur new individual sanction costs each time. When the parties must reciprocally police each other through taking individual initiative to sanction each offense within their group, there is no government over them—even if they outsource powers to monitor infringements to a shared institution, as nations do with IGOs. CP applies when the CAPs causing public harms cannot be sustainably overcome by such reciprocal policing networks among parties—often because voluntary sanctioning involves further CAPs, such as chicken games: most parties wait for one or a few among them to pay the costs of acting as the "policeman" (see chapter three).

Also note that CP does not directly address "principal-agent" problems that arise when agents serving an individual or group (the "principal") act more for the agents' interests than for the principal's good. Such problems are vital in deciding how to make a government maximally responsive to the needs of the people and/or states that it is meant to serve, and thus prevent it from abusing its powers. But CP is only about the general need for government power to overcome some kinds of CAPs; it does not dictate how to avoid "slippage" in agents' priorities. The requirement to avoid excessive discoordination between a people and their government is implied by the democratic requirement in the federalists' argument, but this is compatible with more republican or populist/direct-democratic ways of making officials serve public goods.

Principal-agent issues are indirectly related to CP in two other ways. First, when such problems are serious and unavoidable with feasible NGOs, IGOs, or other civil society groups acting as agents to provide certain public goods, this may disqualify them: then, per CP, only government can reliably secure these goods.[58] Second, sometimes lower-level governing units cannot coordinate sufficiently to act as a "collective principal" to delegate authority to an agent.[59] This is another reason why inter-state or reciprocal solutions may fail. Then CP calls for a new level of government to corral the lower units, rather than merely serving as their agent (as an IGO or treaty organization does). In other words, CP applies precisely when a mere agent with revocable power is not enough to secure the collective good of parties retaining discretion over such an agent's plans.

Still, CP will not entail the need for a supreme power with direct control to provide all goods. In the American case, Hamilton did not take his version of CP to imply that *all* state powers must be consolidated at the federal level; most could remain at the lower levels. But *to fail* "to confer in each case [i.e. on each level of government] a degree of power commensurate to the end" or to the relevant public goods "would be to violate the most obvious rules of prudence and propriety."[60] It is sheer folly to trust our national interests to a government too weak to secure them.[61] The ideas of subsidiarity and consolidation of decision-making power are stated together here: for Hamilton, *both* follow obviously from the more general imperative that "the means ought to be proportioned to the end" or that "every power ought to be commensurate with its object."[62]

Thus CP is a political specification of the fundamental principle that Kant called the Hypothetical Imperative (HI), as distinct from his Categorical Imperative (CI) or substantive moral requirement of universalizability. Kant held that these principles together were constitutive of practical reason, although HI is more obvious[63] (Hobbes and his followers endorse HI but not CI). Of course, dangers come with new powers. But, as John Marshall argued in defending the new constitution proposed by the 1787 convention, it is foolish to make the governing power *less* than adequate to its ends based on speculative fears that such power might be abused. Since *any* power wielded by human persons can be misused, this objection could only be satisfied by the complete absence of any government, which is clearly absurd.[64] Similarly, Hamilton argued that no limitations will be enough if we "imagine an endless train of possible dangers;" every form of government, including the state governments, depends on some virtue in its officers.[65] The design challenge is to include checks and motives that keep the officials/agents responsive to the goods that their principals' need without reducing their powers below what is required to overcome the relevant CAPs. Respondents to the federalists argued for limits protecting individual liberties, which quickly led to the Bill of Rights by late 1791. But they could hardly gainsay Hamilton's main point that the young nation needed a real federal authority with stronger legislative and executive power.

These two principles in the federalist argument are related, because in practice, fulfilling either DP or CP depends partly on fulfilling the other (as Sinclair indicated in discussing Cosmopolitanism: see chapter two). While success sometimes requires consolidation of separate decision-making powers into a *unified* supreme agency that directly addresses each party, this unified authority is legitimate only if it merits the parties' rational consent based on its effectiveness and fairness in its decision-making and enforcement processes. Perceived legitimacy will make a governing authority more effective, but coordinative power depends on other factors too. Similarly, some level of effectiveness is necessary but not sufficient for a government's legitimacy.

With these two principles, we are now in a position to reconstruct the federalist argument in a sufficiently general form that it can also apply to the global level. If its premises can be defended when applied to present-day issues, this form of argument will entail a league of democracies as the solution to today's most pressing global problems.

Federalism, subsidiarity, and the consolidation argument

CP is a fairly conservative principle. It recognizes that some CAPs can only be overcome, and public goods adequately provided, with stable government support—by such methods as subsidies, shared legal standards, or executive mandates. So government ought to be established with such powers at the level (or range over which its acts have force) that is necessary to secure vital public goods that cannot be adequately provided by more informal means, such as private charity, voluntary civic organizations, or free markets. Understood this way, CP accommodates concern for liberties by implying limited government: sovereign authorities should not have powers in excess of what they need to do their proper job, which is to ensure at least the most important public goods (see chapter three). Powers in excess of this would limit individual freedoms to no legitimate end, thereby encouraging corruption. On the other hand, government should not have *less* power than is needed for this vital purpose, or some public goods will be missing or insecure at best. This is the other side of the coin that is forgotten when libertarian ideology claims more for markets, networks, and nonprofit organizations than they can ever provide.

The Consolidation argument

On the basis of CP and DP, the *Federalist Papers* build the paradigm argument entailing higher levels of government with primary sovereignty over matters that must be controlled to secure public goods that lower levels of government cannot provide—because either their laws and policies do not reach a broad enough range of parties, or they cannot sufficiently influence the relevant parties' motives. When Hamilton's central argument is generalized this way to apply to all levels, I call it the *Consolidation argument*. This label refers to a *form* of argument instantiated by particular consolidation arguments for particular governments. The *Federalist* authors, for example, were offering a consolidation argument for an American national government. Here is a first approximation to the general form, with refinements to come:

The Consolidation argument

1 There are various important public goods G1, G2, G3 ... that cannot be achieved in a stable or reliable way without coordination through law or policy backed by supreme enforcement power at a new level L that is higher than extant levels of government (if any). {premise}
2 The Consolidation principle, as part of instrumental reason. {premise}
3 There is strong prima facie reason to establish government at level L with the enumerated powers that are necessary and sufficient to secure public goods G1, G2, G3.... {from 1 and 2 by *modus ponens*}
4 The Democratic principle of legitimacy. {premise, to be further spelled out}
5 There is strong prima facie reason to make the new government at L democratically answerable to all the people who will be its members—which include all citizens of extant governments (if any) at level(s) lower than L that will be consolidated within L. {from 3 and 4 by *modus ponens*}

Thus each argument in this form fills in the first premise with a list of public goods that cannot be secured by sovereign powers that are presently distributed among independent persons or extant governments.

To make this argument-form valid, obviously we have to state CP and DP as if-then claims (conditional propositions). For example,

CP: *if* there are important public goods G that can only be achieved by coordination through law, policy, or cooperation organized through government enforcement powers at level L, *then* there are strong prima facie reasons to give to governing institutions at L primary sovereignty, including powers that are necessary and sufficient to control matters that have to be governed at L in order to secure G.

Likewise, DP holds that government can be legitimate only if citizens autonomously consent to its main powers and procedures. While DP is supported by arguments for democratic rights, more than 200 years after Hamilton anticipated it, CP is now supported by game theory, which indicates what is required to overcome CAPs. CP simply incorporates these insights into Kant's HI. So CP should not be controversial, and the public goods listed in instances of premise [1] are also based partly on the findings of game theory and empirical economics, along with the ethical importance of some goods. The conclusion that follows from these premises is doubly normative: it not only says that *a new government ought to be created* to exercise primary sovereignty over the matters it has to control at L to secure the listed public goods, but also that this government should directly unite the natural authority of *a new people* formed from the individual members of prior political units being consolidated—the correlate of government at L.

Actually, the Consolidation argument in its most general form does not assume that there are any pre-existing institutions with governing powers. In its maximally general form, the Consolidation argument includes Hobbes's consolidation argument for a government at the *first level* above persons in a "state of nature," although Hobbes ignored the democratic requirement (in fact, Hobbes presupposed small fiefdoms: he was really trying to justify a strong national government in opposition to feuding nobles loosely confederated within a weak kingdom).

More clearly than Hobbes, the American federalists also considered possible costs of federal union. The "prima facie" clause in CP is there to recognize that the need for weighty public goods is not a *decisive* reason by itself to justify unifying within government at L the powers needed to secure these goods—powers presently left to the discretion of individuals or to lower levels of government. That is because several kinds of objection to consolidation are possible, such as:

i   independent moral reasons against such a new government in this time and place, or against the only means available to create it, even if it is necessary for achieving the stated public goods;

ii costs in money, time, labor, or human sacrifice that would be needed for government at L to coordinate the relevant public goods, which might outweigh the values of these public goods;

iii other public harms that establishment of this new level of government could cause as side effects, e.g. by contributing to new CAPs or hampering provision of other private or public goods not listed in premise [1].

To what extent government at L can be designed to mitigate principal-agent problems is relevant to such worries. So ideally, we get a sufficient reason to consolidate power in a new government only if all such concerns can be adequately allayed. That does not mean that CP is a utilitarian principle. Although the end (securing public goods) is essential to justifying the primary means (a new government), this may not be a matter of *maximizing* utility provided by private and public goods for all residents. Nonconsequentialist moral theorists can reject any simple utility measure for comparing certain public goods against other costs of government necessary to secure these goods. Or they may regard some public goods as strict obligations that cannot be outweighed by aggregate costs and benefits across different people (at least barring extreme disasters). Moreover, some of the public goods themselves may concern equity among different groups or individuals.

Thus consolidation arguments should address a variety of instrumental and moral considerations against the proposed new level of government, and the Consolidation argument form is compatible with a variety of ethical perspectives on the weight that such considerations should have. However, as a principle for transferring sovereign authority between levels (from natural individuals at L0 to first-level governments at L1 and to federations of these at L2, etc.), CP does imply that when objections of types (i), (ii), or (iii) are absent, weak, or avoidable with smart institutional design, then government at L should be established. This is the further step needed to get beyond the prima facie caveat in CP:

[6] There are no sufficient reasons against government at L: government at L can be structured such that its costs and problems that it causes will be outweighed by the benefits of the public goods that require government at L (in a comparison that may be holistic rather than utility-summing).

Obviously, this step [6] adds a major burden to the argument, which is crucial at the global level: to justify this step will require showing that a proposed global government need not bring undue perils with it. I take up this issue for global consolidation in chapters five and six.

The burdens introduced by step [6] will be met partly through evidence for projected effects that are subject to uncertainties. Still, the breakdown of these steps helps us understand all the considerations that are relevant for so momentous a collective decision as establishing a new level of government. Effective governmental processes are valuable because they constitute a kind of *second-order* public good: systems such as executive orders, majority rule in legislatures, and impartial judicial panels solve CAPs that prevent various first-order public goods from being realized. This is why tradition has recognized just and effective government as a priceless treasure. By contrast, the lack of such institutional capital at any level where it is needed is a disaster of an especially fundamental kind, which must usually be remedied before other problems can be fixed with solutions that get to their roots.

As noted, the first premise of the Consolidation argument also requires evidence that the listed public goods cannot be coordinated through voluntary *civil society* means, such as clubs, NGOs, traditional norms, and informal policing among participants—in short, network approaches. While we lack precise criteria for public harms that are amenable to network solutions (see chapter three),[66] informal expectations and reciprocity clearly work better among smaller networks of individuals who know each other than between millions of people in different states. For example, public condemnation for not following the dictates of the Congress of Confederation was not enough to get the 13 states to contribute their share to national goods, such as a stable federal military and uniform tariff policy. Similarly, scolding nations that do not contribute their fair share of money and peacekeepers to UN operations does little, and shaming the worst rogue regimes often fails to deter them.

Consider in this light the UN's current dependence on wealthy nations for its financing, which makes the UN subject to the lobbying power of elites and the interests of nations that provide significant money and peacekeeping forces. Mark Malloch-Brown, who served as chief of staff to Kofi Annan, notes that everything depends on funding, which makes the UN (like charities) very donor-driven. For example, big donors demand frequent restructuring of the UN's internal bureaucracies, which has often interfered with its ability to address the cascade of crises coming to UN officials for response.[67] Powerful member states can also demand alterations in UN reports or statements. In one recent and scandalous case,

> The United Nations caved in to intense pressure from Saudi Arabia, including the threat of a fatwa, and removed the Kingdom

from a list of countries accused of serious crimes against children, diplomatic sources have revealed. Riyadh is said to have threatened to cut millions of dollars for UN aid programs after it was condemned for its bombing campaign in Yemen.[68]

Amnesty International rightly accused the UN of shameful pandering to the Saudis in this instance, which shows that donor nations can even threaten UN officials personally without suffering any adverse consequences. Such distortions erode the UN's perceived legitimacy: the gridlock between the big UN contributor countries and the rest of the member nations is a core dysfunction that arises from overreliance on networks of donors.[69] I return to prospects for UN reform in the final chapter.

Public rationale, enumeration, and subsidiarity

Federalist proponents of CP also held that unification of powers in higher levels of government is not valuable for its own sake, for symbolic glory, for private gain, or (more controversially) simply to increase sources of (subjective) happiness among people. In this, they follow the broadly republican tradition in political philosophy: the main reasons for establishing any government are the public goods that cannot be realized without it—and especially those with some kind of objective value, such as liberties, security, and the development of distinctively human capabilities. This is roughly the *converse* of CP: if there are no significant public goods recognized by rational members of society that require coordination via sovereign enforcement powers at L, then there are no prima facie reasons for establishing government at L. Let us call this the Public Rationale principle (PR). It might look like an inherently liberal norm requiring minimal government, but it is compatible with communitarian conceptions asserting that some public goods with intrinsic values are only achievable through strong communal ties or group identities. More libertarian conceptions of justified government emerge only if we combine the PR with a less inclusive economic conception of public goods (see chapter three).

Conjoining CP with its converse PR implies the more familiar Principle of Enumeration (PE): the powers granted to any new level L of government, or the matters over which it exercises primary sovereignty, should include *all and only* those powers that are necessary to coordinate parties across L in ways needed to achieve important public goods (or to overcome CAPs that cause public harms). Powers not explicitly granted to government at L on this basis are not consolidated, and thus by implication are retained at lower levels of government, or left to individual decision-making. In American history, this idea is expressed in the Tenth Amendment, which sought to prevent excessive federal authority.[70] Successive application of PE to each level, from the autonomy of every individual to the highest order of government, implies that each matter or issue should be left to decisions at the lowest level possible, consistent with the coordination necessary for adequate provision of vital public goods. This is a simple (instrumental) version of the Principle of Subsidiarity (SB). Hence, CP and PR underlie and explain this familiar idea in natural law: subsidiarity and consolidation are *two sides of the same model of justified sovereignty*.[71] These points provide further support for CP by reflective equilibrium for anyone who already finds SB plausible.

In fact, the traditional conception of SB is a little richer, because it builds in the cosmopolitan idea that legitimate authority to make decisions begins with the individual. As Gregory Beabout puts it, "[e]ach person is endowed with the ability to act with initiative and industry, to make intelligent self-determining choices ordered to the common good."[72] This implies that it would violate individual autonomy to coerce people regarding decisions that they can normally make without endangering common goods. Similarly, it would be wrong for higher levels of government to swamp or crowd out lower levels of collective action, whether undertaken through local government, clubs, or volunteer groups, when these can coordinate actors sufficiently to achieve the relevant common goods. Thus the need for a consolidation argument to show that public goods justifying a new level of government cannot instead be adequately provided by a network or intergovernmental-confederal approach.

However, this conception of SB implicitly depends on DP, because it addresses the sources of rightful authority to make decisions. It is heuristically clearer in constructing a consolidation argument to keep such normative principles concerning autonomy and legitimacy distinct from the instrumental principles concerned with the types and levels of powers needed to coordinate public goods.

When government at one level leaves direct sovereign authority over significant areas of public life and responsibility for public goods in those areas to lower levels of government, we have a "federal" relation between these levels. Such lower levels do not merely derive their authority from a higher level of government, as an administrative bureau does; they retain direct sovereignty over all matters not consolidated in government at the federal level or left to individual self-determination. Thus arguments for robust local government

based on SB and arguments for consolidation at a federal level of government are expressions of the same underlying principles. Still, the
higher-level authorities must also have final say over the division of
labor between the levels, as US federal courts do today: that is part of
federal supremacy.

Thus federal unification is distinct from forming a standard treaty
organization, which derives all its authority from the treaty-makers
as collective entities; its powers will also depend on their continual
consent, as we saw. This was the crucial difference to which James
Madison referred in explaining that the new American constitution
would create "a government established ... by the people at large" as
opposed to a confederation serving only at the pleasure of state governments.[73] In practice, however, federal governments almost always
emerge from weaker leagues or alliances that lack such consolidated
primary sovereignty. This was true in Switzerland, one of the oldest
federations, and also in the Netherlands, which the American founders often had in mind. The same holds for the EU, which illustrates the
lessons derived from the federalist argument. Even though the EU is
one of the strongest treaty organizations ever created, its confederal
aspects still prevent it from solving harmful CAPs, as the next section
argues.

Cautionary lessons for the European Union

After World War II, while NATO provided security, economic cooperation to foster rebuilding and renewal was facilitated through the
European Economic Community. This free trade partnership grew
into a league with deeper and more pervasive forms of cooperation
when it became the EU under the Maastricht Treaty. It moved closer
to a federation with some direct relation to Europeans and a few consolidated powers when it introduced direct election of the European
Parliament and gave EU judges limited authority over member states.
The Schengen agreement on open borders between several European
nations, the monetary union of the Euro across much of the EU, and
the Lisbon Treaty establishing some centralized foreign policy, brought
many European nations into closer relations. As Weiss says, "The
European Union ... has a greater degree of central authority than any
other intergovernmental body."[74] It is far stronger than the Organization
of American States (OAS) or Association of Southeast Asian Nations
(ASEAN), and much broader in functions than NATO. The EU's
governing bodies also enjoy more centralized powers than the US
Confederation had. Yet the EU's remaining flaws have been on glaring

display in recent years, and they should remind us of the problems with the old American Articles.

The free movement of peoples is often a feature of confederations; Europe's 25-nation Schengen area is a good example. But influxes from outside that confederation are a different matter. Revolutionary-era America faced only small numbers of European arrivals, although the forcible importing of African slaves angered northern states, and the new constitution banned it after 1808. Even during this period of relatively stable demographics, xenophobic attitudes prevented the Confederation Congress from formalizing terms for legal immigration and the naturalization of new citizens.[75] Without the stronger central government created by the federalists, the new country would have been pulled apart by fury against later waves of immigrants, such as Germans, Irish, and Scandinavians, and by disagreements over new territories that became home to many immigrants. In the 1850s, beyond the divisions over slavery expansion, a major political party was formed primarily to oppose new immigrants.

In short, large immigrant influxes tend to generate more animosity than a weak confederation can manage. That is exactly what has happened to the EU. Since 2013, the EU has faced a flood of migrants from Syria, Iraq, Iran, Afghanistan, and sub-Saharan Africa, about half of whom might qualify as economic migrants rather than refugees. These migrations are spillover effects from the mass atrocities in Syria and Iraq, the disorder left in Libya, continuing chaos caused by the Taliban in Afghanistan, dangers from jihadi fundamentalist groups in Nigeria, Chad, and Somalia, and civil strife, extreme poverty and oppression across the African Sahel.

The EU lacked the power to coordinate any unified effort sufficient to these challenges. For example, it never tried to take control of the shores of Libya, or stop Assad's mass slaughter in Syria, or pressure Eritrea to end universal conscription, or create a Marshall Plan for Nigeria and the Sahel. Instead, when the EU tried to arrange a fair internal distribution of the refugees, a game of chicken developed with the least receptive nations pushing the burden onto the more receptive, such as Germany and Sweden. A Pew Research Center study found that Germany received 45 percent of all the asylum seekers entering Europe during 2015–2016.[76] Nations on the frontiers, such as Italy and Greece, also received massively disproportionate shares of the burden because of their first-mover disadvantage in this situation. The resulting distributive equity problem generated deep resentments between EU nations. There has also been significant anger at influxes of workers from new EU member nations with lower average incomes, such as Bulgaria; but the main driver of animosities is uninvited migration into the EU.

Disinformation campaigns aided by Moscow and racism add to the problem. Racist parties such as the National Front and skinhead neo-fascist movements used to subsist on the dark fringes of European politics, garnering small fractions of popular votes. But they have now revived across most of Europe, and many of their party leaders are actively courted by Putin, who shores up his popularity by cultivating white nationalism and xenophobia within Russia and in eastern Europe. Worst of all, these visceral reactions proved just barely sufficient for a slim majority of British voters (some possibly influenced by foreign propaganda) to choose to leave the EU in the summer of 2016 referendum.

Brexit reveals the fundamental weakness of confederal arrangements:[77] when a member nation can unilaterally leave—even if the process is complex and difficult—it has insufficient incentive to work with other member nations to overcome the CAPs plaguing their relations. As a result, Britain has weakened the whole EU exactly when it needs greater unity to face Putin's challenges. Although Britain now faces higher transaction costs, if it benefits in the long run, it will succeed in free riding on the EU's other strengths, such as its free trade zone. This will encourage other nations to win the game of chicken by following Britain's example and opting out of most costs while continuing to enjoy much of the benefits. For example, Britain may be able to undercut the whole EU in trade deals with other large nations like the United States, Japan, and China. Britain can act as such a destructive spoiler only because the treaties constituting the EU provide an option for legal separation, rather than forming a "perpetual union," as in the American case. While enormous economic and cultural benefits follow from the free movements of goods and people, it is impossible to sustain these benefits across many states without the central decision and enforcement powers needed to rein in racial tensions and economic temptations to free ride.

The same holds for monetary union. The EU's problems during the recent Greek debt crisis should remind us of the ones that Hamilton and his allies sought to solve: a single currency without oversight by a government with supreme authority to set unified government spending, tax rates, and levels of borrowing leads to discoordination that can be managed only by some minority of the member states (e.g., Germany and France) calling the main shots. This dynamic amounts to what theorists call a "Rambo game" (or "suasion" game) in which asymmetries in bargaining power make smaller parties dependent on one (or a few) leading parties.[78] This can cause divisive resentments over perceived bullying by the "Rambo" player. It also generates a deficit in democratic legitimacy: the people of Greece and Spain did not elect Angela Merkel, the Chancellor of Germany, who took the lead for the EU in negotiating austerity from successive Greek governments.

The roots of these problems lie in the structure of the European Council. The EU Council, consisting of heads of state along with the (non-voting) President of the European Commission and the EU foreign affairs chief, still requires *unanimous consent* for measures on tax consistency, EU finances, foreign policy and common defense, accession of new EU member nations, and harmonization of law on social security, welfare, and family policies.[79] While these last three topics were mainly left to states in the US constitution, the others are exactly the issues that the federal government most needs to control, according to Hamilton, Madison, and Jay. But, among procedures compatible with DP, *simple majority* votes that bind all members have the most coordinative power, while unanimity has the least.

The EU Council votes by "qualified majority" on other topics; under the Lisbon rules, this now requires 55 percent of EU nations representing at least 65 percent of the EU population when the proposal has been approved by the EU Commission (which votes by simple majority with each member state having equal weight, as in the US Senate). If the proposal does not come from the Commission or the High Representative on foreign affairs, it requires 72 percent of EU countries and 65 percent of the population for Council approval.

Moreover, as in the American confederation, such decisions are not always followed. A "European Agenda for Migration" was adopted by qualified majority in September 2015, but the resulting order to relocate 120,000 asylum applicants from Italy and Greece to the other EU nations was widely boycotted. Twenty-one months later, only *2 percent* of these migrants had been relocated while their applications were still pending, and four nations appealed to the European Court of Justice to block the order[80] (a case they ultimately lost in June 2017). In the interim, 1,204,280 asylum applications were filed in the EU during 2016, almost as many as in 2015, with 335,160 coming just from Syria. While the EU is stronger than other confederations in history, its powers to enforce decisions on member nations are still quite limited, as this debacle shows. By December 2017, Germany, Italy, and Greece still hosted grossly disproportionate shares of the roughly four million asylum seekers who came to Europe between 2013 and 2017.[81]

These examples suggest that the EU's decision-making and enforcement mechanisms are not sufficient to overcome certain serious CAPs between its member nations. Hence, CP calls for stronger powers to enforce coordination than the EU presently has. Thus Amanda Taub was exactly right in her analysis that the fundamental problem that gives the EU such bad appearances to many Europeans "is not that the European Union is too strong but that it is too weak." It is united enough to create zones for the free movement of labor and a shared currency, but not sufficiently united to manage those zones effectively.[82] The isolationist solution, namely devolving more powers from the EU to national governments, only makes the relevant CAPs harder to overcome. It is like the old medieval therapy of bleeding a patient already weakened by illness. A federalist diagnosis suggests instead that EU should restructure according to CP and DP, strengthening its coordinative powers and democratic legitimacy, which would bring it closer to a federation with more consolidated authority.

Conclusion

The EU's inability to enforce a coordinated response to the migrant crisis and sovereign debt problems has illustrated the contemporary relevance of American federalist themes. The central argument of the *Federalist Papers* turns on the idea that some public goods may require a higher level of government than presently exists. While some CAPs between states may be mitigated by network solutions, both early American experiences and more recent cases suggest that treaty organizations and confederations with only derivative and revocable powers will not be adequate to overcome many other CAPs that cause serious public harms. We will consider further examples supporting this point in the next two chapters.

Contrary to the current tide, then, the insights of classical federalists are now more important than ever: they need to be explained to wider audiences using all the tools of contemporary social science. Building on the elementary game theory surveyed in this chapter, the next chapter will argue for an expanded conception of public goods, and consider the range of public goods that may now require transnational or global coordination. This will support the first premise in a global analog of Hamilton's consolidation argument.

Notes

1. Peter Singer, *One World*, 2nd ed. (New Haven, Conn: Yale University Press, 2004), 5, citing Kofi Annan, "Two Concepts of Sovereignty," *The Economist* 18 (September 1999).

2. See Thomas G. Weiss, *Global Governance* (Malden, Mass: Polity Press, 2013), esp. ch. 3.
3. Ibid., 20–26.
4. Beck, *Cosmopolitan Vision*, tr. Ciaran Cronin (Malden, Mass: Polity Press, 2006), 44.
5. Emer de Vattel, *The Law of Nations [Le Droit de Gens*, 1758], tr. Thomas Nugent (Indianapolis: Liberty Fund, 2008), Book I, ch. 4, § 53, 289.
6. Immanuel Kant, "Idea for a Universal History with a Cosmopolitan Intent," in *Perpetual Peace and Other Essays*, tr. Ted Humphrey (Indianapolis: Hackett Publishing, 1983), Fifth Thesis, 33 (Ak. 22).
7. Ibid., Sixth Thesis, 33–34 (Ak. 23).
8. Ibid., Seventh Thesis, 34 (Ak. 24).
9. Ibid., 36 (Ak. 26).
10. Immanuel Kant, "To Perpetual Peace: A Philosophical Sketch," in Kant, *Perpetual Peace and Other Essays*, 107–43, Appendix §I, 127–8 (Ak. 371).
11. Ibid., Appendix §II, 138 (Ak. 385).
12. Thus "individual utility maximization" is "non-tuitive": see David Gauthier, *Morals by Agreement* (Oxford, UK: Oxford University Press, 1986, 1988 pb), 61, and 72.
13. Ibid., 83. Similar results follow if we use the Kaldor standard of optimality instead.
14. Ken Binmore, *Game Theory* (New York: Oxford University Press, 2007), 65.
15. Ibid., 17.
16. See Richard McAdams, "Beyond the Prisoner's Dilemma: Coordination, Game Theory, and Law," *Southern California Law Review* 82 (2008–2009): 209–60, 212.
17. Such issues are often called "bargaining" problems and not included among causes of CAPs. However, that label suggests that strategic bargaining is the solution, while fairness considerations are more essential. I agree with Holzinger that distributive issues should be classified as a distinct cause of CAPs because they may prevent parties from reaching any P-optimal outcome: see Katarina Holzinger, *Transnational Public Goods* (New York: Palgrave Macmillan, 2008), 55–56.
18. Ibid., 54.
19. Thomas A. Bailey and David M. Kennedy, *The American Pageant*, 7th ed. (Boston: D.C. Heath and Co., 1983), 123.
20. William Hogeland, *Declaration* (New York: Simon & Schuster, 2010).
21. Catherine Drinker Bowen, *Miracle at Philadelphia* (Boston: Little, Brown, and Co., 1966), 6.
22. Joseph Ellis, *The Quartet: Orchestrating the Second American Revolution, 1783–1789* (New York: Vintage/Penguin Random House, 2015), 17.
23. Or this situation might constitute a BF, because it involves asymmetries between the parties' contributions and payoffs.
24. Ellis, *Quartet*, 5.
25. Ibid., 33–34.
26. Bowen, *Miracle at Philadelphia*, 5.
27. See *The Articles of Confederation and Perpetual Union*, Article XIII and Article IX,§6 respectively.
28. Ellis, *The Quartet*, 6.

29. Ibid., 34.
30. See Emily J. Teipe, *America's First Veterans and the Revolutionary War Pensions* (Lewiston, NY: Edwin Mellen Press, 2002).
31. Ellis, *The Quartet*, 34.
32. Bailey and Kennedy, *The American Pageant*, 127.
33. Bowen, *Miracle at Philadelphia*, 9.
34. See Hamilton's "Letter to James Duane" of 3 September 1780, reprinted in L.U. Reavis, *Alexander Hamilton and the American Republic* (St. Louis, MO: G.A. Pierrot & Sons, 1886): 74–85, 74.
35. Ibid., 75.
36. Ibid., 76–79.
37. See Ellis, *The Quartet*, ch. 4. esp. 107–10.
38. For example, see Thomas Hobbes, *Man and Citizen [De Homine* and *De Cive*], ed. Bernard Gert (Indianapolis, Ind: Hackett Publishing, 1991), *The Citizen*, Letter of Dedication, 93. Compare *The Citizen*, Book II ¶ 2, 123.
39. See Hobbes, *Leviathan* [1651], ed. C.B. Macpherson (New York: Penguin, 1981), Part I, ch. 14.
40. Alexander Hamilton, James Madison, John Jay, *The Federalist Papers*, ed. Clinton Rossiter (New York: New American Library of Penguin Books, 1961), No. 2 [Jay], 39.
41. Ibid., No. 3, 42–44.
42. Ibid., No. 4, 48.
43. Ibid., No. 4, 49.
44. Ibid., No. 6 [Hamilton], 54. Yunker notes the global relevance of this point in "Beyond Global Governance," *International Journal on World Peace*, 26 (June 2009): 7–30.
45. Ibid., No. 6 [Hamilton], 59.
46. Ibid., No. 7, 60–61.
47. Ibid., 111–12. Also see No. 46 [Madison], 298.
48. Bowen, *Miracle at Philadelphia*, 5.
49. Rossiter, ed., *The Federalist Papers*, No. 15, 108. Compare No. 23, 154.
50. Ibid., No. 15 [Hamilton], 109
51. Ibid., No. 16 [Hamilton], 116.
52. Ibid.
53. Timothy Sinclair, *Global Governance* (Malden, Mass: Polity Press, 2012), 28.
54. James A. Yunker, *The Idea of World Government* (New York: Routledge, 2011), 44.
55. Rossiter, ed., *The Federalist Papers*, No. 39 [Madison], 241. For the distinction between republican and direct (or "populist") democracy, see Philip Pettit, *Republicanism* (Oxford UK: Oxford University Press, 1993, 2010 repr), 8.
56. Ibid., No. 46 [Madison], 294.
57. Robert Keohane and Joseph Nye, Jr., "Governance in a Globalizing World," in *Power and Governance in a Partially Globalized World*, ed. Robert Keohane (New York: Routledge, 2002), 193–218, 202.
58. For example, see Duncan Snidal and Henning Tamm, "Rational Choice: From Principal-Agent to Orchestration Theory," in *International Organization and Global Governance*, 2nd ed., ed. Thomas G. Weiss and Rorden

Wilkinson (New York: Routledge, 2018), 135–45. As they note, NGOs often operate "in a context of organizational insecurity" that motivates actions serving their survival even when this does not help the principals (141). By contrast, the central institutions of any government are secure (although its administrative bureaus may alter).

59. Ibid., 140. In extreme cases, the parties may not even be able to articulate their separate and joint interests well without the higher authority acting as trustee.
60. Rossiter, ed., *The Federalist Papers*, No. 23, 155.
61. Ibid., 156–57.
62. Ibid., No. 31, 193.
63. See Christine Korsgaard's influential arguments that the authority of HI is a constitutive condition of a rational will, e.g., in Korsgaard, *Self-Constitution* (New York: Oxford University Press, 2008), 46–47.
64. John Marshall, "Address to the Virginia Ratification Convention," in Lewis Copeland and Lawrence W. Lamb, eds., *World's Great Speeches*, 3rd ed. (New York: Dover Publications, 1973), 242.
65. Rossiter, ed., *The Federalist Papers*, No. 31, 196.
66. The final section of chapter three briefly addresses this topic. I make an attempt at criteria for networkable goods in "Environmental Public Goods not Securable by Markets or Networks," *International Journal of Technoethics* 9 no. 2 (2018), 26–41.
67. Mark Malloch-Brown, *The Unfinished Global Revolution: The Road to International Cooperation* (New York: Penguin, 2011), 181.
68. Bel Trew, "Saudi Threat of Fatwa Made UN Change Child Death Report," *The Times of Australia*, 9 June 2016.
69. Malloch-Brown, *The Unfinished Global Revolution*, 191.
70. It is perhaps ironic that PE follows naturally from Hamilton's premises, as my reconstruction of his logic shows, given the tendency to mischaracterize him as wanting absolute centralized power.
71. In logical form, (CP & PR) ⇒ PE, and PE entails SB through recursion.
72. Gregory Beabout, "Challenges to Using the Principle of Subsidiarity for Environmental Policy," *University of St. Thomas Law Journal* 5, no. 1 (2008): 210–33, esp. 222.
73. James Madison, "Address to the Ratification Convention of Virginia," 238.
74. Thomas G. Weiss, *Governing the World?* (New York: Routledge, 2014), 69.
75. The first federal government under the new constitution passed an act in 1790 limiting legal immigration to "free white persons."
76. Jon Henley, "More Than a Million of Europe's Asylum Seekers Left in Limbo," *The Guardian*, 20 September 2017, www.theguardian.com/world/2017/sep/20/more-than-a-million-of-europes-asylum-seekers-left-in-limbo.
77. It also illustrates why constitutional fundamentals should not be changeable by 51% margins in plebiscites.
78. See Holzinger, *Transnational Common Goods*, 166; and Andreas Hasenclever, Peter Mayer, and Volker Rittberger, *Theories of International Regimes* (Cambridge, UK: Cambridge University Press, 1997), 51. Smaller or seemingly weaker parties may also hold the upper hand in some Rambo games (e.g., when they have less to gain or lose).

79 See the pages on the European Council, europa.eu/european-union/about-eu/institutions-bodies/european council en, and the explanation of the unanimity requirement at http://www.consilium.europa.eu/en/council-eu/voting-system/unanimity/.

80. Barbara Oomen and Ricardo Rodrigues de Oliveira, "Relocation and Its Numbers," 31 May 2017, eumigrationlawblog.eu/2017/05/.

81. See Eurostat, *Asylum Statistics*, http://ec.europa.eu/eurostat/statistics-explained/index.php/Asylum_statistics.

82. Amanda Taub, "The European Union is Democratic, but It May Not Feel That Way," *New York Times*, 30 June 2016, A1 and A6.

3 Market limits and global public goods

- Economic public goods and eight causes of market failures
- Eight categories of transnational and global public goods
- Conclusion: "Government-apt" GPGs

The previous chapter laid out the general form of the Consolidation argument for any level of government and illustrated its logic with examples from the early American confederation and the EU today. This form of argument, reconstructed from the *Federalist Papers*, implies that the robustness of any level of government should be a function of the public goods that cannot be adequately secured without it. Combining this idea with the cosmopolitan framework outlined in chapter one gives us a global version of the consolidation argument that would begin with these three steps:

1 There are vital public goods G1, G2, … G*n* that cannot be reliably secured without coordination through law and government enforcement at the *global level* {a largely empirical premise}
2 The Consolidation principle (CP) {conceptual premise}
3 There is strong prima facie reason to establish government at the global level as a means to the public goods G1, G2, … G*n* {from 1 and 2 by *modus ponens*}

This chapter and the next fill out the first premise of a global consolidation argument by identifying the public goods that require transnational coordination, including global public goods (GPGs) that cosmopolitans should recognize. We might think of premise [1] as conjoining of the conclusions of several subarguments for various GPGs, each with roughly the following form:

1a   G1 is a good either because it is desired by many or all relevant parties [an empirical subjective value premise] or because it has significant objective value [a normative premise].

1b   G1 is a GPG: it cannot be adequately produced through free markets because of market failures and related CAPs between several nations or peoples in all regions.

1c   G1 is also unlikely to be optimally secured by global network actors, given the limits of their enforcement powers and capacities to coordinate the parties involved in the CAPs affecting G1.

1d   Therefore, G1 can only be optimally secured by government enforcement powers with global reach that can overcome the CAPs blocking G1.

As we repeat this argument for other goods G2, G3 … G*n*, the basis for a global level of government becomes stronger. Thus cosmopolitans should be interested in the full range of potential GPGs, and especially those that might exceed the reach of network solutions.

While a full analysis of every major GPG is well beyond the scope of this book, this chapter briefly outlines the standard economic approach to public goods and two important extensions of it. Then it compiles a tentative list of GPGs that are important for justice and well-being around the world today by drawing from the UN's Sustainable Development Goals (SDGs), other recent accounts of GPGs, and further normative and structural considerations. The final section considers evidence that some GPGs are not amenable to network solutions. The next chapter continues this argument with detailed consideration of international security GPGs.

Economic public goods and eight causes of market failures

As Todd Sandler notes, Adam Smith and his followers in neoclassical economics recognized the need for government to organize public goods "in just four areas: defense, a justice system, education, and infrastructure," including basic utilities needed for markets and private exchange to work.[1] This was based on a standard economic account of public goods that cannot be provided well by free market processes—usually because the nature of the good in itself, or its features combined with prevailing social conditions, generates one or more types of CAP. For example, basic infrastructure involves a natural monopoly because a transport, communications, or computer operating system becomes more valuable to each user the more people use it (up to some point where crowding sets in). Such goods are "nonrival" in the economist's sense, i.e., one person's using them does not reduce the value of that good for other potential users. In fact, these goods are *anti-rival*, because they involve a positive "network externality"—each user benefits other users by being on the same network or system.[2]

On this standard economic account, public goods are naturally "nonexcludable" or easily accessible by nonpayers, and/or "nonrival." In free market contexts, typically "[n]onexcludability will result in too little of the good being supplied owing to free riding" by those who pay nothing (or less than the marginal unit cost) of the good, "while nonrivalry means that exclusion, if feasible, will reduce social welfare by denying consumption to those whose derived benefits are less than the price."[3] In other words, when these goods are left to a free market process, the spontaneous equilibrium will be not be Pareto-optimal: the excluded potential users of a nonrival good could have enjoyed it without loss to others, and more people could have been better off if more users of nonexcludable goods paid for them. Paying users may also resent the nonpaying users of nonexcludable or nonrival goods, leading to a distributive equity problem (DEP): at some point, these payers will prefer to go without the good in order to punish those intending to free ride on them. Thus nonexcludability and nonrivalry lead to market failures because they cause various kinds of CAPs (see the taxonomy laid out in chapter two).

Both these aspects of public goods are variable features: there are several gradations from complete rivalry to partial rivalry (being subject to congestion), nonrivalry, and anti-rivalry or "complementarity," as noted; and there are several grades of partial excludability, often resulting from natural relations between of sources of the benefits and persons who enjoy them. For example, human persons have a natural ability to record information of potential instrumental or intrinsic value, but multiple people can do this without degrading the information, making it nonrival. Thus, as Inge Kaul and Ronald Mendosa explain, public goods were traditionally defined in economics by reference to "basic or original properties" of those goods that makes human consumption of them naturally noncompetitive (nonrival) and open to all.[4] In deciding on levels of government, we should focus on goods that are naturally public in this sense, rather than on goods that are only *made* nonexcludable and/or nonrival by political policy regulation, or custom that could be changed (without dramatically impeding other public goods).

There may be exceptions because basic properties of goods often lead to some level of nonexcludability or nonrivalry only in combination with aspects of the prevailing cultural or social context, which act like fixed background conditions. Moreover these conditions, such as basic contract law, may have developed to overcome other CAPs, such as inadequate assurance that business agreements will be honored. Thus basic institutional solutions to one set of CAPs may create circumstances that cause other goods to become more or less nonexcludable and/or nonrival.[5]

Investigation will require us to expand the standard economic criteria for public goods. I begin by noting that the standard three causes of market failures all concern the *demand side* or use of goods. These include:

1 *Externalities*, or links between people's satisfactions through positive or negative effects of one party's activities on others who did not choose them—effects that are "not taken into account" by market transactions.[6]

   • In economic terms, externalities include costs for which producers do not pay (offloading them onto others) or benefits for which they cannot charge (nonvoluntarily giving them for free to others).

2 A *Nonexcludable* goods (or bads),[7] which it is impractical to prevent nonpayers from enjoying (or avoiding) at will, while others may pay the costs of these goods (or of harm-avoidance). These are typically linked to externalities as follows:

   • Producers cannot charge most or all users for these goods, so some will free ride on their positive externalities.
   • When harmful effects are nonexcludable, beyond the buyers of goods connected with these negative side effects, other unwilling parties will suffer harms from them.

   B *Nonrival goods* (or bads), which are not diminished, consumed, or used up by someone's enjoying them (or suffering from them).[8]

   • Because they are nonrival, parties who have paid for such goods have an incentive to share them for free with others whom they like (because this involves no direct costs to them); as a result, some parties get such goods without paying their full value.

- Such goods may still be scarce if they are hard to produce, but it is difficult to charge all users for them: if the first hundred users each paid 100th of the cost, all later would-be users could then free ride. This generates resentment at distributive inequity.

3 *Commons*, or unowned phenomena—such as some land, forests, rivers, atmosphere, fisheries, water cycles, and other natural ecosystem services—that can serve as productive assets for users: access to these resources is not restricted by property rights.[9]

These three categories are closely related. Common pool resources (CPRs), including common property and open access commons, are problematic mainly because they become increasingly rival when aggregate usage exceeds their sustainable yields, thus degrading their productive potential.[10] Yet their relation to property rights and natural processes makes CPRs so significant that it is useful to treat them as a distinct category, together with other goods that are "provided by nature," even if they require some investment to harvest or use.[11] Similarly, external effects of people's market transactions on third parties often involve nonrivalry and nonexcludability in some aspects of a good's effects or usage that law could change. Then we face the question of whether people have a right not to suffer some negative external effect (e.g., pollution or loss of property values) or whether the baseline entitlement is the other way around, so that people ought to pay to avoid these harms.[12] Moreover, while often nonrivalry or nonexcludability come first in the order of explanation, sometimes externalities (causal links beyond voluntary transactions) can reduce excludability or rivalry. For example, when a huge bank fails and drags the market into a free fall by contagion, this negative externality spreads because that bank was too large relative to the size of its whole sector, and thus not easily replaceable.

Thus it is helpful to treat these three features as distinct sources of market failures. They all lead to opportunities for *exploiting others*, either by using something for free that others pay to make, or by foisting onto others some cost of our activities, or both. So free riding is generally not a distinct fourth kind of market failure, but rather a symptom arising from other public features of various goods. Free riding only functions like an independent factor when it creates distributive resentments that may scuttle cooperative efforts to overcome other market failures. A full solution that closes free rider loopholes then brings an additional second-order good of increased *fairness* by preventing exploitation.

As Sandler explains, all of these features (1–3) make it difficult or impossible to trade such goods efficiently in free markets which depend on incentives arising from exclusive use of an asset (or avoidance of a harm) that does not come for free. Sometimes the problem can be fixed by laws that construct new markets, e.g. through establishing property rights over things formerly held in common,[13] or creating new forms of insurance for risks that previously could not be hedged. Sometimes they require pricing various externalities into products, as in the case of regulation to make polluters pay for their pollution costs. These solutions usually require legal enforceability. But it is hard to price in all kinds of pollution, let alone all spillover effects, by law. In the worst cases, Sandler's three causes of market failure combine when somebody is able to externalize a cost by dumping harmful wastes into a commons that it is hard to protect (such as overfished high seas).

As these examples suggest, we could subdivide category (1) into major causes of externalities, which correspond to familiar types of "market failure" described in mainstream media and popular economics works.[14] For example, we already noted that a corporation that is "too big to fail" can externalize some of its risk-costs onto the public. Size-based externalities can also enable various monopoly strategies that violate perfect market conditions, leading to suboptimal results. For example, Amazon has so much market share that it can extract lower prices from suppliers and a larger cut from every transaction than a fungible middleman could. So the familiar forms of market failure turn out to involve externalities and CAPs. But rather than considering all the common types in detail, it will be enough to note five further causes market failures that are relevant to transnational goods and briefly explain each of them:

4 *Production-side interdependencies* or aggregative links between contributors, including threshold effects.
5 *Asymmetries of information* and significant unknowns, including incalculable probabilities.
6 *Rent effects* due to the rarity or unsubstitutability of a production input, especially when this scarcity is unearned.
7 *Basic institutional preconditions* of markets, including legal frameworks and social practices supporting trust.
8 *Objective goods* with an (alleged) importance or significance on bases other than subjective desires or brute preferences (so-called merit goods are a subset of these).[15]

While nonrivalry and nonexclusivity are demand-side features of goods, features on the supply side can also be illuminating. The study of "summation technologies" analyzes patterns in the ways that contributions by different parties involved with a public good determine how much of it is produced.[16] For example, a "weakest link technology" exists when even a single defector or insufficient contributor can spoil the collective good for everyone; this may encourage parties to shore up the weakest link and discourage defection. This pattern is often correlated with an assurance game (AG). By contrast, a "best-shot technology" in which the collective gain depends mainly on the "largest individualized effort" encourages most parties to wait for the best-able or best-situated party to solve the problem for everyone's benefit. In such cases, a chicken game usually results, and the "best shooter" may bear all the costs.[17] A fair resolution may require side payments by the other parties who depend on the most able contributor.

Sometimes these production-side features can reduce below optimal level the profit from providing even goods that are partly excludable and rival. For example, often a certain *threshold* must be passed for enough contributors to make benefits possible, as we saw with AG examples in chapter two. Insurance pools have to reach a certain size and composition to be viable. Many goods, such as basic research and infrastructure, require a *scale* of investment that is too great for for-profit industry to undertake on its own, given the uncertainties about possible end products. Yet viable production of many kinds depends on shared knowledge, infrastructure, and other structural goods: for example, it is hard to set up heavy industry near Goma in the Democratic Republic of Congo (DRC) until Goma has a good electric power grid.

Some of these cases involve related problems of insufficient or asymmetric information. These may have a social basis, e.g. when personal liberties or laws that pool risks allow individuals to hide relevant information from insurers, adverse selection problems occur. Information problems can also result from our natural finitude. When huge up-front investments are required, uncertainty about future benefits may make private funding unfeasible: great gains in technology would probably follow from a successful manned mission to Mars, but the results are so unpredictable that private industry cannot undertake it. Similarly, uncertainty about the safety of consumer products, or costs involved in researching them, will depress sales. A perfect market assumes (in utopian fashion) that all relevant information is equally known by all parties involved. Yet much information about products, pricing, likely returns on investments, and other relevant issues is better known to experts with the right education, or those with the right contacts (social capital). To the extent that important information is rare or privileged, it also creates a *rent effect*, which may need to be governed by normative standards.

Rent effects constitute another pervasive cause of market failures. Whenever production processes depend on scarce inputs, or talents and materials with few viable substitutes, free markets will reach a suboptimal outcome.[18] In some cases, the extra rent returns may be justified because the owner cultivated a rare talent or worked to create a new technology. But often ownership of a rare commodity, such as a natural asset, historically unusual artifact, or insider knowledge, is largely accidental or unearned. In particular, ownership of valuable natural resources often raises questions of historical justice that may cross national boundaries, and efforts to privatize shares of CPRs can be stymied by perceived distributive inequity in the baseline allocation of such scarce natural capital.[19]

Thus institutions determining property rights and patents, along with other conventions and social assurances that secure conditions for efficient free markets, are a special category of public goods. They are constituted by government rules, informal expectations, and shared practices that stabilize expectations: as Gauthier puts it, the Hobbesian war of all against all must be pacified before the invisible hand of markets can do its work.[20] While some social assurances (such as trust within close communities) can be built up by informal networks of individuals, clubs, and other civil society organizations, common expectations among millions of strangers generally require legal underpinnings, such as contract law. Markets are artificial devices that depend on laws, officers to enforce them, and common currencies; informal relations of trust develop within this matrix. National and global markets can function only when maintained by governments, as the wave of panic across global markets in late 2008 reminded us. As a result, Holzinger rightly concludes that even "the privateness of private goods is itself a public good:"[21] we decide collectively (by commission or omission) on property rights and what goods to allocate via markets—and these standards require normative bases.

Institutional preconditions of markets are thus highly relevant to consolidation arguments: they are forms of collective institutional and social capital without which even private goods cannot be left to free markets with near-optimal results. This is clearest in cases such as the economic collapse in Syria when law and order, customary expectations, stable population centers, and infrastructure were all destroyed by mass atrocities. Similarly, problems with property boundaries, reliable currency, and corruption in civil courts will quickly pull the institutional scaffolding from under market transactions. For example, lack of clear title to many lands and buildings in Greece has been an ongoing obstacle to economic recovery. At the global level, theft of patented technology, cybercrime, pirates preying on shipping, difficulties in enforcing international contracts, and the lack of a single global currency all increase transaction costs, acting like sand in the wheels of the market, reducing overall efficiency.

Finally, some goods are also rendered public by their (alleged) objective values, which transcend the consumer preferences that markets can register. Many goods that Kaul and Mendoza regard as rendered public by legal or social decisions, such as norms and standards, basic health care for all, and respect for rights, are protected from market forces largely in response to their perceived *normative* properties, such as some form of "intrinsic value."[22] For example, people may find objective importance in genetic privacy, worker safety, consumer protections, access to clean water, or the survival of endangered species and overall biodiversity—even beyond their ecosystem services to human beings. To that extent, consumer decisions will not accurately reflect judgments about the importance of such goods. As a result, free markets have no way to produce optimal amounts of them, and treating them as market commodities devalues them.[23] Quite a few transnational goods are public partly or wholly on such ethical bases. This is especially clear when they involve moral values, such as goods of justice in relations between nations.

Thus the distributive equity aspect of many CAPs is also an effect of objective values. Widely shared standards of equity and traditions about how to distribute benefits and burdens of collective endeavors are *higher-order* objective public goods, because they help overcome CAPs blocking first-order public goods by facilitating cooperation needed to secure these goods.[24] Fairness to future generations is one example: as work in environmental ethics has especially stressed, our standards must include assurance that current generations will not destroy renewable natural assets that can, if used sustainably, continue providing ecosystem services indefinitely. Fair discount rates for future gains and losses are part of the solution to this DEP. Free markets often fail to secure sustainable usage due both to CPRs and because future persons are not purchasing. Their rights to some share of the unearned bounty of the Earth have to be guaranteed by nonmarket means.

Quite a few public goods have more than one of these eight features. For example, some institutional preconditions of markets embody implicit judgments about a just division of assets. The free market requires what economists call an "initial allocation of factors" to individuals or groups; this requires standards for title or coming to own property, which involve crucial questions of justice.[75] Anger about perceived inequities in initial acquisitions and resulting property distributions create instabilities that can significantly impair market efficiency.

In conclusion, we now have a broader range of market failures and correlated public goods: these include goods that are subjectively desired by all or most persons, or that are objectively important—as part of human well-being, or for their own sake—which require coordination beyond market incentives to be optimally supplied. That can be due to any of the causes 1–8 noted above, or because they are comparative (or tuistic) goods by definition, such as relative opportunity, status, or power. Markets work amazingly well in generating a vast range of goods that add to human welfare, but they cannot produce *all* needed goods; indeed, some of the most important goods have public dimensions, and the remainder are *nested* within an institutional and social matrix constituted by public goods.

Eight categories of transnational and global public goods

Defining GPGs and common examples

As the importance of subsidiarity (SB) implies, many public goods can be supplied at local or national levels: towns can maintain sidewalks, states can stop most noise pollution, and nations can build national monuments and museums. However, it is now a truism that more public goods have come to depend on *transnational* connections (see the summary in chapter one). It becomes ever harder to think of public goods with no significant cross-border effects or supply-conditions. A substandard power grid, train line, official property registry, or highway system in one nation can affect a whole region; a bad healthcare system can lead to infectious outbreaks; even a poor education system in one nation can lead to ideological fanatics who endanger other peoples. And given levels of tourism today, institutions like the Louvre may be considered GPGs.

For the purposes of a global consolidation argument, we do not need a definitive list of GPGs; a plausible set of candidates that probably require coordination by networks or government at the global level will suffice. But we do need a clear distinction between the national, regional, or global "level" of public goods.

Two main ways of defining these levels have become common in recent accounts: they focus on requirements for supply or range of beneficiaries, respectively. For example, Holzinger focuses on the range of externalities in arguing that a public good does not need to be *universal*, naturally benefitting all peoples, nations, and generations, to count as "global" in economic and political analyses. And it certainly need not affect all sub-groups in the same way, or have equal value for all of them. Instead, a public good counts as global if

> the spatial extent of its externalities is global. The collective concerned by the good is scattered over the whole globe—even if not everybody in the world is convinced that the good is really a good. A common [i.e., public] good is transnational if its externalities reach more than one nation-state. ... Thus global common goods are a subset of transnational common goods.[26]

She lists "global warming, biodiversity, and systemic risk in banking" as GPGs, while noting that for some other goods, political decisions may be able to contract the "functional scope" of externalities from global to national ranges.[27] Sandler's definition is similar, focusing on national, regional, and global spillover effects.[28]

For a consolidation argument, however, the most relevant sense concerns the range of agents that must be coordinated to *supply* optimal levels of the public good. TPGs then subdivide into regional goods, inter-regional goods (depending on coordination between select nations in two or more regions), and GPGs that require coordination among (parties within) many nations in all regions. Still, cross-border externalities in the use of goods can also affect supply incentives. Thus, to generate a list of GPGs, we should look for recognized goods that are (according to empirical evidence) subject to market failures and CAPs that only coordination of actors within nations on every continent (if not all nations) can solve.

Usually the implications of this definition will align with the range of spillovers, because most nations significantly affected by a public harm will either need to participate in its amelioration, or want some say over the solutions. Thus in the 2006 report of the International Task Force on Global Public Goods (convened by France and Sweden), both criteria are mentioned:

> The sphere of public goods ... is delineated by issues that are broadly conceived as important to the international community, that for the most part cannot or will not be adequately addressed by individual countries acting alone. ... Global public goods are those whose benefits could in principle be consumed [or enjoyed] by the governments and peoples of all states.[29]

They also mention free rider problems resulting from nonrivalry and nonexcludability, as well as supply aggregation issues. This is slightly more demanding than the definition offered earlier by Inge Kaul, Isabelle Grunberg, and Marc Stern requiring "benefits that are quasi-universal in terms of countries (covering more than one group of countries), people ... and generations."[30] I include issues that affect several nations in every region, even if not all nations; universal public goods are thus a subset of GPGs. Sandler also argues that it is useful to distinguish intergenerational and intragenerational GPGs, and that public goods are not always both completely nonexcludable and non-rival:[31] we need to see how far these features, along with externalities, extend for any particular good.

The Task Force focused on GPGs in six areas: "preventing the emergence and spread of infectious disease; tackling climate change; enhancing international financial stability; strengthening the international trading system; achieving peace and security, which underlies ...all the others," and supporting more forms of freely accessible knowledge (especially in science).[32] These categories clearly include more specific GPGs, such as preventing money-laundering, that affect some nations more than others, although they require cooperation from financial centers in all continents.

Ubiquitous global Connections: Four magnifying factors

Similarly, early this century, Robert Keohane and Joseph Nye recommended thinking of "globalism" in terms of multiple (often interlacing) relationships across continents that may not necessarily affect all nations. They suggested that such connections have thickened in environmental, military, economic, social, and legal domains.[33] We can refine this helpful picture by focusing on intercontinental connections that cause or make possible CAPs that involve parties in many nations across several regions. Processes or factors that *magnify* formerly national or regional market failures to global scales often contribute to such cases. While a given problem may have a local financial, military, or cultural provenance, additional economic, ecological, ideational, and distributive processes may spread its secondary effects across multiple regions.[34] These magnifying and escalating factors thus play a distinctive role in explaining the robust range of GPGs today.

As noted in chapter one, globalization of trade and capital markets seems largely irreversible. Hence we must assess the scope of externalities for all public goods in light of global market forces, which extend local and regional changes through economic multipliers.[35] Market relationships pass along the flourishing and suffering of one nation to other nations that trade with them. Thus Peter Singer rightly cites a 2001 UN High-Level Panel report which notes that "[i]n a global village, someone else's poverty very soon becomes one's own problem: of lack of markets for one's products, illegal immigration, pollution, contagious disease, insecurity, fanaticism, terrorism." The years since this report have amply borne out these predications.[36] For example, the abuse of global communications networks to spread hateful propaganda and steal information are like cyber-analogs to the spread of biological viruses across borders.

As a result, a large public harm anywhere is now more likely to have significant transnational effects, both directly through its intrinsic features and *indirectly* through global trade and medias. For example, disease and invasive species often piggyback on the international transportation of commodities and persons. Similarly, producers motivated by global demand may turn a rare species' habitat to new mines or farms, which arguably harms all who recognize the value of biodiversity around the world. While the benefits of activities causing a public harm may enrich a single area, nation, or sector of business, some of the costs will be dispersed widely onto people and/or companies in many other nations around the world. For instance, industrial toxins can travel through several ecosystems, ending up in polar ice caps; and much of the world's plastic garbage is collecting in major ocean gyres (especially in the north Pacific). Climate change is the easiest example today: via warming caused by human consumption of fossil fuels, deforestation, and soil destruction, Americans, Europeans, Indonesians, Chinese, and Brazilians, many others are displacing huge costs onto nations likely to suffer from rising sea levels, reduced rainfall and glacial river flows, and stronger storms. Fossil fuel users pay much less than the full public cost of their gasoline, coal, natural gas, and agricultural processes, which should include climate-related damages.

The inverse also occurs in "locally unwanted land uses" (such as chemical factories) where widely dispersed consumers need a suitable site for a facility that creates harmful neighborhood effects, such as aesthetic harms that drive down property values.[37] This happens at the global level when nations making and using cell phones, computers, and other advanced electronics buy rare metals that are abundant in the DRC, where the riches flowing from mines inspired a militia culture to control mining areas—part of a series of problems that claimed over *five million lives* in the DRC between 1990 and 2010, largely from disease and malnutrition caused by the fighting.[38] Heavy dependence on oil and natural gas industries also helps foster corruption in many developing nations that supply such fossil fuels (e.g., Nigeria and Russia); this corruption in turn fosters other problems that may spread through destructive ideas and civil conflict. Likewise, expecting developing nations like Ecuador to forego billions of dollars from would-be developers to preserve rainforests that arguably provide nonrival benefits for the whole human race amounts to free riding on Ecuador without paying any of the opportunity costs that it pays for rainforest preservation.

As Sandler explains, there are also scenarios in which richer, developed states pay the price for providing the "best shot" effort needed to promote a GPG: in cases such as "uncovering intelligence, finding cures, isolating bacteria" like Ebola, or "neutralizing a terrorist group," usually "whoever is first to supply the good provides it for everyone."[39] This is the basis for Mancur Olson's "exploitation hypothesis," which suggests that within alliances, the nation with more resources and more at stake will "supply most of the public good" (a Chicken or Rambo/suasion game). For example, the US Centers for Disease Control and Prevention tracks potential epidemics worldwide, which helps other nations.[40] Similarly, the United States has paid high prices for leading interventions to stop brutal dictators, such as Slobodan Milosevic in Yugoslavia, the Taliban in Afghanistan, and Hussein in Iraq. This has caused resentment among Americans who feel too much burden on their nation. Yet the extra leverage that comes with such leadership also causes reverse resentment: when one nation "becomes the world's cop" or controls most military coalitions,[41] other nations protest the hegemon's unfair level of influence. Large nations are also likely to use more global CPRs, thus depriving smaller or weaker nations of future usage, as we see with European fishing trawlers emptying seas around Africa.[42]

Thus both richer/stronger and weaker/poorer nations each get routinely exploited by the other group in different scenarios: DEPs abound in these relationships. Unfortunately, this cause of CAPs is another magnifying factor: while a small set of nations S may have the resources to solve a market failure affecting many other nations around the world, S may insist that all nations benefitting from S's investments in the public good should compensate S proportional to their gain and/or ability. Refusal by many potential beneficiaries to share the costs by side payments may make S, as the potential best-shot provider, resentful enough to forego its own benefits from the public good rather than pay its entire costs.[43] When this happens, it expands the range of nations that must act together to overcome a CAP. For example, understandable western opinion that African nations needed to lead any UN mission in Sierra Leone in the 1990s may have delayed an effective resolution of that crisis.

Thus, fairness in sharing the burdens and benefits of first-order public goods is a key second-order public good that facilitates provision of the first-order ones. When a few nations are left to supply a good for many others, its distribution may also be distorted. As a result, even TPGs that mainly benefit one or two regions may require global cooperation to share their costs in a sustainable way.

In sum, transnational markets, communications networks, biological/ecological systems, and distributive fairness concerns have extended some national and regional public goods, or various means necessary to secure them, to the global level. Similarly, most global harms or CAPs underlying GPGs involve some significant economic effects beyond the immediate effects of their natural features. For example, corruption and kleptocracy in one nation undermine faith in ethical standards that facilitate trust and cooperation, and cause economic spillovers. The looting of Venezuela by Nicholas Maduro's regime may have diverted as much as $300 billion to private accounts and driven over a million Venezuelans into neighboring nations.[44]

Global markets can also provide incentives for rights violations, e.g. by encouraging human trafficking for sex markets and other low-income labor, and rewarding people-smuggling operations that kill innocents and destabilize immigration systems. For-profit media, driven by ratings, also reduce adequate education of citizens and news attention to mass atrocities. Think of American media's almost-exclusive focus on the US elections during 2016 despite the ongoing mass murder in Syria, Myanmar, Yemen, and elsewhere. These examples suggest that virtually every TPG today has some international economic aspects.

Nevertheless, when analyzing likely tasks for a global government, we only need to consider public goods with the most weighty and pervasive global supply conditions and externalities. For example, terrorists getting their hands on old Soviet nuclear weapons would be a huge threat to the whole world. Such an attack would trigger a global economic depression, and potentially a world war. Similarly, setting the precedent in Syria that a ruling regime can kill or drive away a third of its population without international response emboldens would-be dictators in many nations, whose future campaigns of ethnic cleansing will burden or destabilize many other neighboring nations. A plausible inventory of such GPGs may be helpful because extent literature is replete with different examples and categories of global concerns, but few more comprehensive syntheses of putative GPGs. This exercise will at least indicate the range of probable grounds for the first premise in a global consolidation argument.

Candidates for GPGs in recent accounts

Contemporary literature on TPGs suggests many with likely global significance. The list of candidate GPGs below is a synthesis of those suggested in studies by Singer, Keohane and Nye, Malloch-Brown, Sandler, Holzinger, Rischard, Held, Weiss, Pogge, Kaul and Mendoza, and other authors in their United Nations Development Programme (UNDP) collections. My list also builds on the UN's list of SDGs and earlier Millennium Development Goals (MDGs), which both resulted from multiple rounds of negotiations. Thus, while several items in the synthesis list are also supported by my own examples, almost none of the suggested GPGs are original: I am simply organizing them in a clear way to foster discussion and future refinement. This synthesis faithfully indicates the considerable extant convergence among prominent scholars writing on GPGs, although disagreements certainly remain. Eventually, each GPG should be supported by a consensus of economic, sociological, and ethical analysis, but a partial survey of recent work suffices for my purposes.

For example, Keohane has one of the longest records of work on TPGs and GPGs. At the turn of the century, he noted "five key functions" for "regional or global institutions," including to limit "large-scale violence" or cross-border war (the UN's main goal); limit "negative externalities" involved in harboring terrorist groups, displacing pollution onto others, and in protectionist monetary policies; provide shared standards to solve coordination games (e.g., to foster scientific collaboration across nations); stop cascading financial failures (like the Asian financial crisis of 1997–1998 that helped cause Russia's default and currency devaluation); and prevent mass atrocities and alleviate the worst poverty.[45] This taxonomy groups some GPGs by structurally similar causes and others by similar kinds of outcome; but because so many different types of CAPs underlie various GPGs, it may be heuristically clearer to group them by area of global concern or effect-categories.

Thomas G. Weiss's accounts of "global governance gaps" imply a similar set of GPGs. These problem areas calling for better ways of organizing global coordination include, for example, the need for reliable and widely respected reporting on casualties in wars and tactics being employed, and more support for UN peacekeeping operations; better understanding of the causes of terrorism, consensus on definitions of terrorism and national self-defense, and efforts to prevent abuses of these labels; more consensus on human rights, deeper commitment to R2P, support for the ICC and norms regarding humanitarian aid operations, and better documentation of rights violations; clearer agreement on the best anti-poverty policies, climate science, and ways to combine human development with sustainability (the goal of the Global Compact among corporations and NPOs); and international financial institutions that are more responsive to developing nations, along with transnational sources of revenue for the most effective kinds of development aid.[46] Weiss also notes the goals of many global governance mechanisms that are already in place, from technical standards in telecommunications to treaties to criminalize different forms of attacks on civilians and transportation.[47]

Malloch-Brown provides another representative sample in his reflections on the 2000 summit when leaders thought the UN might be able to tackle issues such as "failing states that became havens for international terrorists, environment-destroying practices, from industrial smokestacks to burning rainforest, and little-researched communicable diseases in the third world," all of which can affect other nations across the world.[48] He also notes problems deriving from global trade, competition over fossil fuel resources, and people living on under two dollars per day. A bit more systematically, he lists four categories of issues that "a global executive or parliament" would need to address if it existed: problems deriving from fast economic and population growth; how to foster integration of cultures without "ruinous backlash;" physical limits to energy sources and environmental capital; and the "problems of those left behind" in poverty as the global middle class advances.[49] Then he turns to the UN's eight MDGs, most of which concerned health and education.

These MDGs have now been succeeded by the UN's slate of 17 broad SDGs (adopted in September 2015). This landmark agreement is a political compromise rather than a consensus among scholars, and it focuses on human development variables. Nevertheless, it clearly indicates a widely shared sense that many goods within these 17 categories require cooperation across multiple nations and regions—and in some cases, fully global partnerships.[50] I will flag the connections between each SDG and my proposed categories of GPGs so that it is clear how my synthesis list incorporates these UN goals. To meet these SDGs, the UN is clearly relying on network solutions, including voluntary cooperation of nations and help from NGOs, public-private partnerships, issue campaigns, etc. Social scientists typically agree that some TPGs can be provided by individual national initiatives and voluntary coordination among nations.[51] However, as noted earlier, it is safest to survey the whole landscape of GPGs before trying to determine which GPGs may be better secured through global networks or global government.

The terminology employed in my list is largely a matter of convention and effort to clarify distinctions. Candidate GPGs can be defined in more abstract terms, or by particular sub-goods making up a larger general good; so the groupings and level of detail in the taxonomy could vary depending on heuristic considerations. I also include some suggested institutional fixes, which are technically "intermediate" GPGs,[52] i.e., instrumental to other final goods desired for their own sake. Given distributive equity, as we saw, this consideration of necessary means is sometimes important to understand why a public good is global; and it helps to clarify potential implications of some GPGs. With these caveats, here is a preliminary synthesis of GPGs stated or implied in many recent accounts:

List 3.1 60 likely global public goods

---

1 Security from foreign invasion by national governments

a deterring nations from starting wars aimed at territorial acquisition;
b freeing occupied lands and rebuilding nations damaged by hostile takeover;
c protection of lives and property from targeted attacks by rogue regimes;
d strong limits on sovereign cyberattacks, a system to track their sources, and guaranteed proportional countermeasures; punitive sanctions against states harboring or encouraging massive hacking and cybercrimes campaigns (linked with 8e);
e strict limits on use of armed satellites, space-based weapons, and nano and robotic weaponry—including unmanned ground vehicles, air drones, battle droids, and similar automated military technology;
f reliable and impartial systems for arbitrating territorial grievances, border disputes, and petitions for regional autonomy or secession.

2 Protection against nongovernmental threats and highly destructive weapons

a protection from transnational piracy, hijacking, and kidnapping;
b protection against terrorist groups inspired by religious and political ideologies, including radicalization through the internet by ultra-fundamentalists and hate groups;

List 3.1 (Continued)

  c preventing powerful gangs and criminal organizations from taking over parts of sovereign nations;
  d controls on weapons trading, an end to land mine usage, and stringent bans on biological and chemical weapons;
  e nuclear nonproliferation and security of all nuclear material on the planet.

3 Recognition and legal establishment of fundamental human rights

  a rights to life and basic liberties of conscience, religion, speech, association, and privacy;
  b rights to freedom of movement, freedom to emigrate, to asylum, and to bodily integrity;
  c freedom from war crimes including torture and killing of prisoners of war and noncombatants; freedom from genocide, ethnic cleansing, persecution, and other mass atrocity crimes;
  d freedoms from slavery, child prostitution and pornography, and child factory labor;
  e equality of rights to education, basic health care, employment opportunity, and to run for political office; equality before the law regardless of gender, race, ethnicity or religious background [compare SDG 5: achieve gender equality, and SDG 16: provide justice for all, accountable and inclusive institutions];
  f rights to popular sovereignty through deliberative democracy strengthened by medias funded to serve the public good;
  g freedom from extreme genetic competition introduced by genetic engineering (whether direct or via fetal selection) to enhance physical or mental capacities beyond their normal human range.

4 Poverty reduction, basic needs, and response to natural disasters

  a alleviating dire poverty and managing urbanization in developing nations in ways consistent with local autonomy [compare SDG 1: end poverty in all its forms, and SDG 11: make cities inclusive and safe];
  b building stable governments in developing nations; increasing capacities to resist corruption and military coups; establishing impartial independent judiciaries and stable rule of law;
  c basic medical care for all; eradication of chronic diseases that reduce human capabilities and child survival rates [compare SDG 3: ensure healthy lives, and SDG 6: safe water and sanitation];
  d curing or controlling diseases with potential to become epidemic or even global pandemics, by curtailing their spread at their points of origin;

List 3.1 (*Continued*)

e   global lending and resource trading systems that encourage democracy by refusing to reward authoritarian regimes—especially after dictators overrule legitimate election results, overthrow democratic governments, or suppress democratic reformers with terror tactics;

f   infrastructure building in poor nations; universal access to internet communication; renewable energy sources with efficient distribution; financial reform and widely accessible credit; stable banking systems in developing nations [compare SDG 9: build resilient infrastructure, and SDG 7: ensure access to affordable, reliable, and sustainable modern energy];

g   universal basic education for all children, including basic skills, objective history, and recognized science [compare SDG 4: promote inclusive and equitable quality education for all];

h   stability in global commodities markets—especially secure food supplies—with global reserves for crises and inventory controls to prevent wild price swings (linked to sustainable agriculture in category 7) [compare SDG 2: end hunger, achieve stable food supplies];

i   unified, rapid, reliable responses to natural disasters, drawing on the resources of all nations well-placed to help, and sharing the costs fairly among all nations;

j   development of international systems to prevent or mitigate massive natural disasters, including early warning systems for tsunamis and earthquakes, evacuation plans for typhoons, etc.; rapid-insertion emergency relief teams to rescue large numbers of people quickly after disasters;

k   authority to coordinate the many aid charities that come to help after large natural disasters.

5   Immigration and global labor markets

a   fair immigration laws to regulate the movement of people between states, and coordination among nations to protect asylum seekers without overburdening particular nations through fair distribution;

b   fair terms for seasonal labor or guest worker programs short of permanent resident status;

c   systems for placement, support, education, and integration of new immigrants to avoid high concentrations leading to urban poverty zones, gang violence, etc. (linked with 4a);

d   minimal standards for fair labor and safe work conditions in all nations [compare SDG 8: decent work for all];

List 3.1 (Continued)

e strong provisions against people-trafficking in all nations; protections for victims of trafficking and their relatives;

f protection of minority subcultures, languages, and group affiliations to the extent possible without compromising other basic human rights.

6 Management of a global economy for sustainable development and fairness

a elimination of tax havens in small states; reform of corrupt banking centers that serve kleptocracies; tax rate harmonization to create a level playing field;

b a global system to detect and prosecute theft, fraud, money-laundering and drug trading across borders, and to coordinate national police responses to transnational racketeering and crime rings;

c coordination among currencies, banking, and finance systems to reduce transaction costs, provide stability, and enable unified responses to regional crises that prevent cascading market crashes;

d eventually, a central authority to determine interest rates and monetary policy for a global currency to further reduce transaction costs and control transnational business cycles;

e enforceable global minimum property rules, including a patent regime to protect intellectual property from cybercrime and thereby encourage invention, while setting reasonable limits to patents to ensure access by developing nations [compare SDG 9: develop infrastructure and foster innovation];

f strengthening WTO capacity to open markets to imports and resolve trade disputes with binding authority, while protecting worker safety, labor rights, and environmental standards in all nations [compare SDG 8: sustainable economic growth and SDG 10: reduce inequality];

g a global regime to police e-commerce to prevent fraud and make possible an international internet sales tax;

h international antitrust law to prevent the emergence of multinational companies with excessive market share or undue influence; a general system for regulating multinational corporations for the sake of other GPGs [compare SDG 8: sustainable economic growth];

i coherent global limitations on levels and speed of capital flow between nations to improve stability and lower the advantages that capital currently enjoys over labor;

List 3.1 (Continued)

    j   addressing other market failures that cause imbalances and unnecessary risk, especially to more vulnerable developing nations [compare SDG 8: sustainable economic growth].

7 The world environment and natural resources

    a   sustainable use and preservation of commons in which the whole world has a stake, e.g. clean air, healthy marine environments, protection of the polar regions from ozone depletion and destructive development; stable fisheries via fair limits on fishing with international cost-sharing [compare SDG 14: conserve and sustainably use oceans, and SDG 12: sustainable consumption and production];

    b   preservation of rainforests and wetland environments to maintain their biodiversity [compare SDG 15: sustainably manage forests ... and halt biodiversity loss];

    c   healthy watersheds, sustainable use of rivers and aquifers, and improved reservoirs and irrigation systems to preserve adequate freshwater supplies for all [compare SDG 6: ensure availability and sustainable management of water];

    d   stable agricultural systems to preserve productivity in perpetuity, meet the needs of rising populations, and reduce incentives for "land grabs" by powerful nations [compare SDG 2: food security];

    e   global limits on the most destructive pesticides, herbicides, and fertilizers that harm water sources, with funding to install more sustainable alternatives [compare SDG 6: clean water, and SDG 3: healthy lives];

    f   soil preservation through improved farming technologies (e.g., biochar and no-till seeding), limits to grazing herd sizes and maintenance of green land cover [compare SDG 15: combat desertification, halt and reverse land degradation...];

    g   maintenance of endangered animals, habitats, and natural wonders through international parks;

    h   a global system to charge nations for negative environmental externalities; a global cap-and-trade system to limit emissions of greenhouse gases, together with preservation of forests, peat lands, and arable soils to sequester carbon [compare SDG 13: combat climate change];

    i   a global fund to compensate nations when they accept large opportunity costs to preserve environmental goods that benefit larger regions or the whole world—e.g., preserving wetlands, tropical forests, and other wilderness (for their ecosystem services, pharmaceutical potential, and intrinsic value of their biodiversity).

List 3.1 (Continued)

---

8   Science, communications, education

    a managing systems for international telecommunications, from bandwidth in the spectrum to the functioning of the internet; management of web domains to ensure the free flow of information across borders without blockage by repressive governments;

    b communication initiatives to counter malicious indoctrination regimes; sanctions to stop cyber-troll farms and cyber-propaganda mills; limits on government monitoring of individual communications to protect privacy (connected with 3f);

    c assuring freedom of speech, protecting journalistic privileges, balanced with the need to protect vital state secrets for security to operate effectively under democratic control (see 2b);

    d promoting academic exchanges and expansion of global educational opportunities for talented students, especially from poor nations;

    e basic scientific research that benefits the whole of humanity, or which can be done most efficiently by avoiding duplication and achieving economies of scale, e.g., particle accelerators, space stations and space exploration, genetic databases, etc.

Obviously, several items on this list might be debated; some of these alleged GPGs, or parts of them, might be interpreted as national, regional, or inter-regional goods for select nations. My goal is not to argue for each of these candidates but rather to emphasize the plausibility of the eight categories (given the convergence in recent scholarship), and thus the daunting range of needs calling for global cooperation.

The next two sections offer more evidence for several GPGs from further expert accounts and consider the limits of the SDGs as a guide. But first, the category for human rights needs a brief clarification. While most accounts of GPGs include protections of the most basic human rights, this might seem dubious if we think of rights as simply abstract ideals that can gain strong followings in some regions while being ignored in others: why, then, would they require global coordination? The linkage theory outlined earlier (see chapter one) helps here. Basic human rights involve especially weighty objective value-judgments (one cause of public status); in each case, they are entitlements *to* some type of good—a negative liberty, material good, or positive opportunity. So systems that secure these rights and define their scopes by legal establishment or social practices are intermediate or instrumental public goods, and the need for such institutional embodiments reflects back into the content of the rights.

Although often local practices, informal customs, state police and judges, and national laws may look sufficient to protect most human rights of a nation's citizens, those systems can fail, be corrupted, and turn against innocent persons whom they should be protecting. Hence the secure establishment of basic human rights is an institutional GPG, occasionally requiring intervention by other nations as a backstop in the most extreme cases.

Moreover, serious and ongoing violations of human rights in one nation can endanger nearby nations, and weaken the confidence of people everywhere in human rights standards. All normative standards, including human rights and distributive equity principles, are *anti-rival* epistemic and social goods that grow in collective value the more people, groups, and nations believe in them: thus they are most beneficial when globally supported.[53] Mass atrocities, propaganda wars against democratic norms, and attempts to legitimate soft despotism (see the Introduction) all undermine such anti-rival goods. They weaken moral ideals that every nation needs to be widely shared. This is why totalitarian regimes have recognized spreading respect for rights standards in other nations as a threat to their own viability. As a result, cultures focused on defense of human rights in constitutional law and social practices cannot remain merely national or regional public goods: they require global support.

Limitations of the SDGs

Although the UN's SDGs were never intended to be a comprehensive list of global goods, they clearly support several GPGs in categories (4) and (7), i.e., poverty-reduction and environmental challenges (many of the prior MDGs had a similar focus). This reflects a "development before democracy" approach needed to gain consensus in the UN negotiations. Thus virtually all the SDGs, and most of their more specific targets, look compatible with China's soft despotism (see the Introduction). The only SDG targets that allude to democracy concern goal 16, which Putin quickly rejected.[54] Thus the SDGs risk giving the impression that "ending poverty in all forms everywhere" does not require such public goods as civil and political rights, independent judiciaries, management of the global economy to stop kleptocrats and crony oligarchies, independent media and open internet access, freedom from fake news campaigns designed to target liberals or destroy media reliability, or objective education that frees minds from extreme ideologies Yet incompetence and corruption in governments is the single largest cause of poverty in most developing nations today.[55]

Thus, while they include many laudable goals, the overall framework of the SDGs occludes the roots of some global and national problems. Below the level of global goods, many of the national, regional, and inter-regional environmental problems addressed within the SDGs derive partly from bad or absent government at these levels, which leaves dictators free to conduct scorched earth campaigns, or to enrich their families by selling natural resources rather than spending the earnings on infrastructure, green technology, or education and health institutions that lower birth rates. For example, would Goma be so poor if the Kabila regime used the money it reaps from selling rainforest to China to finance a geothermal power plant and electric grid in Goma, and stopped local officials from extorting bribes that prevent businesses from growing?[56] If there were civilian control of the military in Burma/Myanmar, could the military get away with driving over 600,000 Rohingya Muslims off their lands in favor of generals who will sell or develop these lands?

The SDG plan also says too little about how the goals and their targets should be reached beyond suggesting more development aid. It does not even sketch out a fair and viable system for sharing responsibility for the steps necessary to reach these goals.[57] Without addressing this crucial distributive equity issue, it is not evident that much new collective action among governments will result. If governments do not change their priorities due to the collective decision on SDGs, the whole exercise is in danger of being reduced to a mere PR campaign.

Pogge and Sengupta argue that the SDG program is weakened by failing to specify responsibilities for specific actions and failing to "call for structural reforms of the global institutional order" that underlies many aspects of poverty and environmental harms today. As they note, government-financed and charity-provided development aid will not be enough; stopping tax-dodging and illicit financial flows are crucial.[58] They also call for an independent body of experts to monitor progress toward the goals, and recommend adding a goal to reduce violence and discrimination based on sexual orientation. Perhaps most importantly, they also criticize the lack of sufficient emphasis on human rights, including rights to food, water, sanitation, and basic medical care,[59] and they call for a stronger set of targets on reducing inequality within and among nations.[60] These objections support several items on my synthesis list given above.

Further support: Held, Rischard, and the UNDP project

Further support can be found in other prominent studies. David Held's extensive work defends human rights based on the moral importance of each individual, as we saw (chapter one). Like other cosmopolitans, he argues that the development of customary international law and treaty law has limited national sovereignty by protecting rights to life and effective opportunities.[61] He also notes several security issues, including the need for shared militaries and peacekeeping forces rather than unsustainable growth in national militaries; multilateral decision-making and international security forces for "last resort" enforcement of R2P; support for the ICC and international criminal law; and strong protections from nuclear and biological weapons.[62] He also rightly stresses the need for democratic institutions at all levels, including accountability for global governance networks.[63]

Held focuses most on a panoply of problems involving globalized economic forces (which appear in various categories in my list, where they are mostly classified by results rather than causes). These include environmental externalities involved in rapid growth; "inadequate development of nonmarket social factors" or civil society institutions to support education, employment, and heath care; extreme poverty and regulatory deficits that allow major financial crises; and the need for uniform global health, environmental, and labor codes for businesses to prevent regulatory races to the bottom.[64] He also discusses global environmental goods, the need for a "fair regime for transnational migration," and several other GPGs supported by the UN system, such as "control of contagious diseases [and] humanitarian relief for refugees."[65] In sum, most items on my synthesis list are mentioned in Held's work, though without the same emphasis on CAPs between national governments that impede them.

Held often cites the 2002 list offered by World Bank scholar J.F. Rischard, which detailed twenty "inherently global issues" that are "insoluble outside a framework of collective global action involving all nations of the world."[66] This criterion, while stronger than mine, also looks beyond the scope of externalities to the scale of coordination required to secure the GPG. In particular, these 20 goods lie beyond the reach of free markets and the steering power of single national governments.[67] He focuses on global public harms instead of their correlate goods; e.g., under environmental problems, he includes climate change, "biodiversity and ecosystem losses, fisheries depletion, deforestation, water deficits, maritime safety and pollution" (see my category 7). Rischard also lists problems in the global economy and trade that correspond to most items in my categories (4) and (6), as well as (8e). In a set of items focused on building human capabilities, he includes "education for all," which is a top priority in many poor nations; a massive increase in poverty-reduction programs, closing the "digital divide" between rich and poor nations; preventing and mitigating natural disasters; and preventing the spread of infectious diseases.[68] These correspond to parts of my categories (4), (5), and (6).

Yet Rischard conspicuously leaves out enforcement of basic human rights,[69] perhaps because he assumes that "we cannot have global government" and so does not consider options that would strengthen mechanisms for protecting human rights.[70] I have argued instead that we should first propose a plausible set of global needs, assess what kind of government they require, and only then ask whether such a government is feasible. If we curtail the list to suit preconceptions about what can be achieved, we presumptively cut off what a global consolidation argument can teach us.

The two volumes on GPGs edited by Inge Kaul and colleagues with the support of the UNDP emphasize many of the same categories. The case studies include infectious disease control, free dissemination of basic information, an intact ozone layer, effective ways of defusing conflicts before they lead to civil war, stability in global finance,[71] poverty relief, distributive justice in global trade systems,[72] and "cultural heritage" as GPGs.[73] Mohan Rao's essay was unusual for its time in focusing explicitly on the way that disagreement about fair divisions of costs and benefits can block cooperation needed for some public goods, especially if economic bargaining strength is abused: we need equity norms because "[t]he size of the pie is not independent of the way the pie is sliced."[74] The editors also rightly stress connections between national, regional, and global goods (often due to magnifying factors): for example, poverty alleviation in sub-Saharan Africa could become a GPG if, by meeting the needs of regional populations, it were also to help prevent conflicts, reduce environmental degradation with international consequences, and lower risks to global health.[75] It could also promote economic growth in nations trading with sub-Saharan Africa.

The second UNDP volume largely confirms the same categories of GPGs, while focusing more on how they can be coordinated and financed.[76] Thus its essays discuss in detail how to improve the WTO and multilateral trade regimes; fair governance of the IMF; the high costs of corruption in political and business sectors within some developing nations; promoting broader public health agendas; intellectual property laws; conserving biodiversity; and the critical issue of water rights.[77] The volume also includes an essay on fairness and inclusiveness in decision making on GPG provision,[78] as well as detailed recommendations on how NGOs and other civil society actors can enhance efforts by national governments and intergovernmental groups to secure GPGs.

The range of GPGs is similar in other prominent collections, such as Held and McGrew's *Governing Globalization*. In this work, in addition to essays on multilateral decision-making, we find essays on problems in the global financial system, transnational crime, transnational regulation of digital communications, intellectual property rights, newer UN "peace support" and enforcement operations, and the threat of global pandemics (with slow responses to the spread of AIDS as an example).[79] Similarly, the recent book on global cooperation failures by Held, Thomas Hale, and Kevin Young focuses on transnational security, management of environmental problems such as climate and deforestation, and dangers related to trade negotiations and global financial governance.[80]

These works, like the second UNDP collection, concentrate on both the potentials and limits of network solutions to such global problems, including NGO- and IGO-facilitated efforts. This brings us to the final necessary step in the analysis of GPGs—namely dividing "networkable" GPGs from those that cannot be adequately secured without sovereign government powers.

Conclusion: "Government-apt" GPGs

With a plausible list of GPGs in hand, we can move to step (c1) in the global consolidation argument begun at this chapter's outset. This involves identifying GPGs that are better provided by a global government than by inter-state agencies and international civil society networks. As with the sense of "global" in GPGs, "global government" here refers to a sovereign authority that can coordinate multiple nations on all continents with the force of law (see chapter two on primary sovereignty). We have already encountered strong evidence that networks cannot provide all crucial public goods—especially at regional and global levels. In chapter two, the limitations of confederal systems and structurally similar inter-state coordination regimes showed that supremacy or governmental enforcement is sometimes needed. Several other examples in this chapter point in the same direction.

Yet, as I noted in chapter two, there is a theoretical difficulty here: despite much valuable recent work on achievements and deficits in governance networks, we seem to lack precise criteria for "networkable" goods—although have clear criteria for public goods more generally (as we saw in the first section). There is not even a standard terminology, given the "widespread misconception that public goods are state-provided;"[81] thus the need for expressions like "government-apt" versus "network-apt" public goods. This distinction cuts across all levels, and there are several kinds of agents in the middle category between markets and governments.

Of course, we can use case studies to evaluate the feasibility of network solutions for GPGs: the next chapter focuses on GPGs related to international security and terrorism (categories 1 and 2), with some attention to prevention of mass atrocities (category 3). Some GPGs in these categories may require military force or sanctions. For example, NGOs may be able to improve education for tolerance in areas where young people are instead being radicalized, and IGOs may help reduce flows of money and weapons to terrorist groups; but once a group like ISIS holds cities, only military power can dislodge it. Similarly, immigration is at least partly controlled by national governments, which need to coordinate their laws if a fair global system is ever to exist. Case studies for the other categories of GPGs must await further work.

However, there are four more general reasons to expect network governance solutions to be inadequate for several GPGs within categories 4–8. First, as the examples in Table 3.1 illustrate, various

Table 3.1 Levels and kinds of goods

Potential suppliers → Level of beneficiaries ↓	Providable by markets	Providable by networks (a) IGOs and treaties (b) NGOs/civil society	Some coordination via government enforcement is needed
National	Education	Basic education for all	Legal rights to equal opportunity education
Regional	Tradeable quota system for Scandinavian fisheries	Transnational lake cleanup and protection; EU scholarships	Fair apportionment of refugees granted asylum within Europe
Inter-regional	Trade within the western hemisphere	NAFTA trade treaty; Fair trade regime for US imports from Amazon	ASEAN food reserve system for Asian nations
Global	Efficient agricultural production	Limits on CFCs to protect ozone layer; global scientific partnerships	Stable ice-pack for spring river flows via stable climate

intermediate public goods are government-supplied by definition: legal enforcement of equal opportunity can only be achieved by government. But this is relevant in the examples given because it is believed that informal customs and network efforts, such as foundation-funded scholarships for minority students, are not enough to eliminate obstacles like residual effects of past racism. Similarly, free markets may tend toward efficient farming; but firms maximize profits as they approach zero inventories, so they do not hold years of excess food supplies. Voluntary efforts by charities can enable short-term emergency food aid, and inter-state agencies like the World Food Programme can help build more resilience in developing nations and assist long-term refugees, such as the millions now exiled from Somalia, Myanmar, and Syria. But if people in a nation that imports much of its food want a *firm guarantee* that shocks to the world agriculture market (e.g., from natural disasters) cannot impose a famine on them, then their national government must hold a sizeable food reserve. The ASEAN example is useful because its rice reserves are held within each member-nation, which is less efficient than a single unified system would be (as in most insurance schemes). In the United States, the federal government is able provide this food security for all the states, and a unified global food security system would be even better. But fair distribution of food reserves in a multi-region food emergency would have to be legally guaranteed to provide this GPG.

Second, there are well-known problems with the proliferation of IGOs, treaty regimes, and NGOs involved in global governance. The editors of the second UNDP volume suggest that an "advisory panels" like the Intergovernmental Panel on Climate Change should be "formed for all key global issues;" they also note Lyla Mehta's proposal for a "world water parliament," and the idea of a "world financial authority"[82] that could supersede the IMF and World Bank. I mentioned the need for a globally financed biodiversity fund to compensate developing nations for opportunity costs of tropical forest and wetland preservation. There have been many calls to revamp the UN Economic and Social Council or to create another intergovernmental "apex body"[83] to tackle the worst poverty issues (in addition to other SDGs). Kaul and Le Goulven even proposed an "ambassador," "CEO," and "implementation council" for each major GPG to connect national ministries, civil society agents, epistemic communities (expert groups), and businesses with interests in that GPG—a governance network presumably without a treaty basis (in most cases).[84]

The combination of such suggestions looks like the network approach run amok, spawning ever more panels, working groups, and advocates. More charitably, it seems like a herculean series of contortions to compensate for the absence of a unified global government. Even though networks make the provision of GPGs much less scattered than they would be with random national efforts, a profound fragmentation still results. It is as if, for every major GPG, we had a free-floating administration running largely on reputation and the goodwill of stakeholders, unattached to any central source of authority. In their insightful warnings about fragmentation as a source of global gridlock, Hale, Held, and Young note that by 2011, there were 7,608 IGOs and 56,834 international NGOs, with 700 agreements negotiated on environmental issues, and 319 preferential trade agreements (the numbers, of course, have risen sharply since then). That is a lot of transaction costs, potential for uncertainty, and lobby power for special interests, even if it allows beneficial experimentation and flexibility on some issues.[85] More importantly, such a division of labor is only efficient on "many small, specific problems," leaving "large, overarching ones"—the shared structural roots of many global harms—unresolved. Amid the "redundancy and navelgazing" within this "proliferation of institutional bodies," any nascent "political will" to coordinate a large number of nations to solve the largest or most fundamental problems is diffused.[86]

Fragmentation through many network agents can also mean that effort and resources go more toward areas with more influential NGOs and donors behind them, rather than being systematically decided by a fair political process. As Colin Bradford and Johannes Linn note in calling for global governance reform, "[t]he interrelationship among institutions are ultimately political problems because they entail determining relative priorities among areas of health, education, gender equality, the environment, poverty, finance, trade, growth, and security"—tradeoffs that require collective value-judgments. Thus they regret "the absence of a truly representative, globally inclusive steering group ... at the apex of the international system."[87] Of course, such a group could do better at steering the whole system if it worked by majority rule and had legal enforcement powers.

Third, there are technical problems arising from the market failures blocking various GPGs, including supply aggregation, the type of parties to be coordinated, and information limits that can stymie network provision of goods. This is too complex a topic to summarize briefly, but here are a few insights from Sandler with my tentative additions.

Information asymmetries are common in international relations because "national sovereignty limits information;" this is one reason why states chose to delegate monitoring to IGOs that have more expert knowledge,[88] But IGOs and independent watchdogs have limited capacities to fix resulting moral hazard and adverse selection problems. National governments can do much more, e.g. by compelling firms to give accurate accounting statements, refrain from deceptive advertising, and reveal true risks involved in products they offer. Similarly, a global government could compel national authorities, multinational corporations, and international NGOs to reveal facts about their holdings, policies, and interests—information needed in creating sustainable systems that secure GPGs by coordinating diverse sets of nations.[89]

As this suggests, it is often harder to coordinate larger rather than smaller groups of parties, and harder to coordinate groups that are quite heterogeneous in preferences and capacities. By contrast, volunteer groups, clubs, and other NGOs tend to unite parties with similar interests and resources. But global coordination needed for GPGs must frequently involve many nations (or parties within nations) of different sizes, cultures, interests, and wealth—making it less likely that network coordination will be sufficient. In a few cases, large "disparity among potential contributors" may help move them toward actions favoring the public good, e.g. when the richest party gains so much that they are willing to shoulder most of the costs.[90] But as I argued, this holds in such chicken or Rambo CAPs only up to the point that distributive inequity becomes too salient: then, only force of law may be sufficient to distribute costs and benefits fairly enough to restart cooperation.

This brings us to the way that contributions by different parties "aggregate" to generate the collective good.[91] Generally we might expect networks to do well in solving AGs by offering focal points, as many international organizations have done. Yet when asymmetry among the parties makes one (or a few) of them into "weakest links," a network fix will succeed only if it can shore up the capacities of the weakest contributors. As we have seen, in global cases, this means that a few nations lacking the capacity, assurance, or good will to do their part can block a GPG for everyone. If networks cannot overcome the doubts, incapacity, or recalcitrance in these weakest contributors, a stronger authority may be needed. As the Task Force on GPGs puts it "Some global public goods can only be produced when every government fully complies with a common approach ... This makes for arduous long-term problems of cooperation" because the risk of failure undermines the needed assurance.[92]

Such challenges can be met by networks and IGOs in certain discrete cases, as the eradication of diseases like polio and smallpox show. But it is very hard to maintain ongoing efforts from all necessary parties. When a high threshold level of total contribution is needed to make the joint effort worthwhile, IGOs may be able to organize a conditional contract among nations to provide them assurance. But if reaching the threshold itself involves a game of chicken, BF, Rambo, or PD, it may not be reached (as in some UN peacekeeping requests): an authority with legal enforcement powers may then be needed.

Even best shot cases, as Sandler explains, tend to supply public goods spontaneously (or without binding agreements) only intermittently; it is harder to supply "continuous goods" this way. "Summation" scenarios where the public goods (shared benefits) increase with each contributing party are also difficult:[93] in that case, if only a few among the many parties contribute, the public good will be woefully undersupplied. This often involves a PD, which may be overcome with reciprocity through repeated rounds. But with many parties, repeated failure due to enough free-riding spoilers may also kill chances of an informal, voluntary, or network solution (as seen in "public goods contributions games"). The usual example is the elusiveness of a truly binding, enforceable climate treaty; but a global fund for biodiversity, general contributions to the UN, and contributions to IMF funds are structurally similar.

Moreover, for all the supply aggregation challenges just reviewed, a global government would have far more capacity than diverse networks to *link* the efforts that discrete nations make toward different GPGs—so that if nation A (as a better shooter) needs to provide most of good G1, and nation B (currently a weak link) needs to step up for G2, nation C can compensate A and B by contributing more to G3 (a summation case). In this way, an overarching scorekeeper can promote an efficient division of labor in supporting diverse GPGs while also increasing distributive equity—the indispensable lubricant of all cooperative schemes. Such links would also make it easier to incentivize long-term support for intergenerational public goods, which are among the toughest to coordinate.

As noted, we should also consider impure GPGs and transnational club goods. Sandler is well-known for arguing that club goods, which are largely excludable but only partly rival, can usually be provided to club members without needing higher-level coercive authorities.[94] Thus regional and global goods, such as the Panama Canal, transnational electric grids, and informational networks, will not require transnational government intervention unless they start to involve significant externalities beyond the club, or large upfront costs and uncertain payoffs. By contrast, nonexcludable but partly rival GPGs, such as transnational policing to control organized crime, will be overused and undersupplied unless a few contributors pay most of the costs; enforcement is needed to limit free riders. Similarly, excluda-ble but nonrival GPGs, like valuable information and technology won through costly scientific work (e.g., detailed atmospheric satellite data and lifesaving medicines), will be under-accessed unless there is a fair and reliable way for most potential beneficiaries to pay the providers or received subsidized usage.

Finally, some GPGs may be supplied by activities that also produce other private, club, or national goods. For example, foreign aid may help the donor get military intelligence from the receiving nation, or maintaining a nation's wetlands that preserve biodiversity for the whole world may also help that nation's tourism industry. A voluntary, informal, or network approach may work for such GPGs when the "joint product" gives the provider enough benefit. But when the pro-vider's local gain is small compared to the collective benefit, as it often will be for GPGs, this incentive may be insufficient.[95] Moreover, even when it works, other beneficiaries of the GPG are free riding, leading to potential resentments; and the provider's nonglobal incentives can distort their activities in ways that reduce the GPG provision (as has often been the case in foreign aid or in military interventions with mixed humanitarian and economic motives).

These problems would be avoided by a more impartial global authority to distribute the costs and benefits of GPGs with joint prod-ucts. Weiss sums up the situation well: while we certainly need "more robust intergovernmental organizations to foster greater compliance" with policies that benefit many nations around the world, IGO and network fixes "cannot replace the compliance functions of a global government."[96]

The three types of drawback with network solutions just reviewed mostly concern coordinative power—the aspect to which CP applies. The fourth problem directly concerns legitimacy. Even when IGOs, NGOs, expert groups, issue campaigns, and other civil society actors can secure some parts of various GPGs, it may not be right to let them do this without global government oversight. For then they are not directly answerable to the world's peoples. Accountability is diffused when IGOs answer only to national governments, while NGOs and issue groups answer to their main sponsors; however well-meaning, these elites thereby gain far more leverage. In fact, this is another instance of problematic privileges that accrue to a hegemon on whom most others free ride. Thus Kaul and colleagues argue, following Held and McGrew, that the power now wielded by multinational "civil society organizations and corporations" needs more formal legiti-mation: only governments can "turn decisions into firm and binding agreements. And only through government can voting power temper the influence of private purchasing power" (of both for-profit and nonprofit actors). The visible hand "must be the public's hand" to be legitimate, on this democratic view.[97] Equitable distribution will be more likely if "publicness in decision-making" (a version of DP) is respected, giving all stakeholders a fair role in processes to decide on GPG provision.[98]

Obviously control of GPG provision through intergovernmental regimes and networks dominated by a few nations will not meet this standard.[99] When "nongovernmental bodies and multinational companies" strongly influence decisions about global issues, new "rules of the game are being written without the involvement of many players and teams." Hence, these sub-democratic systems will not do well in overcoming global CAPs involving DEPs.[100] But greater legitimacy in the process and equity in the results indirectly increases coordinative power: parties are more likely to accept decisions for a collective if the process signals group inclusion, giving each party significant voice.[101]

However, why not think of charities, advocacy groups, professional societies, clubs, churches, and even corporations as other conduits through which "democratic" opinions are formed and expressed? For example, like many recent champions of global network solutions, Amartya Sen's "plural affiliation" approach celebrates the roles of civil society groups transcending national boundaries, such as political parties and issue-focused initiatives, professional organizations (e.g., medical societies), educational foundations, and other NGOs.[102] Such collectives form a crucial part of any social order, as G.W.F. Hegel famously argued (and much work on "social capital" has now confirmed).

I do not deny their value as potential pathways for deliberation and expression of opinion, but it should concern us when civil society groups effectively become the ultimate authorities. At any level, systems in which public goods are mostly provided by charities, volunteer groups, foundations, professional organizations, and other NGOs tend to let many beneficiaries free ride for too long, resulting in a kind of *philanthropocracy* that breeds dependency. Moreover, even if more individuals are actively engaged in such a system, it will constitute a consociation in which people can only be represented via membership in various groups. Thus choice is reduced: if you want any voice, you have to work through the dominant groups within an international order capped by a kind of "États Généraux." The direct relation to individual people needed for primary sovereignty is the remedy for this problem.

In sum, networks are not the panacea that many have imagined. As Niall Ferguson explains, unfortunately, many network systems have inherently anti-egalitarian tendencies because a few nodes with slightly more connections at the outset attract geometrically more connections as the system develops.[103] This dramatic threshold effect is due to the phenomenon of "network externalities" explained earlier. In practice, this means that more influential civil society organizations come to benefit from a natural monopoly and tend to become dominant in their niches—operating like central hubs in a web.

Thus, effective coordinative power achieved by networks tends to be concentrated in fewer *private* hands over time, compounding the consociation problem. When instead their power remains dispersed among many network agents in a sector, it is fragmented and less effective.[104] Just as Hamilton said, for some public goods, only republican-democratic government can combine the unity needed for effective coordination and the broad accountability to stakeholders needed for legitimacy.

∞

In conclusion, it seems likely that several GPGs within the eight-category taxonomy cannot be adequately secured and legitimated without the stronger kinds of coordination afforded by a global government. While governance networks can do a lot, and our existing IGOs could be strengthened to protect some GPGs more fully, there are technical limits to the CAPs that they can overcome—especially when consistent, long-term cooperation requires more equitable divisions of labor and payoffs. However, to make a decisive case for league of democracies, it will be enough to show that neither the UN inter-state system nor transnational networks are sufficient to secure the first three categories of GPGs. That is the topic of the next chapter. Analogous arguments may be added later for other GPGs to strengthen the central case made on the basis of categories 1–3.

Notes

1. Todd Sandler, *Global Challenges* (Cambridge, UK: Cambridge University Press, 1998), 9.
2. Katarina Holzinger, *Transnational Common Goods* (New York: Palgrave Macmillan, 2008), 17.
3. Sander, *Global Collective Action* (Cambridge, UK: Cambridge University Press, 2004), 17–18. Compare Thomas Weiss, *Global Governance* (Malden, Mass: Polity Press, 2013), 40.
4. Inge Kaul and Ronald Mendoza, "Advancing the Concept of Public Goods," in *Providing Global Public Goods*, ed. Inge Kaul, Pedro Conceição, Katell Le Gouven, and Ronald Mendoza (New York: Oxford University Press, 2003): 78–111, 79–80.
5. See Holzinger, 19–21.

6. Sandler, *Global Challenges*, 9.

7. Holzinger says that nonexludability is "the most problematic property in the production of common goods:" see *Transnational Common Goods*, 143.

8. Ibid., 10.

9. Ibid., 11.

10. Here I follow Holzinger's definitions and "Traditional Taxonomy of Public Goods" in *Transnational Common Goods*, 15. Also see her definition of CPRs as "rival and nonexclusive goods" (29). Some authors distinguish between open access commons and "common property" which is only accessible to a "well-defined group:" see Gary Liebcap, "Conditions for Successful Collective Action," in *Local Commons and Global Interdependence*, ed. Robert Keohane and Elinor Ostrom (London: Sage, 1995), 161–90, 163.

11. Ibid., 20.

12. See Gijs van Donselaar, *The Right to Exploit* (New York: Oxford University Press, 2009), ch. 2.

13. But this involves a normative judgment concerning initial ownership, as discussed later. See analysis in "Why Habermas Needs Distributive Equity Principles," *Constellations* (2019), forthcoming.

14. For example, see Joseph Stiglitz's analysis of approximately ten distinct types of market failures in his popular work, *The Price of Inequality* (New York: W.W. Norton, 2012), chs. 2–4. Also see Stiglitz, *The Great Divide* (New York: W.W. Norton, 2015), Part IV.

15. Compare the seven types of market failure listed in Ruben Mendez, "Peace as a Global Public Good," in *Global Public Goods*, ed. Inge Kaul, Isabelle Grunberg, and Marc Stern (New York: Oxford University Press, 1999), 382–416, 386. Mendez includes merit goods, information asymmetries, and incomplete markets, but not rents or institutional preconditions.

16. Sandler, *Global Challenges*, 46–49, and Kaul and Mendoza, "Advancing the Concept of Public Goods," 93.

17. "Summation" technologies usually leads to a PD, weakest-link to an AG, and best-shot to chicken: see Holzinger, *Transnational Common Goods*, 70.

18. See Gauthier, *Morals by Agreement*, 98–99.

19. Liebcap, "Conditions for Successful Collective Action," 165–67.

20. See Gauthier, *Morals by Agreement*, 85 and 102 on the market as nested within a moral framework.

21. Holzinger, *Transnational Common Goods*, 16.

22. See Kaul and Mendoza, "Advancing the Concept of Public Goods," 85. Although they are correct that some naturally private goods are made public by custom or law, I regard objective value as a natural basis for publicity that is prior to "policy design" (87).

23. For prominent arguments for objective goods, see Mark Sagoff, *The Economy of the Earth* (Cambridge: Cambridge University Press, 1994); Michael Sandel, *What Money Can't Buy* (New York: Penguin Books, 2012); Debra Satz, *Why Some Things Should Not be for Sale* (New York: Oxford University Press, 2010); and Elizabeth Anderson, *Value in Ethics and Economics* (Cambridge, Mass: Harvard University Press, 1993).

24. Cecilia Albin gives a helpful summary of such equity norms in "Getting to Fairness: Negotiations over Global Public Goods," in *Providing Global Public Goods*, ed. Kaul et al., 263–79, 267.

25. See Gauthier, *Morals by Agreement*, 94–95.

26. Holzinger, *Transnational Common Goods*, 165.

27. Ibid., 165–67.

28. Sandler, *Global Collective Action*, 75–76. However he also argues that in some cases, in order to attain economies of scale or scope, public goods should be provided by authorities reaching more widely than their spill-over effects (85–86).

29. International Task Force on Global Public Goods, *Summary: Meeting Global Challenges* (Stockholm, Sweden: Erlanders Infologistics, 2006), 2; www.gpgtaskforce.org.

30. Inge Kaul, Isabelle Grunberg, and Marc Stern, "Defining Global Public Goods," in *Global Public Goods*, ed. Kaul, Grunberg, and Stern (New York: Oxford University Press, 1999), 2–19, 3.

31. Todd Sandler, "Intergenerational Public Goods," in *Global Public Goods*, ed. Kaul, Grunberg, and Stern, 20–50.

32. Task Force on GPGs, *Summary*, 5.

33. Robert Keohane and Joseph Nye, Jr., "Governance in a Globalizing World," in *Power and Governance in a Partially Globalized World*, ed. Robert Keohane (New York: Routledge, 2002), 193–218, 193–98.

34. Compare Weiss, *Global Governance*, 43.

35. Sandler, *Global Collective Action*, 201.

36. Peter Singer, *One World*, 2nd ed. (New Haven, Conn: Yale University Press, 2004), 7.

37. Holzinger analyzes these as games of chicken involving both a coordination problem and a distributive problem, as each (informed) party wants some town, just not their own town, to host the facility: see Holzinger, *Transnational Common Goods*, 80–81.

38. Thomas G. Weiss, *Humanitarian Intervention*, 2nd ed. (Malden, Mass: Polity Press, 2014), 56. Also see CongoJustice.org; and Robert Draper, "Rift in Paradise," *National Geographic* 220 (November 2011): 82–117.

39. Sandler, *Global Collective Action*, 27 and 66 (in discussing coordination games).

40. Ibid., 34–35.

41. Ibid., 35.

42. Ibid., 60 (my examples).

43. Thus Lisa Martin notes that "bargaining problems [i.e. distributive issues] can be just as devastating to prospects for international cooperation as can collaboration problems [i.e. social dilemmas]": see Martin, "The Political Economy of International Cooperation," in *Global Public Goods*, ed. Kaul, Grunberg, and Stern, 51–64, 56.

44. R. Evan Ellis, "The Collapse of Venezuela and Its Impact on the Region," *Military Review* (July–August 2017), 22–33.

45. Robert Keohane, "Governance in a Partially Globalized World," in *Power and Governance in a Partially Globalized World*, ed. Keohane, 245–67, 248–49.

46. These are among 30 (partly overlapping) issues that Weiss discusses in *Global Governance*, chs. 4–8.

47 Ibid., 119–20, 111, 172, and 208 note 5.
48. Mark Malloch-Brown, *The Unfinished Global Revolution*, 184.
49. Ibid., 187–88.
50. See the list and explanation at www.un.org/sustainabledevelopment/sustainabledevelopment-goals/. The targets under each goal are also easily read at sustainabledevelopment.un.org/?menu=1300.
51. See Holzinger, *Transnational Common Goods*, 33–36. Yet some of her cases, like Sandler's, assume that in chicken scenarios, certain parties will provide the public good (34); compare Weiss, *Global Governance*, 174. In fact, such cases raise DEPs that may make non-governmental solutions unsustainable.
52. This concept comes from Kaul, Grunberg, and Stern, "Defining Global Public Goods," 13.
53. The benefits of human rights, like distributive equity principles and other ethical norms, lies partly in their second-order or adverbial function, modifying the ways that other first-order goods may be pursued or produced.
54. Graham Long, "The Idea of Universality in the Sustainable Development Goals," *Ethics and International Affairs*, 29, no. 2 (2015): 203–22, 211.
55. See Daron Acemoglu and James Robinson, *Why Nations Fail* (New York: Random House, 2012), esp. chs. 11–14.
56. See Pádriag Carmody, *The New Scramble for Africa* (Malden, Mass: Polity Press, 2011), 171–73; and Jonathan Rosen's story on Goma, america.aljazeera.com/articles/2015/2/14/after-decades-of-war-goma-drc-is-open-for-business.html.
57. Long, "The Idea of Universality in the Sustainable Development Goals," 213–14. However, I agree with Long that the SDGs have a cosmopolitan aspect in setting goals for all persons as individuals.
58. Thomas Pogge and Mitu Sengupta, "The Sustainable Development Goals: A Plan for Building a Better World?" *Journal of Global Ethics* 11, no. 1 (2015): 56–64, 57.
59. Ibid., 58–59.
60. Ibid., 60. Some of their concerns thus relate to the first-order goals within the SDGs, while others concern the governance needed to secure the first-order public goods.
61. David Held, *Cosmopolitanism* (Malden, Mass: Polity Press, 2010), 50–56 and 124.
62. Ibid., 8–10, 107, 120–24, 145, 155, 171, 178, 195–98.
63. Ibid., ch. 7.
64. Ibid., 5–7, 59–63, 108–10, 149, 188–94.
65. Ibid., 113, 143, and ch. 7. He offers helpful summaries on 166 and 181–83.
66. J.F. Rischard, *High Noon: 20 Global Issues and 20 Years to Solve Them* (New York: Basic Books, 2002), 65.
67. Ibid., 12, 34 and.46.
68. Ibid., 66.
69. Ibid., 66.
70. Ibid., xi, 166.
71. Charles Wyplosz, "International Financial Instability," in *Global Public Goods*, ed. Kaul, Grunberg, and Stern, 152–89, 177; also see Nancy Birdsall and Robert Lawrence, "Deep Integration and Trade Agreement: Good for Developing Countries?," in ibid., 128–50.

72. E.g., Ethan Kapstein, "Distributive Justice as a Global Public Good," in *Global Public Goods*, ed. Kaul, Grunberg, and Stern, 88–115. Also see the editors' summary of categories in their "Conclusion," 450–504, 454.
73. This item is rarer on lists of GPGs; but given the benefits that everyone may gain from exposure to a wide variety of cultures, and the objective values in much cultural heritage, a case can be made for it.
74. J. Mohan Rao, "Equity in a Global Public Goods Framework," in *Global Public Goods*, ed. Kaul, Grunberg, and Stern, 68–87, esp. 68–69.
75. Kaul, Grunberg, and Stern, "Defining Global Public Goods," 12.
76. For example, the editors note ten public goods in the Secretary-General's "Roadmap" for implementing the MDGs, including basic dignity, education, health care, global public health, global security and peace, transport and communication systems harmonized across borders, accessible knowledge with respect for intellectual property, transparent and accountable government, and sustainable use of natural commons. See Kaul et al., "How to Improve the Provision of Global Public Goods," 45.
77. Kaul et al., eds., *Providing Global Public Goods*, 263–79.
78. Albin, "Getting to Fairness," 263–79.
79. David Held and Anthony McGrew, *Governing Globalization* (Malden, Mass: Polity Press, 2002): 209–33, 209–10.
80. Thomas Hale, David Held, and Kevin Young, *Gridlock: Why Global Cooperation Is Failing When We Need it Most* (Malden, Mass: Polity Press, 2013), 55.
81. Kaul, Conceição, Gouven, and Mendoza, "How to Improve the Provision of Global Public Goods," in *Providing Global Public Goods*, ed. Kaul et al., 21–58, 23.
82. Ibid., 34 and 52.
83. Ibid., 53.
84. Inge Kaul and Katell Le Goulven, "Institutional Options for Producing Global Public Goods," in *Providing Global Public Goods*, ed. Kaul, Conceição, et al., 371–409, 395.
85. Hale, Held, and Young, *Gridlock*, 45–46 (my italics).
86. Ibid., 47.
87. Colin Bradford, Jr. and Johannes Lynn, "Global Governance Reform: Conclusions and Implications," in *Global Governance Reform*, ed. Bradford and Linn (Washington, DC: Brookings Institution Press, 2007): 115–31, 127–28. They think the most realistic option is a revamped G-8, but I argue against that option in chapter six.
88. Sandler, *Global Collective Action*, 72 and 96. Keohane has made similar arguments.
89. Ibid., 73.
90. Ibid., 32–35. Fortunately, this dynamic makes it more likely that like-minded democracies could unite.
91. Ibid., 61–68 (the table on 68 offers a helpful summary).
92. The International Task Force on GPGs, *Summary*, 3. Compare Weiss's discussion of Scott Barrett's analysis in Weiss, *Global Governance*, 41.
93. Sandler, *Global Collective Action*, 61–68. He notes that in "weighted sum" scenarios, efforts by different contributors are not perfectly substitutable

(61 and 67); thus it may help to redistribute resources to parties whose efforts have more positive impact.

94. Todd Sandler, "Intergenerational Public Goods," in *Global Public Goods*, ed. Kaul, Grunberg, and Stern, 20–50, 22–23.
95. Sandler, *Global Collective Action*, 49–55.
96. Weiss, *Global Governance*, 60.
97. Kaul et al., "How to Improve the Provision of Global Public Goods," 29.
98. Ibid., 24, 30, 35.
99. Inge Kaul and Ronald Mendoza, "Advancing the Concept of Public Goods," 102–4.
100. J. Mohan Rao, "Equity in a Global Public Goods Framework," 70 and 73.
101. Tom Tyler and Stephen Blader, "The Group Engagement Model: Procedural justice, social identity, and cooperative behavior," *Personality and Social Psychology Review*, 7 no. 4 (2003): 349–361.
102. Amartya Sen, "Global Justice: Beyond International Equity," in *Global Public Goods*, ed. Kaul, Grunberg, and Stern, 88–115 and 116–125, esp. 120–22.
103. Niall Ferguson, "The False Prophecy of Hyperconnection," *Foreign Affairs* 96 (September–October, 2017): 68–79, 76.
104. See my essay, "Environmental Public Goods Not Securable by Markets or Networks," *International Journal of Technoethics* 9 no. 2 (2018): 26–40, esp. 34–36.

4 The failure of the United Nations to deliver international security

- Preventing aggression: Why the UN could not fulfill its main goal
- Weapons proliferation and the limits of treaty processes
- Cyberwar, satellites, and robotic weapons
- Stopping the causes of terrorism and sharing the costs of nation-building
- Conclusion

In the previous chapter, we surveyed a wide range of global public goods (GPGs) that now lie beyond ability of nations to secure without a global government. This has been increasingly clear since the 1990s. As Thomas McCarthy summarized, globalization of markets, communication, and "technological and cultural flows" pose ever more problems "that cannot be resolved within the borders of individual states or with the traditional means of interstate treaties." Cosmopolitans thus maintain that better "supranational" political institutions are needed[1]—even if they hope that the network approach may work for quite a few GPGs.

Among global treaty organizations, the UN was created primarily to provide global security goods by stopping international wars and also nonstate threats (the first two categories of GPGs). More recently, there have also been efforts to adapt the UN framework to stop civil wars and secure basic human rights against threats of mass atrocities. The R2P resolutions of 2005 are the formal result of this initiative.

Yet unfortunately, as this chapter will show, the UN's Westphalian basis disables it from providing these GPGs. I argue that world war has been avoided by other processes, and that weapons proliferation has not been sufficiently contained. While some treaty regimes on weapons have been more effective, treaty processes are ultimately insufficient because of their case-by-case nature and limited enforcement capacities. As a result, new technologies have put us on the road to massive new arms races. Thus, even for the oldest recognized categories of GPGs, the inter-state system under the UNSC has proven dangerously inadequate.

Preventing aggression: Why the UN could not fulfill its main goal

Structural problems in the UN's design

Common criticisms of the UN are often naive: people assume that it is too idealistic without examining its structural problems, or revile its bureaucratic waste without appreciating the difficulties that dedicated the UN's professional civil servants face, and how much expertise is gathered within the UN agencies. Some critics are ideological ultra-nationalists who see the UN as some kind of nefarious foreign agent; fanatical fringe groups have even spread myths that the UN intends to conquer America.

My critique is in a different spirit entirely from these shallow dismissals. Like virtually all cosmopolitans, I regard the founding of the UN as a great step forward in history, and I endorse the main aims of its founders. In particular, I agree with Gareth Evans that skeptics underestimate how many valuable tasks different UN agencies undertake, and overestimate its costs:

> The core functions of the UN ... engage some 37,000 people at a cost of just over $2 billion a year—about the same number of employees it takes, at rather higher cost ($3.7 billion), to run the New York City Police Department ... If to the UN's core functions are added its related programs and organs (like the UNDP and UNHCR), the other specialized programs and agencies of the entire UN family (like the FAO and WHO), and its peacekeeping activities, the total UN system cost is still no more than $15 billion.[2]

Evans is right: this is a lot of professional service for the common good of the world at a very modest price (and the more informal benefits of bringing together people from every nation on Earth is also worth a little bureaucratic redundancy). The terrible irony is that UN specialized programs and agencies in development, public health, culture, and environment, are far more successful than the Security Council. It is like a solar system with largely healthy planets orbiting a feeble, corrupted star.

Peacekeeping and peace enforcement missions have a more mixed record. Evans argues that the statistically real reduction in the number of conflict-related deaths in the world is "largely attributable to the huge upsurge in activity in conflict prevention, conflict management, negotiated peacemaking, and post-conflict peacebuilding," much of it "spearheaded by the maligned UN."[3] This is more controversial: while UN peacekeeping efforts have played a major role in conflict reduction, especially since 1989, there are many cases in which UN peacekeepers were sorely needed but never deployed—for example, in Libya after Qaddafi's fall. Moreover, such examples as the rise of terrorism in the Sahel, Assad's slaughter of Sunnis in Syria, and the uncontested Russian invasion of Crimea still show that the UNSC fails dramatically in the biggest cases—often because at least one veto-wielding member has a strategic interest in the injustices. This is not the fault of UN staff: Evans rightly cites Shashi Tharoor's distinction "between the UN as stage" for national governments to act, and "the secretariat and agencies" that have little control over the national leaders. He blames the failure to reform the system on groups of member nations[4] that like to hide behind a weak UN—in particular, the incentives that permanent five (P5) nations have to keep the Security Council ineffective.

My critique is focused on the UN as an institution and legal framework, as distinct from the execrable behavior of some nations or groups of states playing their parts on the UN stage. It is the *institutional design* that enables particular nations and groups to prevent effective UN action on major global problems. As with the US Articles of Confederation, the compromises made at the UN's founding rendered its decision-procedures and enforcement powers largely inadequate to its tasks. The core principles on which the UN architecture is based empower too many nations that are not committed to democratic values, or even (in the extreme cases) to the ideals of peace, basic security, minimal rights for civilians, and international rule of law.

Technically its charter allows the UN to exclude regimes that are too offensive to humanity; but as Orend notes, from an early point, it was "decided that it's better for everyone to be 'inside the tent,' so to speak," for fear that an excluded nation might get even worse.[5] That gamble proved to be a historic mistake. It prevented the benefits of UN membership from being used as an incentive, as it has been for EU or NATO membership. The *universal inclusion* of all nations, no matter how illegitimate their regimes are, is the UN's deepest flaw, to which the absolute veto power of the P5—one of Joseph Stalin's lasting gifts to humanity— is secondary.[6] While the distinctive status of five nations looks utterly outdated, the need for unanimous consent of the "great powers" in 1945 is a symptom of the underlying Westphalian principle: the UN's main goal is to preserve nation-states against threats of attack, rather than to uphold individual rights.

This was Franklin Roosevelt's idea, following Woodrow Wilson's intentions: as Meisler reports, Roosevelt thought that "[i]f some aggressor 'started to run amok and seeks to grab territory or invade its neighbors,' the new organization 'would stop them before they got started.'"[7] After the horrors of two world wars, it made perfect sense for the Allied leaders to prioritize preventing cross-border aggression. Still, Roosevelt gave too little weight to individual human rights, as he also showed in refusing Jewish refugees. Might makes right in the Security Council because the Council's main purpose is to defend the *de facto* existence of all nonaggressive national governments against external threats. But unfortunately this gambit, which compromised the UN's moral legitimacy to achieve the limited albeit noble goal of international security, has failed—as I argue next.

The Westphalian UN and the integrity of borders

The UN followed earlier efforts to secure the first category of GPGs concerning international security. Following the League of Nations, which was supposed to prevent aggressive war, the 1928 Kellogg-Briand Pact fundamentally changed international law: the parties—including the United States, all the major European nations, and Russia—rejected the realist view that sovereigns may make war at will to settle disputes or advance national interests.[8] Among other things, this made it illegal for nations to add territory or expand their borders through war, although that "crime against peace" was not fully articulated until the Nuremberg and Tokyo Tribunals. The same ban on aggression forms the core of the most important international treaty to date, i.e., the UN Charter—although the League Covenant was arguably stronger in one respect, demanding military cooperation when necessary to enforce the League of Nations' decisions.[9] UN expert Thomas G. Weiss confirms this assessment: the UN's "overarching policy goal is maintaining international peace by preventing the use of military force as an instrument of unilateral state policy;" more broadly, "[a] reliable system of collective security" was the "original raison d'être of the UN."[10] Its deeper normative goal was to reinforce the much older idea of international law as a constraint on the customary rights of nations.

These goals were not simply strategic, they were inspired by classical modern cosmopolitans such as Kant, as we saw (chapter two). For example, in the late eighteenth century, J.G. Fichte argued for a world system in which each nation has a "cosmopolitan right" to demand reciprocal recognition as sovereign as long as it respects the sovereignty of other nations and maintains a stable government—failed states being a threat to other nations, which therefore have the right to stabilize them. Fichte argued that a "confederation" of legitimate nations has the right to stop aggressive war, and may raise armies for this purpose. Thus, "[a]s this confederation expands and gradually encompasses the entire earth, the result will be *perpetual peace*, which is the only rightful relation among states."[11] Like Kant however, Fichte never imagined this permanent coalition of nations including tyrannical regimes: they never squarely faced the potential conflict between protecting nations as collective entities and defending the individual rights of their residents.

Thus the Westphalian tradition appeared for a time to be in concord with cosmopolitan thought while actually proceeding from a weaker normative basis. As Hale, Held, and Young note, the Westphalian limit on national sovereignty was "inherent in the idea" of a global order capable of maintaining peace and security: the unlimited right to war in a Hobbesian state of nature must be given up.[12] As Al Gore summarizes, the Treaty of Westphalia in 1648 "formalized the construction of a new order in Europe based on the primacy of nation-states, and the principle of noninterference by any nation-state in the affairs of another."[13] The League of Nations and the UN brought this idea to fruition: international law acquired far more normative weight (and attention) than it had prior to 1919 as a loose assemblage of treaties and customary norms. And yet, although it was a monumental achievement to give the Westphalian norms the peremptory legal force they now enjoy, the steps taken in 1945 were not ultimately effective in delivering peace. For its design makes the UN dependent on consensus among powerful nation-states to enforce these norms against war, thus diluting its coordinative capacity. It also defends national governments, no matter what their makeup or moral orientation, as presumptively expressing the collective cultural will of their people. As a result, antidemocratic regimes can exercise considerably weight within the UN, and especially on the Security Council.

At the end of the twentieth century, leading just war theorist James T. Johnson noted that the UN lacks the kind of final authority and responsibility for the common good traditionally required for a proper authority to declare war or use military force.[14] This is a point about sovereignty in Hamilton's sense: the UN's derivative nature, which gives it little control over armed forces, undermines its standing to wage war. Johnson argues that the Westphalian world order grossly fails to achieve public goods in the areas of security and justice in armed conflicts.[15] War has continued since the founding of the UN, and become even more violent with the rise of religious fundamentalism and the breakup of communist conglomerates previously held together by dictatorships.[16] This view is echoed by a growing chorus of critics in recent years. Political philosopher Fred Dallmayr explains that the inter-state system does not secure us from terrorist threats or deter and prevent crimes against humanity because it was only designed to secure borders from territorial aggression by other states.[17] More than seven decades after the UN's founding, our world system is still dominated by nations claiming unlimited sovereignty over their own lands and peoples.[18]

Admittedly, as Weiss argues, states are more pragmatically constrained now by many interdependencies, monitoring and lobbying by NGOs and inter-state agencies, and by bilateral and multilateral treaties with rare influence from UNSC resolutions. But these constraints, important as they are, have not prevented over a hundred smaller wars since the UN was formed, including many civil conflicts involving systemic attacks on civilians. The UN has been especially weak in defending the central provisions of the UDHR. As Burleigh Wilkins points out, the UN Charter made the protection of human rights "rest on the governments of the states where the violation of these rights occurs."[19] In practice that has meant that the Declaration and its two associated treaties amount to noble rhetoric with little enforcement. Similarly, the UN's International Court of Justice (ICJ) does not review General Assembly acts or Security Council resolutions—let alone laws of member nations—for consistency with human rights law. The ICJ only arbitrates disputes between nation-states that willingly submit a case to it; in 1945, no founding member of the UN would have allowed the ICJ to act like court of review.

Orend also emphasizes that "the UN is a voluntary association of states, and thus is ultimately their creature," protecting their "rights to political sovereignty and territorial integrity."[20] The compromise reached in founding the UN gave national governments virtually *absolute* sovereignty over their "internal affairs." Stalin was given a veto-wielding seat despite killing almost four million people by famine in Ukraine a decade earlier: he would not have joined without the promise that the UN would look the other way while he signed thousands of death warrants and carried out purges and pogroms. We can summarize the precepts guiding this design as follows:[21]

1 In order to secure peaceful coexistence, to avoid a devastating third world war, and to promote global trade and commerce, every national government accepts the right of every other to control its internal affairs as long as it does not act aggressively against other sovereign states.

2 The central purpose of the UN (and especially the enforcement powers vested in the Security Council) is to stabilize relations among nations of many different cultures, to secure their existing borders by deterring aggression, and when feasible, to restore these borders in response to invasions breaking the peace.

3 National rights of "self-determination" are irreducibly collective: they do not necessarily derive from each individual's right to autonomy. While colonial mandates should end, the collective right of whole peoples can be expressed through any type of regime and takes precedence over individual rights.

4 *De facto* control is the standard for recognition of national governments as sovereign; and each sovereign has unlimited original authority over its natural and monetary resources, limited only by its treaties. This holds whether or not the government is democratic, or grants equal basic liberties, or demonstrates even minimal concern for the common good of its citizens.

5 Thus any national government, however unjust it may be to its own people, will be accepted as a member of the UN, if it refrains from aggression toward foreign nations. Even governments committing mass atrocities can be members of the Security Council.

This blend of norms implicit within the UN Charter deeply conflicts with cosmopolitan ideals. Its associationist conception of collective self-determination puts it on the side of Westphalian statism against the rising paradigm that I called Rights-based sovereignty (RBS), based on the Enlightenment Principle, which makes individual rights and other public goods the justifying bases of political power. (The democratic requirements we considered in chapter two are a demanding version of generic RBS).

Thus the UN framework aims primarily at "peace" in the *negative, minimal sense* of security from wars of conquest, severed from the broader requirements of justice that were linked with peace in the Just War tradition.[22] This reflects the fact that wars for territorial gain had been the greatest cause of human suffering for centuries. But the UN was not designed this way because ideals of global justice went no further in 1945: the importance of the basic human rights was already recognized in the Charter of the Nuremberg Tribunal, in prior international conventions against war crimes, and soon after within the UDHR. Instead, the UN was so limited in its main goal for reasons of pure realpolitik: after surviving the confrontation with the Axis powers, leading nations had ample reason to settle for a *modus vivendi* relation among nations stabilized by the promise of UN action against aggression. If the threat of total war could be could be overcome by allowing bad regimes to act with impunity at home, it was worth it— especially to avoid nuclear holocaust. Any rational person would have made this choice in 1945. But the strategic situation is very different now (see the Introduction and chapter five).

The failure of the Westphalian paradigm

It is also clear now that the worthy compromise made in founding the UN has largely failed in its central purpose—even though many more treaties have followed in effort to control causes of war. This failure is due to problems very similar to those we found in the US Confederation (see chapter two). In particular the weakness of the Security Council results from four *central flaws*:

First, the infamous vetoes of the five permanent members prevents the UNSC from overcoming transnational CAPs. In general, the closer an authority is to making decisions on the basis of simple majority rule, the more effectively it can overcome CAPs of almost all kinds by coordinating enough parties.[23] Enforceable majority rule is thus a second-order public good: it can stop would-be spoilers and free riders whenever they are in a minority. By contrast, the higher that supermajority requirements get, the easier it is for a few holdouts to block any cooperative effort, no matter how important it may be to all others. The UN offers an extreme illustration of this problem: any CAP in which even one of the P5 nations has incentives to defect makes the UNSC totally ineffective.

Second, as noted above, because the UN is designed for universal inclusion of all *de facto* governments, the members of the Security Council need not be democratic or even rights-respecting regimes. The ten elected members, which currently include Kazakhstan and Kuwait, are chosen by UN nations on the basis of strategic interests, and sometimes back allied nations even when they are launching aggressive wars in violation of the UN Charter. This also applies to nations gaining membership on other influential bodies within the UN system such as the Human Rights Council, which currently include massive rights-violators like the regimes of Venezuela and the DRC.

Third, the Security Council lacks any real enforcement power of its own; even if it votes to use "all necessary measures" to combat some aggression or stop enormous atrocity, it can still only act *through* the operation of its most powerful members—usually via coalitions of nations willing to risk their troops as peacekeepers, or via other regional bodies (such as the African Union [AU] or NATO in recent years). This introduces a second level at which CAPs can block action necessary to secure peace or other GPGs: defectors may prevent willing nations from reaching the necessary threshold commitment of troops and resources (a losing AG), or cause resentment by free riding on a few nations who do all the work (an inequity problem).

For example, everybody recognizes that it was really the United States and Britain, not the UN, fighting in the Korean War; likewise, it was Britain, France and America rather than the UN that conducted the air war against Qaddafi's forces in Libya. As Evans puts it, the UN has no "peace enforcement" capacity of its own; "these operations are now universally seen as the province of specially created coalitions of the willing."[24] Gore concurs: when the diplomatic efforts of the UN and NGOs do not succeed and "sustained military operations are necessary ... 'coalitions of the willing' have been formed."[25] The UNSC merely authorizes enforcement actions by groups of nations, over which it then has little control. The most likely result is a chicken game, with all nations that benefit from enforcement actions (as moral goods or via other material side effects) hoping to free ride on the few willing nations. As a result of these three flaws, the Security Council is a veto-stymied paper tiger that can rarely do more than issue verbal criticism of injustices.

Alexander Hamilton could have diagnosed these problems instantly. Recall his insight in *Federalist* 15 that the fundamental failure of the American Confederation lay in its operation solely through the agency of the several states (see chapter two): the UN's system of *indirect enforcement* is the same flaw at the global level. Hamilton saw that this indirection in executive power arose from the Congress of Confederation having no direct relation to individual Americans in either direction—as a body authorized by them, or as a power coordinating them via legislation. Similarly, the UN's *derivative sovereignty* makes it entirely beholden to nation-states with no direct relation to their citizens. This is the UN's fourth central flaw: it has no primary sovereignty. Because of this, the UN cannot directly levy taxes on peoples or businesses, or raise its own armed forces for peace enforcement, or "speak" directly to citizens over the heads of national governments and gain their direct support.

Here we arrive at the heart of the matter: this fatal flaw of indirection, from which the others derive, is too deeply embedded in the UN's design and practice to be fixable. The universal inclusion of all nations makes it impossible to reform the UN so that its representatives are directly elected; but without direct election, the UN cannot build independent enforcement powers by legislating directly for citizens (e.g., by enforcing a trade embargo). How could representatives in a reformed General Assembly, let alone Security Council, ever be elected by citizens in nondemocratic nations who do not even get to elect their national government? In US history, the deep reforms of 1787 advocated by the federalists were possible only because all the states were (at least partly) democratic: despite serious flaws, they could hold elections for federal officers without wholly changing their nature. This also made later reforms, like expansions of suffrage and the direct election of senators, feasible in time. An analogous reform is not possible for over half the UN member nations today.

This analysis differs from more common critiques in arguing that the P5 veto problem is a symptom rather than the root the UN's powerlessness: the origin lies in the Westphalian spirit that led to the UN's confederal form and inclusion of horrendous regimes. Thus Daalder and Lindsay are correct to reject the common fallacy that "the universalism of the UN" is the "gold standard of legitimacy." On the contrary, it is the UN's worst feature. The nature of the sovereign agents acting to make decisions in the UN system is crucial, and at least half of the governments who send ambassadors to the UN are *morally illegitimate*: "Most states in the world today, including a majority of UN members, do not represent the interests or perspectives of the people they rule."[26] The Security Council's weakness arises partly from the veto system and lack of direct enforcement functions, both of which sap its coordinative power; but its most damning flaw is moral hollowness. Rather than drawing authority directly from the world's peoples, it gives voice and leverage to their oppressors.

This scandalous situation has, tragically, made the UN a losing bargain: while protecting dictators, the UN has proven unable to provide international security. The UN's founders optimistically underestimated the toll that Stalin and his successors would take, and they could not foresee Mao's actions. As Weiss notes, the original "idea that the Security Council would automatically mobilize dedicated UN forces against aggression foundered on the shoals of Cold War rivalries," and it never returned; "peacekeeping" missions were a stopgap invention of UN pioneers during the 1950s.[27] Thus the UNSC never acquired the dedicated and fully equipped armed forces that it was supposed to have under control of its military secretariat. And even on rare occasions when the UNSC agrees on strong enforcement measures, national governments have often insisted on retaining active control of their own forces in UN combat missions authorized under Chapter VII of the charter.[28]

As a result, during the Cold War, the UN could do little to deter, stop, or reverse most wars of aggression since 1945. Of course, the roughly 91,699 peacekeeping military personnel and civilian support staff deployed around the world in 22 operations (with most in seven missions) as of June 2018[29] do much good, and have helped calm many small-scale conflicts and prevent hostilities in other tense regions from leading to new violence.[30] But these peacekeeping missions are rarely coupled with robust nation-building programs that are needed to root out the corruption dogging many developing nations. For example, despite decades of UN peacekeeping missions in the DRC and over $100 billion in foreign aid, 17 years of Joseph Kabila's rule have left chaos, little growth, and almost four million internally displaced persons (IDPs)—5 percent of the nation.[31] Peacekeeping forces are also largely limited to civil conflict zones; they are not designed to stop large-scale wars between nations, or to take back unjustly-gotten territory from aggressors. That kind of combat mission has been carried out by other nations authorized by the UNSC, such as the United States with a few allies liberating Kuwait from Saddam Hussein in 1991. At most, UN peacekeepers occasionally help stabilize a peace that resulted from a negotiated settlement between the factions after a war has ended.

Thus, despite the best intentions in its design and heroic efforts of its diplomats, the UN is *not* among the main reasons that classical wars started by aggressive invasion have declined since World War II. Post-1945, Europe avoided repeating the mistakes made after World War I by accepting the Marshall Plan, which was largely an American initiative.[32] Building on this reconstruction, European nations established the European Economic Community, which has grown into the EU—a stronger regional community with a common market, shared cultural and educational programs, and a currency shared among most EU nations (see chapter two). Nuclear war between NATO and the Soviet Union was (barely) prevented by bilateral deterrence and the Kennedy-Khrushchev diplomacy during the Cuban Missile Crisis. As Yunker notes, this "cannot reasonably be attributed to the existence and activities of the United Nations."[33] Moreover, later de-escalations of the nuclear threat were largely achieved through bilateral arms control treaties like START I and II.

Regional organizations have also sometimes acted to prevent or undo crimes of aggression; for example, since it succeeded the Organization of African Unity in 2001, the AU has established some credibility by stopping Eritrea's efforts to undermine the transitional government in Somalia, and by resisting Al-Shabab militants there.[34] Similarly a subset of ECOWAS nations (the Economic Community of West African States) took some military action in effort to stop the Sierra Leone conflict during the 1990s, although ultimately UK military intervention was necessary to end the atrocities.[35]

Some multilateral treaties have also helped decrease risks of international war: for example, the Nuclear Nonproliferation Treaty (NPT) of 1970, which came from a UN process, gets significant credit for the fact that only a handful of states possess nuclear weapons over four decades later.[36] Yet the acquisition of nuclear weapons by Israel, Pakistan, and North Korea illustrate again the limits of UN control. North Korea is one of the worst tyrannies in the world, yet it is protected by China against UN intervention.

Meanwhile, many wars have occurred since the Security Council's creation without its effective involvement. Since 1948, there have been 17 major wars with only four Security Council authorizations for countermeasures (plus the partial authorization of NATO action against the Taliban in Afghanistan).[37] This tally includes the long war of attrition in Vietnam, when French and US vetoes would have blocked any UNSC opposition; but it leaves out several smaller wars in which nations intervened unilaterally to stop massacres because the UNSC was doing nothing—such as India intervening in East Pakistan in 1971, or Vietnam invading Cambodia in late 1978 to stop the Khmer Rouge's mass murder, and Tanzania's counter-invasion of Uganda to stop Idi Amin's brutal regime, also in late 1978.[38]

This count also omits some others conflicts in which potential P5 vetoes made it impossible for the UNSC to turn back aggression across borders, such as the invasion of Hungary by the Soviet Union in 1956 and American actions to support US-friendly military dictatorships in Guatemala or Nicaragua. The UN did authorize force to turn back the 1950 invasion from the north in Korea, but this was possible only because the Soviet Union was boycotting the Security Council to protest Taiwan holding the Chinese seat. While distracted by Korea, the UNSC did nothing when Mao's new People's Republic invaded and annexed Tibet in 1950. Instead, it eventually rewarded them by giving Mao's aggressive regime the P5 seat. Similarly, the UNSC cannot act to counter new Chinese aggressions in the south Asian seas, and it will be powerless if China ever invades Taiwan. This has been prevented so far only by the deterrent threat of American forces.

More recently, Russian opposition again prevented the Security Council from acting to stop Serbian aggression and mass murder in Bosnia and Kosovo in the 1990s. A game of chicken between nations unwilling to put their forces at risk led to inaction during the Rwandan genocide; the Hutu militants calculated correctly that killing Belgian peacekeepers would prompt a UN withdrawal rather than a punishing UN response.[39] China and Russia have blocked action against the regimes in north Sudan and Syria that have killed hundreds of thousands (see chapter six).[40] Obviously the UN was powerless when Russia seized Crimea and fostered a proxy war in eastern Ukraine. And the Security Council has done little more than issue paper condemnations in response to several other bloody conflicts in Asia and Africa in the last half-century. Even the UNSC's authorization of a joint Australian-New Zealander force to protect East Timor in 1999 came only after the Indonesian government had stopped its attacks on civilians there under pressure from US President Bill Clinton. Here again, two nations did most of the work.

Finally and most critically, the Security Council did not do nearly enough when the 1948–1949 Arab-Israeli war prevented the establishment of *both* states mandated by the General Assembly act that created Israel. This may be the failure of greatest historical ramifications, because the UN's refusal to enforce the two-nation plan and to manage division of Jewish and Arab populations opened the door to decades of bloody conflict that have helped spawn fundamentalist jihadi terror movements that now threaten many nations around the world. The UN only sent emissaries to the Middle East to negotiate armistices between Israel and its enemies, including the heroic diplomat Ralph Bunche; but war-weary P5 nations sent no troops.[41] If instead the UNSC had defended Israel in 1948, compensated displaced Arab residents, and ensured that a Palestinian state was created—with Jerusalem as a shared "international city" as originally proposed—it might have prevented the subsequent wars against Israel, and avoided Israeli settlements illegally built on conquered territory, which have prolonged the conflict. The original World Trade Center might still be standing today if the UN had worked effectively in 1948–1949.

This tragic record of UN failure shows how vetoes and lack of direct control destroy coordinative power. After reviewing such cases, along with civil conflicts like Russia's brutal assault on Chechnya, Hale, Held, and Young rightly conclude that

> the entrenchment of privilege for leading states [on the UNSC], which was once necessary to foster participation and legitimacy, now stands in the way of Security Council action on matters of life and death. . . . The threat and use of a Security Council veto has transformed that body into a typical state of inertia wherein very little progress is made on many pressing issues. . . . In effect, the Security Council has become locked into this hierarchy of power.[42]

The result is that national governments have lost faith in the UN's ability even to protect the integrity of borders, let alone help secure other GPGs. So far, the only major alternative has been the notion, reinvented under George W. Bush, that America could act by default as the world's policeman.[43] Yet this unilateral approach has also proven hopeless. As Thomas Magnell warned in 2002, the idea that the United States may intervene unilaterally in any nation when we think this necessary for our national security or the world's good "abrogates accepted notions of sovereignty" and violates the requirement of UNSC approval for all military actions beyond immediate self-defense.[44] If universalized, this unilateralist policy would unravel what little coordinating power remains within the UN framework. One nation, no matter how mighty, can never garner the legitimacy to act as the world's policeman. Acting without perceived international authorization draws fire from alienated allies and provides easy fodder for propaganda by Russia and terrorist groups.

Moreover, American power is now manifestly insufficient to provide GPGs related to security, and lukewarm support from other NATO nations will not fill the vacuum. As Philip Breedlove notes, NATO's military budget has declined since 1990 despite its additional members and Russia's "enduring existential threat;" few NATO nations can conduct "full spectrum combat operations," and only the United States can do so for extended periods.[45] US unilateralism amounts to paying most of the costs for maintaining stability across the whole globe, while other nations, including many rich ones, free ride on our $695 billion defense budget (fiscal 2018). This habit of expecting America to take the lead in every crisis means that when the United States balks, no one acts—so the dictators causing the crisis win the chicken game. After the wars in Iraq and Afghanistan, Americans lack both the resources and collective will to continue massive interventions: that is the main reason why NATO nations have not organized a coalition (with Egypt, Jordan, and Saudi Arabia) to stop Assad's mass murder in Syria, and relied mainly on Kurdish forces to fight ISIS. The US military budget is already unsustainably high, larger than the next nine national militaries combined, adding to an enormous annual deficit that is ballooning due to huge tax cuts in December 2017. Clearly, America is no longer willing or stable enough to provide the bulk of global security. But when the world has no policeman, aggressive invasions like Russia seizing Crimea and atrocities like those in Syria, with all their knock-on effects, will become more regular events.

Weapons proliferation and the limits of treaty processes

The spread of WMDs

While armed invasion by belligerent governments seeking territorial gain was the primary bane of European history until 1945, democratic nations are now threatened by nonstate actors such as terrorist groups who wish to establish fundamentalist theocracies and commit endless small-scale attacks in western cities. The increasing accessibility of more powerful weapons emboldens smaller rogue regimes as well. John Lango points out that over a hundred nations are already capable of manufacturing biological weapons, and as more use this capability, the probability that a plague will result from accidental release or intentional attack magnifies.[46] Given "terrible and unavoidable uncertainties about WMD [weapons of mass destruction] possession by nongovernmental agents, such as revolutionaries, mercenaries, arms dealers, and of course, terrorists," the mere possession of WMDs, especially by weak states, is a threat to the security of all peoples.[47] Similarly, Thomas Magnell argues that WMDs "have become cheap enough for small nations, poor nations, like-minded bands of individuals, even prosaic criminal organizations to seriously menace large, wealthy, militarily strong nations."[48]

This problem is increased when tyrannical regimes are overthrown without sufficient plans, as part of reconstruction, to repossess the regime's armaments. For example, too much of Qaddafi's weapons stockpile has ended up on the black market. This would not have happened if a large coalition of nations, perhaps acting as UN peacekeepers, had taken responsibility for securing Libya and stabilizing its new caretaker government after Qaddafi's fall. As their power expands, smaller rogue states and large terrorist groups empowered by black market weaponry edge international relations closer to a Hobbesian state of nature: this "predicament of nation states calls for a global authority with sufficient power to redress or prevent attacks on themselves. This requires a transfer of power and a relinquishment of significant elements of sovereignty" to consolidate sufficient authority in the global institution to counter these threats.[49]

To this argument, Magnell adds that life and liberty are "preeminent among prudential values and, together with justice, preeminent among moral values;" but today they cannot adequately be secured for anyone without a stronger global authority.[50] Like international money laundering and human trafficking, the fabrication and spread of weapons of mass and moderate destructiveness is now a global public harm that lies beyond the power of national governments and their IGOs to contain. Because each nation has a short-term economic interest in selling sophisticated weapons, a PD prevails: even morally motivated nations will not accept a ban on exporting such weapons without a system for assuring that all others will do likewise. Without such a system, there can be little control on the global free market in guns, bombs, missiles, land mines, improvised explosive device (IED) components, military aircraft, and even the materials and knowledge necessary to make chemical and biological weapons.

Illegal arms shipments are also hard to stop because controlling them can be a weakest-link CAP: like cocaine and heroin, they can move through the nations or ports with the least internal policing. Only very high-tech materials such as nuclear and nerve gas weapons remain hard for terrorist groups and their state sponsors to get, and for how long? Without authoritative global coordination, sufficient control cannot be maintained over stockpiles of nuclear materials to prevent all such materials from falling into the hands of ideological fanatics. Assad's success may also encourage more tyrannical regimes to build chemical stockpiles. As Magnell says, a world in which such WMDs could end up in the hands of dictators and zealots across all continents "should be unthinkable," but that is the highly suboptimal result to which the invisible hand of the current global weapons market is leading.[51]

Treaties for arms control

The history recounted above acknowledges UN success in facilitating arms control treaties between governments; but given black markets and rogue regimes, such treaties have proven insufficient to halt the global spread of powerful weapons. Another weakness in this intergovernmental approach is that nations can withdraw from most treaties at will (making them essentially confederal arrangements at best). For example, North Korea has exited the NPT,[52] despite sanctions imposed by US allies. Often no serious penalties follow treaty exit or violation, in which case the treaty has correspondingly little power to overcome PD or chicken CAPs, which are common in arms races. The International Atomic Energy Agency (IAEA) provides an inspection system that can be engaged by the UN; but this makes little difference if nations can prevent the IAEA from doing its job at key uranium enrichment facilities within their territory.

Iran remains a member of the NPT, and UNSC-approved sanctions against Iran since 2006 did apply real pressure in their case, leading to the landmark 2015 nuclear control deal with Tehran (the Joint Comprehensive Plan of Action). But this is a rare exception because, as noted in chapter two, coordinating broad sanctions is very difficult: each nation hopes that a sufficient number of others will pay the costs to sanction the offender while they still trade with the offender. Thus within a mutual policing network, secondary sanctions may be necessary to overcome the CAP involved making primary sanctions effective.

Hale, Held, and Young note the comparatively stronger enforcement system built into the Chemical Weapons Convention of 1997 (CWC), which commits members to accept inspections without warning.[53] But the refusal of Hussein's regime in Iraq to allow inspectors immediate access to suspected chemical and biological weapons sites did not provoke anything close to sufficient UNSC action to enforce inspections. This is a crucial forgotten cause of the US invasion of Iraq in 2003, as Michael Walzer rightly stressed in a series of papers leading up to that fateful decision.[54] In 2013, the Assad regime's repeated use of chemical weapons against Sunni civilians in Syria also met with little response—a threat by the United States proved hollow. Russia then brokered an insincere promise from Assad to hand over all his chemical weapons. Despite Russian pronouncements that Assad had complied, he launched further chemical attacks (e.g., with concentrated chlorine) repeatedly in 2017 and 2018. As this illustrates, because enforcement of a treaty like the CWC is left to the voluntary initiative of member states, it involves a chicken CAP.

The situation with biological weapons is even more worrying because the 1975 convention against their use does not include mandatory inspections and enforcement. Attempts have been made to strengthen the convention, which includes 178 state parties—most of the world— but support for the small IGO established by the treaty has actually weakened in recent years.[55] Still, upholding this treaty may be an AG among governments, which fear to use biological weapons: their external harms are less predictable or controllable than chemical weapons, and could include fouling one's own nest. But terrorists with anthrax would be quite different; those willing to die for their cause will not be deterred by the fear of becoming infected themselves. Thus governments must strictly limit the technology to grow and concentrate deadly viruses or bacteria, especially now that scientists working on vaccines have been able to reconstruct pandemic threats like the 1918 flu virus.[56]

The proliferation of weapons of moderate destruction, such as military aircraft, rockets, conventional bombs, shorter-range missiles, mines, and IED components is immediately relevant for terrorist threats, as the recent history of conflicts in the Middle East shows. One of the few bright spots is the Mine Ban Treaty of 1997 (also called the Ottawa Convention), with 164 state parties. Land mines cause extensive and long-term risks of injury and death to millions of civilians,[57] and "major social and economic burdens" on nations with high rates of injury (such as Cambodia), leaving "large tracts of land…useless for cultivation and grazing."[58] These are enormous indiscriminate externalities. Thus the push to stop future land mine-laying was promoted by many NGOs such as the International Campaign to Ban Land Mines (ICBL) championed by the late Princess Diana Spencer. *Human Rights Watch* reports that this treaty has brought real benefits:

> Since the treaty went into effect on March 1, 1999, more than 46 million stockpiled antipersonnel mines have been destroyed, 23 countries have completed mine clearance to become mine-free, and the annual number of casualties from landmines and explosive remnants of war has decreased dramatically. In recent years, antipersonnel landmines have been used only by Syria, Burma, Israel, and Libya, none of which have joined the Mine Ban Treaty, as well as [by] a small number of rebel groups.[59]

Yet the United States has still not ratified the treaty, largely due to insistence on using mines to protect South Korea from North Korea—despite the availability of newer technology for this task. Bill Clinton imposed a six-year moratorium on the "export, sale, or transfer of antipersonnel land mines abroad,"[60] but this ban was reversed under George W. Bush. In 2014, the Obama administration announced that it would not acquire or produce new land mines, but the Trump administration is already restocking cluster munitions. Among the 34 other nations that still have not ratified the Mine Ban treaty are China, India, Pakistan, the Russian Federation and Iran; and the treaty does not ban anti-vehicle mines. Moreover, to get it done, promoters of the Mine Ban Treaty had to take it outside the UN's Conference on Disarmament framework, which is gridlocked by the need for consensus from all minor participants.

Unfortunately, recent conflicts in Afghanistan, Libya, Ukraine and Yemen have led to increased causalities from land mines, with 8605 reported in 2016 (80 percent suffered by civilians).[61] And the limits on high-tech land mines in circulation have not stopped ISIS and Taliban forces from acquiring or making their own versions of land mines, leaving IED booby-traps all over towns they have vacated. The technology to make low-grade buried explosives is now too widely accessible to be stopped by the massive quarter-century of work to outlaw mines. As with guns, 3d printing will only make this problem worse. The same applies to vehicular bombs, suicide vests, and makeshift mortars used by terrorist groups.

There are myriad other efforts to control small arms such as small missiles and powerful firearms, but they are generally less effective. As Gore rightly complains, "[w]hen a new generation of weapons is manufactured, the older generation is not destroyed," but instead sold at bargain prices to warlords and unjust regimes in conflict zones.[62] UN-backed efforts, including the new Arms Trade Treaty passed by the General Assembly in April 2013,[63] are laudable but likely to produce only marginal reductions in the illicit trade in these weapons.[64] This treaty hopes to limit tanks and armored vehicles, artillery, combat aircraft, warships, missiles and small arms; and it sets up a Secretariat to implement the treaty. But the limits it sets are too subjective: states party to the treaty must judge whether their own sales of these weapons could facilitate breaches of peace or violations of international humanitarian law.[65] Moreover, only 94 states have ratified this treaty (as of December 2017); and among the large exporters of arms, this includes only Britain, France, and Germany. Most of Asia is not party to this treaty; China, Russia, India, and Pakistan have not even signed it, and chances for US ratification seem slim. Small-arms shipments continue to fragile states fraught with corruption and violent militias.[66]

Clearly, strict controls on exports of large firearms and artillery weapons are crucial to making any real dent in their availability on the global market, but influential nations such as the United States and Russia have vested interests in companies that profit hugely from these exports—an appalling side effect of a large military-related sector in their economies. Gore points directly to this "military-industrial complex," blaming "the lobbying power and political influence of gun manufacturers and defense companies" for "this spread of weapons around the world." This holds especially in America, which supplied 52 percent of "all the military weapons sold" to importing countries in 2010.[67] A CNN article reported that arms exports jumped over 30 percent just from 2008 to 2012, with the United States providing 39 percent of the supply and Russia 14 percent,[68] followed by Germany, France, China, Britain, and other developed nations.[69] Official arms sales by all nations jumped from a total of $17.5 billion in 2003 to $49 billion by 2009 and to $71.8 billion by 2014.[70] That is a steep rate of increase at more than twice average inflation. This diffusion of firepower in planes, tanks, bombs, missiles, and guns is a disaster for the world. The global lure of profits is clearly swamping arms control efforts in these crucial areas.

This is one of the starkest illustrations of how relatively helpless treaty regimes are in the face of PD-type dynamics: leaders in weapons-manufacturing nations know that if they do not secure sales contracts for their military industries, competing nations will just take up the slack; thus they gain little from holding off unless *every* potential supplier joins them in export limits. The problem is exacerbated by outdated national accounting standards that count these arms sales as credits in national GDP figures and world economic growth, although they are (at best) costs of containing threats that are pure negative externalities, much like the costs of running prisons. A league of democracies could get a handle on this enormous problem by constraining all member nations to limit their weapons sales and sanctioning non-members who send arms into conflict zones: when enough nations complied with stricter limits, either voluntarily or by force, the opportunity costs in lost revenue to any one nation would much less than its benefits in reduced dangers later on.

Cyberwar, satellites, and robotic weapons

The difficulty of deterring cyberattacks

The world also faces a new generation of military technologies that will raise the stakes even further. We have no major treaty that tries to rein in the growing threats of cyberattacks of all the following kinds:

- massive data thefts by government-sponsored agents for espionage, to supply domestic industries with secret technologies, and to fuel crippling levels of cybercrime;
- political sabotage via data theft, planting false stories, trolling social media sites to push propaganda, and using bots to plant fake comments and attack opposing media sources;
- use of software to sabotage infrastructure, transport systems, communication networks, or military machines (like the Iranian centrifuges attacked by the US-Israeli "Stuxnet" virus).

While western governments have focused mainly on the third category until 2016, it is now clear that all three kinds of cyberattack are being directly promoted by hostile states to undermine democratic nations (see the Introduction). It is not clear that a treaty to address them could be enforced, because assessing violations of it might prove technically impossible if hackers could beat monitoring systems and make it look as though their attacks came from other countries.

There are at least four massive CAPs that the world faces in this area. First, cyberwar represents a new frontier in arms races, with all sides suffering rising costs that may leave them in roughly the same comparative relations of power after the expensive and dangerous escalation. Richard Clarke argues that a lot of cyber-weapons are already locked and loaded, ready to be triggered: for example, "Chinese, and presumably US decision makers have authorized placing logic bombs" into each other's military and utility systems, such as those running power grids.[71] Unfortunately in preparation for cyberwar, the natural tendency to end mutually counterproductive escalation through a tit-for-tat strategy may not hold if there is enough doubt about what cyberattack capabilities the other side has built, and difficulty in tracing an attack's origin with sufficient certainty.[72]

Second, the lack of credible deterrence makes a multilateral balance of threats difficult to craft. China was able to steal the personal information of four million US government employees in a 2015 breach with no significant response. Direct Russian attacks have brought down banking and media systems in Estonia, the power grid and election systems in Ukraine, and communications networks in Georgia, all without suffering any material consequences. US sanctions against Russia announced in March 2018 were partly in response to Russian efforts to plant malware in systems controlling our power grids.[73] But this may not be sufficient: there is a clear need for a stronger coordinated deterrence against cyberattacks and policies to punish offending regimes based on the preponderance of evidence even when they deny launching the attack.

Yet lack of transparency distinguishes cyber-powers from traditional nuclear capacities. As Clarke stresses, the most effective cyberattack capabilities may be kept totally clandestine until used: "The potential surprise capability" of a new computer virus that could shut down key computer systems, and cyber-defenses unknown to the attacker, "makes deterrence in cyberwar theory fundamentally different" from conventional and nuclear deterrence.[74] The attacker may be able to neutralize the enemy's offensive systems (almost) entirely and then disconnect his own country from the global internet—or he may be overconfident that he can. This amounts to a real or imagined first-mover advantage that makes a tit-for-tat strategy unable to overcome the CAP. As Gore notes, "some Chinese military strategists have written that a well-planned cyberattack on the United States could allow China to 'gain equal footing' with the U.S. in spite of U.S. superiority in conventional and nuclear weaponry."[75] Such enthusiasm could encourage aggressive moves in a Pacific conflict. NATO nations could only build up a deterrent to cyberwar strategies by credible threat of a massive response to any (successful or attempted) first cyber-strike on us.

Third, there are tipping point problems. As Clarke explains, the first-striker's potential advantages may force a quick decision by the victim nation who sees the first strike coming or unfolding; but a hasty decision may be an overreaction.[76] Although NATO itself has no coordinated "offensive cyberforces" to counter Russian hackers who increasingly target NATO systems, NATO declared in 2014 that "it could rule a cyberattack on one of its member states to be the equivalent of an armed attack, which would lead to a commitment by all NATO members to respond."[77] There is thus a clear risk of rapid escalation into a new scenario with which world leaders have little experience. Clarke also notes that some cyber-weapon "such as worms, can spread globally in minutes," potentially imposing collateral damage on many innocent third parties,[78] somewhat like a biological attack.

Thus again the need to deter cyber-sabotage *before* it happens. Given the potential that a cyber-response might fail, a guaranteed kinetic response may be the only effective deterrent, as it proved to be with nuclear arms. For example, NATO policy could promise that a cyberattack on our stock market, power grid, or communications systems would be met by sinking naval vessels or destroying air force bases in the attacking nation, in addition to cyber-sabotage measures. Yet this tough approach demands confidence in attribution, which in turn requires international agreements on networking protocols that make tracing easier.[79] Nations refusing to participate in such systems that enable attribution would be suspect and thus blamable with lower levels of evidence.

If such a policy sounds disproportionate, we should remember that lack of deterrence may lead to far worse outcomes. Still, a broad democratic league would offer the alternative of potent economic sanctions against nations launching first cyberstrikes, and might eventually be able to close off large portions of the internet for months to any nation that originated or frequently acted as a conduit for serious cyberattacks. A similar response might deter systemic cybercrime causing large economic harms. A league of democracies could also share the massive costs of cyber-shields that can effectively defend civilian infrastruc-ture, financial networks, and transportation systems—including ways to switch such systems quickly to "a non-networked" backup control once it is evident that a cyberwar is underway.[80]

Fourth, as noted in the Introduction, Putin's regime has opened a whole new front with cyberattacks on democratic systems across the western world, and paid little price for these acts of war. This extends far beyond supporting particular candidates like Marine Le Pen or Donald Trump and undermining their opponents; it is a new kind of cyberwar aimed at "discrediting the entire idea of a free and fair election."[81] This wide effort to destroy our news media and essential political institutions might be far more damaging in the long run than a cyberattack on military bases or infrastructure. The Russians have done much more than launch cyberbots and pay small armies of Macedonians to spread false news stories that harm Putin's polit-ical opponents abroad.[82] In Poland, they eavesdropped on politi-cians to promote a right-wing party that has since taken over public medias and tried to dissolve the constitutional court.[83] Russian cyber-mercenaries and bots are posting thousands of artificial comments on social media to shape coverage of Russia and inflame social rifts and tensions within democratic nations.[84]

This danger is growing, *whether or not* any official in the Trump circle directly colluded by encouraging Russians to steal their oppo-sition's emails. Five months before the US midterm elections of 2018, Facebook is scrambling to take down hundreds of new propaganda pages apparently started by Russian interests. Putin's massive cam-paign to corrupt democratic processes and public trust in free media systems will never be stopped without an equally massive response. In my opinion, a declaration of war against Russia followed by a wide spectrum of conventional military strikes would be justified to pun-ish and deter these continuing attacks on our social fabric. However, a wide league of democracies would be able to punish Putin's regime with proportionately crippling financial and trade sanctions—along with initiatives to make Europe independent of Russian gas.

Arms races in space and robotics

Other developing technologies create further challenges. We have a new arms race in military satellites as Russia and China catch up with the US. Without an enforceable treaty limiting space-based weap-ons, China and Russia have already deployed satellites that can move next to enemy satellites and then explode. Next we may see missile arrays and lasers on satellites that can hit ground targets and ground-launched missiles, and threaten other satellites on which vital military navigation and civilian communications depend. Ground-based missiles and lasers can also hit strategically valuable satellites.[85] Of course such kinetic assaults could be combined with cyberattacks on satellites as well. But the arduous process of creating a treaty to control space-based weapons has not even begun, and verifying compliance would require inspecting each satellite before it is launched.

A new horizon also looms in robotic weaponry; drone technology is only the tip of the iceberg. In the next three decades, we may see weaponized driverless ground vehicles and seagoing vessels that are operated remotely. While the era of droid armies may be a bit farther off, advances made in commercial robotics will eventually make this feasible too. Nanotechnology adds the disturbing possibility of miniaturized flying drones, swarms of computerized metal insects, and even microscopic devices that mimic a bacterial attack. Aside from the risk that such weapons might be hacked by opponents, they share with drones and cyber-weapons the danger of making it seemingly low-cost or easy to attack. While such technology may help in the fight against terrorism in the near term, over the long run, it could lead to new arms races, with trillions of dollars that could be spent on human welfare and the environment diverted to weapons that become outdated almost as quickly as our cell phones. Gore notes a Brookings estimate that "since 1940, the United States has spent $5.5 *trillion* on its nuclear war fighting capability—more than on any other program other than Social Security."[86] Imagine how much better off the country would be if just half of that money—almost $36 billion a year—had gone into education, infrastructure, or even nuclear power stations instead. We do not want to repeat this waste in the robotic age, but we may be doomed to do so without the coordinating power of a strong transnational government to enforce strict global limits on robotic, nano, and space weapons.

The superiority of government over multiple self-policing treaty regimes

All these cases underline the grave limits of international treaties as a means to securing GPGs related to security. Treaty-making processes are slow and also subject to CAPs; only in cases where the problem approximates toward an AG, or a tit-for-tat strategy is possible in response to a PD, do they stand much chance. Even then, arms control treaties need big public campaigns to get them adopted. In this respect, making treaties is like taking a vote that extends over years and requires a very large supermajority of all the relevant agents, often approaching 100 percent of the major contributors to the transnational harm that is being corrected. As the prior chapter stressed, even when such a bargain succeeds, nations can often invoke an exit procedure at minimal costs, or abrogate a treaty they have ratified, or refuse to do their part in punishing treaty violations. Without a system to make such spoilers pay large costs, even the most important treaties lack real teeth. As Sandler says, the lack of enforcement mechanisms is the chief problem "plaguing many international agreements or protocols."[87] Yet a system powerful enough to overcome this problem (as CP requires) should also be democratically answerable to all the peoples affected (per DP). Treaty regimes often meet neither of these crucial conditions.

Of course, the alternative of forming a democratic transnational union with revenue-raising and enforcement powers would also require resolving significant CAPs. Sandler rightly notes that creating a robust enforcement mechanism often "poses its own Prisoner's Dilemma;"[88] thus forming a supranational structure requires overcoming significant inertia,[89] as with any institutional public good. But the difference is that the CAPs blocking formation of a higher level of government only have to be overcome once. The stakes are large and so the resistance will be high, as the American case in 1787 showed. But if the new government is created, it can then overcome lots of other CAPs, securing *many different* TPGs and GPGs, e.g., by assuring enforcement of many treaties. By contrast, organizing different IGOs to enforce each treaty, or distinct networks of transnational NGOs or similar clubs for each TPG, requires overcoming different CAPs in each case—and then overcoming new CAPs every time the self-policing network needs enforcement actions. As noted in chapters two and three, this is like trying to solve each problem with a separate mini-government and finding new volunteers to punish each violation.

So while the difficulty and costs of creating a single strong transnational government might be twenty times higher than forming an intergovernmental treaty or club solution to provide a single GPG (e.g., security from weaponized satellites), the transnational government is a flexible multipurpose solution for a hundred such GPGs. It could also tie different TPGs together: if you accept costs to support this one TPG, you get more access to another. For example, a democratic league could enact favorable bargains with nonmember nations by ensuring that a massive block of large-economy nations would be more open to trade with them when they comply. A government system acting to secure different TPGs can create such links, while largely autonomous nodes in a loose transnational network can only cobble together temporary or *ad hoc* support for each TPG one by one.

Stopping the causes of terrorism and sharing the costs of nation-building

The United States spent about $1,500 billion on "global war on terror" operations between 2001–2014,[90] only then to see the rise of ISIS across parts of Iraq and Syria. Growing terrorist groups in the Sahel in Africa and northwest Pakistan, and the lone-wolf attacks they inspire in other nations, are even harder to stop than the spread of powerful weapons. Terrorism can be defined as the intentional targeting of multiple civilians (for death, injury, or capture) by combatants in order to evoke fear, panic, or flight, as a means to political ends. It is mass violence and murder to cause terror among civilians as a means to reach ideological goals. Terrorism so defined violates all the rules of war that have become part of the peremptory law of nations over time. It is a method of war comparable to the repression tactics of tyrants, utterly without honor, worse than piracy, no matter what military disadvantages or ultimate goals are cited to justify it. Religious sects that valorize it are corrupt, even barbaric in their disregard for children pressed into service as suicide bombers. But the problem is too large for individual nations to conquer one by one, especially in areas where this cultural virus is rampant. Unfortunately it is also largely beyond the power of the UN and related regional organizations to contain.

Thomas G. Weiss notes that the UN has adopted a strong convention to criminalize acts that could lead to the ultimate nightmare of nuclear terrorism, but the convention relies on nations to enforce it with their own justice systems. Real action to prevent weapons-grade materials from falling into terrorist hands is done by direct multilateral cooperation among nations in Europe, North America, Russia, and former Soviet states. But proliferation of nuclear technology still poses a huge danger: for example, Gore notes that "the former head of Pakistan's nuclear program... developed extensive ties with Islamic militant groups."[91] Still, Weiss emphasizes that despite weaknesses in some nations' laws, "13 global treaties constitute a composite policy to define, proscribe, and punish such individual categories of terrorism as hijacking, piracy, hostage-taking, bombing civilians, procuring nuclear materials, and financing terrorist activities."[92]

This is an impressive accomplishment. Yet such treaties do little to pressure nations that fail to uphold treaty provisions; the inter-state approach relies largely on moral suasion and shaming. The difficulty of getting nations to cooperate in relatively simple cases like suppressing piracy off the Somali coast illustrates the temptation to free ride on nations with more to lose. Even when cooperation against terrorism is a win-win for most governments (a harmony game, not a CAP), particular regimes may think they stand to gain from religiously inspired violence or from the social divisions that terrorist groups help to reinforce. For example, the weak government of Lebanon cannot resist Hezbollah forces that control parts of that nation. Iran supports Hezbollah along with Shia militias in Syria and Houthis rebels in Yemen, all to weaken rival Sunni-led governments in Jordan and Saudi Arabia. The result in Yemen has been a civil war threatening hundreds of thousands with more malnutrition and disease. Existing agreements among nations do not put the necessary pressures on regimes of this kind. Nor do they solve the problem for governments that are willing in principle to stop terrorists but lack the means (e.g., Libya or Nigeria).

However, I agree with Weiss that a truly effective response to the rise of terrorism requires addressing its causes rather than only its symptoms. He cites Kofi Annan's smart approach, embodied in the 2006 Global Counter-Terrorism strategy focusing on "dissuasion of people from resorting to or supporting terrorism; deterrence of states from sponsoring terrorism; capacity development so states can defeat terrorism [within their nations]; and defense of human rights..."[93] But when we look more deeply into the root causes, they require nation-building initiatives well beyond the capacity of current international treaty regimes, IGOs, NGOs, and traditional aid programs. Though reining in weapons trafficking and corruption in financial markets would help a lot in limiting the capabilities of terrorist organizations, ultimately the ethnic or religious groups that currently supply people, money, and know-how to terrorists have to be won over.

That is the central lesson of Michael Weiss and Hassan Hassan's detailed history of ISIS, which explains how different segments of Sunni communities in Iraq and Syria were effectively driven toward self-imported foreigners serving Al Qaeda, even while many of their tribal elders recognized Al Qaeda's ideology as poison.[94] When regimes oppress and tyrannize sections of their own nation, young men in these groups may be tempted to turn to terrorists promising a way to resist—especially if democracies do not support any legitimate rebel groups. To prevent this requires a transnational order strong enough to force governments in nations like Yemen and Syria to stop their oppressions, or even to negotiate new partitions.

More generally, terrorism is motivated and made possible by four main factors: (i) failing or weak governments that leave effectively lawless regions—like the Sinai, northeast Nigeria, northeast Syria, and Waziristan; (ii) structural injustices and oppression of particular groups, along with poverty that leaves young people few good options; (iii) the new medias resulting from the internet that allow websites to popularize and normalize terror tactics; (iv) and the effects of extreme religious ideology on young people's natural desire to dedicate themselves to some cause that seems noble, higher, or glorious. Many accounts miss this last factor, but Lisa Monaco rightly emphasizes ISIS magazines and messages "serving up an intoxicating narrative that followers can belong to a cause greater than themselves."[95] When adolescents are offered no healthy models of a noble life to compete with terrorist propaganda, the poisoned simulacrum of a fundamentalist warrior-martyr can seem inspiring. To reverse this requires deep structural changes in the nations where they grow up, including much better education systems and limits on the most extremist clerics.

We also have to focus on the internet platforms that terrorist groups use to spread their wide propaganda nets. This requires new tools when these groups use more encrypted communications to further radicalize and instruct alienated individuals who fall for their rhetoric. Unregulated global electronic communications is no longer a viable option, but we have developed no alternative set of global policies for the internet, let alone ways to enforce them. We have almost total internet freedom in democratic nations, and extremely limiting controls and surveillance under dictatorial regimes like China's: a league of democracies could rein in both these extremes, and perhaps even build an internet 2.0 designed to be safe from cybercrime, terrorism, and human trafficking.

The UN, its agencies, existing IGOs, and inter-state task forces are woefully insufficient to solve these four root causes of the upsurge in terrorism. When a state F is failing or massively oppressing one ethnic or religious group, restoring it cannot wait for years of slow internal development aided by charities: minimal justice requires systemic intervention by a powerful coalition to enforce power-sharing between all major groups, to strengthen F's police and army, to help new, less corrupt officials professionalize F's civil service and schools, to reduce crime and lay a foundation for the most basic social services, and to plan a viable economy. Such complex tasks cannot be accomplished just by bombing terrorist camps or even by sending in a few expert advisors to help shore up basic banking and financial systems that enable fledgling businesses. Our transnational networks are full of NGOs that try to help with bits and pieces of this work, but a global authority to rescue failing states would need 20–30 times the resources that today's collection of NGOs and IGOs bring to such tasks.

In some cases, transformation into a sustainable state also requires credible military backing. For example, terrorist groups in Somalia understand that if an effective government is ever established, they will lose areas in which they control the local population, extract profits, and operate with impunity. They will not allow this without a hard fight. Yet few nations have they military power to strengthen a failing foreign government, and they would all rather see some other state shoulder that burden. For instance, France has taken on the task in Mali and the Central African Republic, and rightly feels betrayed by other NATO members who have not stepped up to help it. The United States feels abandoned in Afghanistan, and the AU needs a much larger force in Somalia, where not enough African nations are contributing. Such betrayal is the rule in games of chicken, which are among the hardest for network solutions to fix. Only a very large coalition of strong nations could both ensure that long-term missions to rescue failing states have adequate resources *and* spread their costs effectively.

There are similar challenges with military occupation of a nation that has initiated large-scale attacks on other states, or humanitarian intervention to stop mass atrocities in civil conflicts. Both kinds of military intervention require a process of reconstruction following the invasion and occupation; like restoring a failing state, this requires a large and extended presence. But members of the Security Council and other leading nations do not want their troops to get bogged down in a conquered nation, especially if militias and terror groups operate there. This is a double threshold problem: we need many nations to contribute for the burden on each to be small enough to be tolerable and the total to be large enough for the task. That is why, for example, Kenya has not occupied southern Somalia even though this is the only way it could really stop Al-Shabab (at this point, Kenya is more interested in simply kicking out Somalia refugees). It is easier to dither with endless resolutions at multilateral conferences or meetings on the problem and try to pass the buck to others. But Kenya might well agree to contribute to an Operation Somalia as a member of a league of democracies in which this burden was fairly shared among (say) *30* other member states: it would then be assured that its contribution would not be wasted, *and* that its involvement would not become an overburdening quagmire.

The hardest challenge for effective global counterterrorism is to resist ultra-fundamentalist perversions of nobility. Distortions of culture, whatever their historical origin, are partly to blame; but culture is the hardest of all human phenomena to change through force, incentive, law or even dialogue. Our experience with Germany and Japan following World War II showed that changing the cultural soil from which fanaticism grows requires changing the educational system; this is hard, but *it can be done*, with incalculably large resulting benefits across the whole world for many generations. Indeed there are few public goods with such pervasive intergenerational impacts as rooting out cultural memes that can start fanatical movements and huge wars. The problem is that future generations cannot pay us back for the costs involved in this Herculean task.

Though it would be difficult even for a well-functioning league of democracies to tackle such deep cultural problems in areas like north Pakistan and southwest Afghanistan, a democratic league would stand a much better chance of helping these nations effectively than the UN umbrella or small groups of nations in direct multilateral partnerships (or both). Terrorist groups will not be party to any new agreement or convention; because they value destruction of "enemy" civilian populations above their own life and liberty and sometimes even that of their children, no morally acceptable deterrents are likely to sway them. And as we have seen, the small arms and weapons of moderate destruction commonly used by terrorist groups are ever-harder to embargo effectively.[96]

To respond adequately, then, a new transnational government would have to work with the relevant nations to dismantle networks of fundamentalist madrasas and online propaganda that are providing such terrorist groups with most of their recruits. It would have to set up new systems to support education for women, moderate religious leaders, and toleration of other groups. Yet to be perceived as *legitimate* around the world, rather than simply condemned as a new "crusade," any such deep cultural intervention would have to be recognized on all sides as justified by the basic rights of children and undertaken by a coalition clearly independent of western strategic or business interests. This case illustrates especially well why the coordinative power and legitimacy that comes from broad multilateral support are both so crucial. A democratic league could draw on Islamic-majority member nations like Bosnia, Jordan, and Indonesia (and eventually Pakistan and Malaysia) to help; and it could effectively demand protection of both Sunni and Shia groups, along with smaller minorities, in nations where one or the other holds more political power.

Conclusion

This chapter has synthesized evidence that the UN network and inter-governmental treaty regimes are insufficient to provide GPGs related to international security. The UN has been largely unable to secure borders, deter aggression, control the proliferation of most WMDs, and protect human rights not only because it requires P5 consensus but also because it cannot ensure a fair sharing of burdens and costs for treaty enforcement, rescue of failing states, and post-conflict reconstruction. Similarly, treaties, IGOs, informal networks of NGOs, and other international civil society actors will not be enough to overcome the root causes of terrorism, or prevent new arms races in cyber, satellite, and robotic weapons. Centralized legal authority and force are required to overcome the CAPs that allow such global harms to grow. Only a new union of the world's democracies is proportioned to such needs.

This finding is a key part of the global consolidation argument begun in chapter three. But the overall argument for a democratic league is sound only if the proposed institution is viable— i.e., if it would be politically possible to construct it and run it without unjust side effects or costs that are too excessive. Showing that a league of democracies is viable in this sense is the task of the final two chapters.

Notes

1. Thomas McCarthy, "On Reconciling Cosmopolitan Unity and National Diversity," in *Global Justice and Transnational Politics* (Cambridge, Mass: MIT Press, 2002): 234-74, 239-40.
2. Gareth Evans, *The Responsibility to Protect: Ending Mass Atrocity Crimes Once and For All* (Washington, DC: Brookings Institution Press, 2008), 176.
3. Ibid., 176–77.
4. Ibid., 179.
5. Brian Orend, *The Morality of War*, 2nd ed. (Peterborough, Ont: Broadview Press), 37.
6. On the development of the P5 veto, see Stanley Meisler, *The United Nations: A History*, rev. ed. (New York: Grove Press, 2011), 9–14.
7. Ibid., 3.
8. Oona Hathaway and Scott Shapiro argue that the ideas leading to the Kellogg-Briand (a.k.a. Pact of Paris) derived from Grotius: see *The Internationalists: How a Radical Plan to Outlaw War Remade the World* (New York: Simon & Schuster, 2017).
9. Ibid., 161–62. Article 16 of the League Covenant also required members to cooperate in trade sanctions and other measures to completely isolate a nation initiating aggressive war against any league member.
10. Thomas G. Weiss, *Global Governance* (Malden, Mass: Polity Press, 2013), 106–7.

11. J.G. Fichte, "Outline of the Right of Nations and Cosmopolitan Right," in *Foundations of Natural Right* [1796], ed. Frederick Neuhouser, tr. Michael Baur (Cambridge, UK: Cambridge University Press, 2000): 320–34, 331.

12. Thomas Hale, David Held, and Kevin Young, *Gridlock* (Malden, Mass: Polity Press, 2013), 55.

13. Albert Gore, *The Future: Six Drivers of Global Change* (New York: Random House, 2013), 128.

14. James T. Johnson, *Morality and Contemporary Warfare* (New Haven, Conn.: Yale University Press, 1999), 32-33.

15. James T. Johnson, "Just War, as It Was and Is," *First Things* 149 (January 2005).

16. Gore, *The Future*, 129–31.

17. Fred Dallmayr, *Peace Talks—Who Will Listen?* (Notre Dame, Ind.: University of Notre Dame Press, 2004).

18. Brian Orend, *Human Rights: Concept and Context* (Peterborough, Ont.: Broadview Press, 2002), ch.7.

19. Burleigh Wilkins, "Introduction" to *Humanitarian Intervention*, ed. Aleksandar Jokic (Peterborough, Ont.: Broadview Press, 2003), 9.

20. Orend, *The Morality of War*, 56.

21. Contrast the list provided by Hale, Held, and Young (*Gridlock* 58), which exaggerates the extent to which the UN Charter recognizes individual rights as limiting state sovereignty.

22. Johnson, *Morality and Contemporary Warfare*, 49–50.

23. The only exception is distributive inequity that occurs when a permanent minority is continually exploited by various majorities—an abuse that can largely be prevented by minority rights.

24. Evans, *The Responsibility to Protect,* 177. There was more direct UN control during the Congo operations in 1960–1964: see Meisler, *The United Nations*, 121–33.

25. Gore, *The Future*, 135.

26. Ivo Daalder and James Lindsay, "Democracies of the World Unite," *The American Interest* 3, no. 1 (2007): 1–17, 5–6.

27. Weiss, *Global Governance*, 107–8.

28. Ibid., 109.

29. See United Nations Peacekeeping, www.un.org/en/peacekeeping/resources/statistics/factsheet.shtml.

30. Weiss, *Global Governance*, 109.

31. Stuart A. Reid, "Congo's Slide into Chaos," *Foreign Affairs* 97, no. 1 (2018): 97–117.

32. See Orend's argument for the rehabilitation approach to *jus post bellum* in *The Morality of War*, 2nd ed., ch.7.

33. James Yunker, "Evolutionary World Government," *Peace Research* 44, no. 1 (2012): 95–126, 99.

34. But the AU's criticism of the ICC for issuing an arrest warrant for President Bashir of Sudan show its limits.

35. See Melissa Labonte, *Human Rights, Humanitarian Norms, Strategic Framing, and Intervention* (New York: Routledge, 2013), ch. 5. This was partly because some Nigerian troops engaged in widespread abuses such as looting in Sierra Leone.

36. Hale, Held, and Young on this point (*Gridlock* 69–70).
37. Ibid. Table 2.1 counts 13 major wars (60–61) with Libya, Syria, Ukraine, and Yemen added since 2012.
38. See Michael Walzer's rightly famous discussion of these cases in his *Just and Unjust Wars*, 2nd ed. (New York: Basic Books, 1992), ch. 6 and xviii.
39. See Samantha Power's shocking history in *A Problem from Hell* (New York: Basic Books, 2002), ch.10.
40. Hale, Held, and Young, *Gridlock*, 86. Compare Weiss, *Global Governance*, 116–17.
41. A helpful account of these events can be found in Stanley Meisler, *United Nations*, 43–54.
42. Ibid., 86–87.
43. For example, this unilateralist approach was advocated by neoconservatives such as Jean Elshtain in her *Just War Against Terror* (New York: Basic Books, 2003).
44. Thomas Magnell, "Vulnerability, Global Authority, and Moving Away from a Local Maximum of Value," *Journal of Value Inquiry* 36 (2002): 2.
45. Philip Breedlove, "NATO's Next Act: How to Handle Russia and Other Threats," *Foreign Affairs* 95 (July–August, 2016): 96–105, 99, 102.
46. John Lango, "Preventative Wars, Just Wars, and the United Nations," *The Journal of Ethics* 9 (2005): 247-68, 255.
47. Ibid., 256.
48. Magnell, "Vulnerability…," 4.
49. Ibid., 5.
50. Thomas Magnell, "Life and Liberty on a Global Scale," *Journal of Value Inquiry* 37 (2003): 1.
51. Ibid., 8.
52. Hale, Held, and Young, *Gridlock*, 91.
53. Ibid., 70.
54. Walzer, "Five on Iraq," in Walzer, *Arguing About War* (New Haven, Conn: Yale University Press, 2004), 143-70. The suspicions had a clear basis: Hussein had repeatedly used massive chemical attacks against Iranian forces and Kurdish civilians in the 1980s and 1990s.
55. Bonnie Jenkins, "The Biological Weapons Convention at a Crossroads," *Brookings*, 6 September 2017, www.brookings.edu/blog/order-from-chaos/2017/09/06/the-biological-weapons-convention-at-a-crossroad/.
56. Maryn McKenna, "How to Stop a Deadly Virus," *Smithsonian* 48 (November 2017): 52-61.
57. Anita Parlow, "Banning Land Mines," *Human Rights Quarterly* 16 (1994), 715-39, 718.
58. Ibid., 721. Parlow notes that Angola, for example, had 33 percent of its land littered with mines at one point.
59. Mary Wareham, "Time for the US to Embrace the Ban on Landmines," *Human Rights Watch*, 4 March 2013, www.hrw.org/news/2013/03/04/time-us-embrace-ban-landmines.
60. Parlow, "Banning Land Mines," 724–26.
61. Rick Gladstone, "Casualties Surge from Land Mines and Improvised Explosives," *New York Times*, 14 December 2017, https://www.nytimes.com/2017/12/14/world/middleeast/land-mines-casualties.html.

62. Gore, *The Future*, 136.
63. See the report from the UN Office for Disarmament Affairs, www.un.org/disarmament/ATT/.
64. Hale, Held, and Young praise these efforts (*Gridlock*, 70).
65. See the text of the treaty at www.un.org/disarmament/ATT/.
66. See Mark Bromley et al., "Transfer of Small Arms and Light Weapons to Fragile States," *SIPRI Insights on Peace and Security* (January 2013), books.sipri.org/product_info?c_product_id=453.
67. Gore, *The Future*, 136.
68. Steve Hargreaves, "US Leads Global Arms Exports," *CNN Money*, 23 June 2013, economy.money.cnn.com/2013/06/27/weapons-exports/.
69. Also see the current statistics at the website of the Stockholm International Peace Research Institute, www.sipri.org.
70. Compare Jansesen, ed., *The World Almanac and Book of Facts 2017*, 166. Also compare SIPRI data showing the recent uptick after years of decline during the Clinton presidency.
71. Richard Clarke, *Cyber War* (New York: HarperCollins, 2010), 198–99.
72. Ibid., 214–15.
73. Sophie Tatum, "US Accuses Russia of Cyberattacks on Power Grid," www.cnn.com/2018/03/15/politics/dhs-fbi-russia-power-grid/index.html.
74. Clarke, *Cyber War*, 192–93.
75. Gore, *The Future*, 134.
76. Clarke, *Cyber War*, 215–17.
77. David Sanger, "As Russian Hackers Attack, NATO Lacks a Clear Cyberwar Strategy," *New York Times*, 17 June 2016, A13.
78. Clarke, *Cyber War*, 201.
79. Patrick Lin, Fritz Allhoff, and Neil Rowe, "Is It Possible to Wage a Just Cyberwar?" *The Atlantic*, 5 June 2012.
80. Ibid., 217.
81. Massimo Calabresi, "Hacking the Election," *Time*, 10 October 2016, 30–35, 32 (quoting Dmitri Alperovitch).
82. See, for example, Andrew Byrne, "Macedonia's Fake News Industry Sets Sights on Europe," *Financial Times*, 15 December 2016, www.ft.com/content/333fe6bc-c1ea-11e6-81c2-f57d90f6741a.
83. See Anne Applebaum, "Poles Fought the Nationalist Government with Mass Protests," *Washington Post*, 24 July 2017.
84. Scott Shane and Mike Isaac, "Facebook to Give Ads to Congress in Russia Inquiry," *New York Times*, 22 September 2017, A1. Also see Neil MacFarquhar, "Russia's Powerful Weapon to Weaken Rivals: Spread False Stories" *New York Times*, 29 August 2016, A1 and A8.
85. Jonathan Broder, "Pearl Harbor in Outer Space," *Newsweek* (May 13, 2016): 12–16.
86. Gore, *The Future*, 135. Microwave technology used by China and Cuba to attack US diplomats is another emerging threat.
87. Todd Sandler, *Global Challenges* (Cambridge, UK: Cambridge University Press, 1998), 32.
88. Ibid., and Sandler, *Global Collective Action* (Cambridge, UK: Cambridge University Press, 2004), 85.
89. Sandler, *Global Collective Action*, 95.
90. Janssen, ed., *The World Almanac and Book of Facts 2017*, 165.

91. Gore, *The Future*, 137.
92. Weiss, *Global Governance*, 111.
93. Ibid.
94. See Michael Weiss and Hassan Hassan, *ISIS: Inside the Army of Terror*, 2nd ed. (New York: Regan Arts, 2016 pb), chs. 3–9.
95. Lisa Monaco, "Preventing the Next Attack," *Foreign Affairs* 96 (November–December, 2017): 23–29, 27. Monaco's analysis includes all four key factors.
96. Magnell, "Vulnerability,…" 7.

5 How to design an effective league of democracies

> One of [our] responsibilities is to be a good and reliable ally to our fellow democracies. We cannot build an enduring peace based on freedom by ourselves. ... We have to strengthen our global alliances as the core of a new global compact—a League of Democracies— that can harness the vast influence of the more than one hundred democratic nations around the world to advance our values and defend our shared interests.
>
> —Senator John McCain (R-Ariz), 1 May 2007

The main goal in this chapter is to explain how a United Democratic League (UDL) is feasible. The objection that it is impossible really summarizes the sense that there are no politically viable and morally acceptable solutions to several more specific problems that this league would have to overcome, such as that

- there is no fair way to structure representation within such a UDL that would be acceptable to enough prospective member nations;
- given their importance, we could not justify excluding China and Russia at the start, and
- if we did exclude China and Russia, this would restart the Cold War;
- there is no fair and objective way to decide which nations could join, and what the criteria for membership would be;

- we cannot give a coherent account of the UDL's enumerated powers without making it into a world government, an ultimate Leviathan potentially threatening all national sovereignty;
- there is no way of achieving sufficient solidarity among peoples in enough potential founding nations;
- non-western nations would rightly see a democratic league as pure western hegemony, another bid by the United States with Britain and France to control the world; and
- many nations would be very upset if the UDL threatened to replace the UN.

These and other related questions must all be answered to show that there is a politically feasible road toward a league of democracies that could be morally viable and effective in securing GPGs—especially those related to security that were reviewed in chapter four. Because answers to any of these objections depend in part on the responses to others, we have to consider the whole proposal to judge whether the potential costs and dangers of such a UDL are clearly outweighed by the GPGs that it can secure.

Answering these concerns corresponds to the final step in a global version of the federalist's consolidation argument (see chapter two). In the process, related proposals—some of which were reviewed in chapter one—serve as foils that help clarify my suggestions. The closest is Allan Buchanan's conclusion that in place of "UN-based law," humanitarian interventions and contested secessions should be decided by a "law-governed regime ... consisting of the most democratic, rights-respecting states."[1] Buchanan thinks a treaty organization requiring supermajority votes for intervention might be the best alternative, and I will follow this suggestion,[2] combining it with ideas from Pogge and others. While space does not permit an analysis of secession crises, Buchanan is also right that the world needs an institution that could arbitrate such issues objectively and (unlike the ICJ) reliably enforce its rulings.

The paramount point throughout my defense and elucidation of the UDL idea is that it only has to be better than the current UN structure, or than any feasible reformed version of the UN, or proposed concert of a few leading nations such as a "Democratic 10" (D10);[3] the league proposal does not have to be perfect to be worth serious attention. At many points throughout this book, I have contrasted what a democratic league could do with the potential of a UN Security Council hampered by CAPs. It is crucial that a UDL would be able to stop mass atrocities by carrying out preventative nation-building, armed humanitarian interventions, and postwar reconstructions better and more legitimately than ad hoc UNSC-coalitions ever could. Without repeating prior examples, I will defend this claim with a more detailed institutional proposal that helps address the main objections. However, we should bear in mind that there are several possible ways of structuring a UDL; my version is only one illustration.

A United Democratic League: Outline of an institutional structure and functions

This section will fill out the earlier sketch of the league proposal emphasizing the need for a grand compromise between Europe, the United States, and non-western democracies, which sketched a plausible pathway toward a UDL (see the Introduction). Also see the summary of other recent versions of the league proposal, and my arguments against building the UDL out of NATO, or running it as a "D-60" coalition within the UN, or as a concert of democracies operating as a backup to the UNSC (chapter one). I will extend these earlier points when relevant.

Here I lay out a specific institutional proposal informed by the lessons of game theory and the American federalists (see chapter two). The next chapter then refines these ideas in response to the standard objections. The overall goal is to defend the most ideal design that is practically feasible. This structure is not a utopian world federation of perfect nations. On the other hand, deviations from the ideal articulated here may result in an institution that is adequate for some purposes, but less than it could and should be. The goal is simultaneously to satisfy (a) the CP, which demands the sovereign powers needed to secure many GPGs, and (b) the DP's demand that such powers be authorized by the originary sovereignty of a combined "people."

Design of the main bodies to represent both small and large nations

CP and DP, together with the list of the relevant GPGs (see chapter three), imply that we need to coordinate the sovereign powers of as many of the world's democratic nations as possible—especially including its leading economic powers—to solve global CAPs and secure the most vital human rights, in particular by stopping mass atrocity crimes. The UNSC lacks this capacity because it cannot draw on the resources of enough member nations via *binding majority votes*, or *enforce* its decisions with independent executive power (chapter four). To solve this problem, I propose five innovations listed as (A) to (E).

(A) The UDL needs a separate, strong executive branch to enforce its edicts. According to DP, both this executive power and the UDL legislature should be *directly elected* in an adequately deliberative and fair democratic process in order to be fully legitimate: because this executive and legislature may place burdens on individuals (e.g., through transnational taxes) rather than operating only through the intermediary of national governments, they need to be directly answerable to the individuals affected.[4] Similarly, independent courts in this system need to become real courts of review, able to check the powers of the legislative and executive branches by interpreting the league's charter and list of basic rights. Such courts need to be answerable to the people through an executive that appoints them and a legislature that confirms them.

(B) Membership in a democratic league needs to be permanent in the sense that there is no unilateral abrogation: it requires approval from other members for any one nation to leave the league. Without this feature, as we saw, the precommitment needed to overcome many CAPs is missing; the problems this causes are now evident in the EU, whose members would work much harder to find full solutions to their immigration, fiscal, and tax policy problems if they were unable to exit by unilateral decision (chapter two).

In his work, James Yunker has argued that freedom to leave his proposed federation of democracies (FUDN) would be essential to persuading peoples that they had nothing to fear from the FUDN. He is certainly correct that sovereignty does not require extreme measures to prevent secession or to preserve "territorial integrity at all costs."[5] However, low-cost exit would move a democratic league toward a confederation of convenience without sufficient stability to overcome assurance problems and similar CAPs among its members. The constant threat of exit can act almost like a veto power.

Still, Yunker thinks his FUDN could exclude any exiting member from its common market.[6] However, the current brinksmanship between Britain and the EU shows that, despite leaving a confederal alliance, a nation may still manage to retain many benefits of its common market. At most, the UDL could allow a nation N to annul their membership after N's national referendum favoring exit by a two-thirds majority, with approval from at least two-thirds of the other member nations. Perhaps the league could allow easier exit terms within its first 20 years to reassure founding members; but after a short window, leaving should be much harder than joining.

In that sense, the UDL would be more than an ordinary treaty organization, committing member nations to significant responsibilities.

In joining, nations would hand over, in a semi-permanent way, a few of their sovereign functions to the league bodies; their powers to resist the democratic league on these few central issues would be quite limited. The league would also possess enforcement powers not dependent on particular nations volunteering for enforcement actions (see chapters two and four). This would be the UDL's most fundamental difference from the UN, i.e., a real consolidation of a handful of sovereign powers meeting the requirements of CP. In terms of DP, its basic superiority lies in the direct answerability of its chief officers to the peoples of all member nations.[7]

Such a *perpetually binding alliance* of many democracies would be far more legitimate and much more powerful than the UN Security Council, and could fulfill most of the promises that the UN has been unable to keep. Of course conflict between league members would still be possible; but nations guilty of severe and protracted violations of league terms could be expelled. It is also unlikely that nations invited to join the league would degrade to the point where they were on the brink of mass atrocities, because league support would help prevent this.

(C) I assume that like the UNSC, the EU's Council, and the North Atlantic Council, a Democratic Council (DC) would be the core of the UDL. The simplest model would give each member nation one seat on the DC; but this model is flawed for several reasons. First, state equality would carry the confederal implication that the UDL-DC is just another meeting of ambassadors or chief executives from each member. On the contrary, I have argued that UDL councilors should answer directly to their nation's people to emphasize their partial independence from their national governments. It would be even better if some councilors were elected at large by all the citizens of the member nations, but I will assume that this is impossible in the immediate future.

Second, national equality in the DC would greatly disadvantage nations with large populations, including India, Indonesia, and the United States as likely founding members. The numerical gaps between these nations and, say, Iceland or Luxembourg, are even more radical than between California and Wyoming in the US Senate, where state equality has become a grave injustice and hindrance to progress. We should not look to repeat this antifederalist error, which is now very hard to reverse, at the global level.

Thus I propose that nations should have a vote on the DC *partially* proportional to their populations, with upper and lower thresholds. Thus for example, nations with residents numbering between 1 and 10 million could have a weighted vote of 1 unit, while the largest nations like India could have a weighted vote of perhaps 30 units, with steps in between. At the next step down in population, the United States and

Europe (collectively) could have perhaps 25 votes each in the DC, with steps between populations of 320 and 1 million assigned votes between 25 and 1. This would prevent the largest nations from totally swamping the others, while still giving them larger voting strength in the DC.[8] The details are not crucial here, as long as there are upper and lower limits on the votes going to any one nation, with compression to account for the large population gap between India and the rest.

On the other side, large-population nations should be further protected by a lower house, or UDL Parliament, in which they would have nearly proportional representation, with some upper limit. This is crucial in my view to be fair to India, the United States, and Indonesia, and to provide China a strong incentive to become sufficiently democratic to join—which would give China a weight roughly equal to India's. The league could establish qualifications for these positions, perhaps allowing national governments some say on the field of candidates, and encouraging them to nominate elder statespersons for the DC in particular.

(D) Coming to the executive branch, I have argued that one of the greatest flaws with the UN, inevitable at the time of its founding, is its lack of any strong and independent executive agents. Hamilton saw this problem correctly in the American case, and our nation might not have survived if the convention had not largely taken his advice to create a strong presidency. The same seems essential for a democratic league: only a single directly elected leader, such as a chancellor, could enable the UDL, when necessary, to prevail *even in overruling the President of the United States.* To make such an option feasible, given the vast scope of peoples and nations to whom this chancellor would answer, it might be necessary at first to have some system of rotation—perhaps with all candidates coming from Asia for one term, from the Americas for another term, from Africa in a third term, and Europe and the Middle East in a fourth, for example. To allow a great chancellor to be reelected one time, another option would be simply to apportion candidates to regions, ensuring that enough are fielded from the Americas, Asia, Africa, Europe, and the Middle East each time.

In one attractive initial system, national governments would nominate one of their former or present councilors from the DC to stand each time, with the field to be narrowed in two runoff elections before the final election—perhaps with the first operating as a negative runoff to eliminate candidates who are too unpopular within any single region.[9] I am assuming that at the start, candidates for chancellor would be running not as members of a particular political party, even if such parties exist in the league bodies. Inevitably party associations will arise; as the American experiment showed, they are a spontaneous phenomenon. But it would be highly desirable in its early years if the league were led by chancellors who cared more about establishing the league's value and credibility.

(E) I suggested earlier that the UDL Charter could link with the ICC, relying in particular on the ICC's definitions of war crimes and crimes against humanity. While the ICC has state parties that might not be initial founding members of the UDL (see below), the UDL could still enforce ICC orders, subpoenas and indictments, as well as refer cases to the ICC, as the UNSC does. Still, the league would have its own bill of Basic Democratic Rights (BDR), which would include those implied in the ICC Statute along with fundamental rights necessary for popular sovereignty. The UDL also needs a League Court of Review (LCR) to interpret the consistency of league actions with its charter and BDR. Unlike the ICJ, this court could rule on disputes between member nations without their prior consent each time, and it would have greater enforcement powers. However, to avoid divisive problems the EU has experienced, the LCR should not rule directly on internal laws of its member nations; it should instead refer cases warranting censure or more dramatic penalties to the DC for judgment when needed. It would be the job of the DC to discipline members when their national laws violate the league's terms, and pass ultimate judgment on the fitness of a nation to continue as a member if it refuses to fix such problems.

The UDL armed forces: Rapid deployment and long-term volunteers

The UDL Chancellor's most important role would be to organize and direct nation-building and humanitarian intervention actions undertaken by the UDL. It is crucial that the chancellor can respond quickly and forcefully to humanitarian emergencies with council approval (perhaps by a three-fifths supermajority for combat missions, especially if ground troops are envisioned). For most purposes, the league would not need a very large military of its own—or more likely, military forces on semi-permanent loan from the member nations, as the UN Charter initially intended. The UDL only needs *rapid deployment forces* of perhaps 25,000 to 35,000 with roughly 40 to 50 larger ships, 150 to 200 fighter and bomber aircraft, hundreds of helicopters for rapid movement of material, and supplies commensurate to these forces. This is double the number that some scholars have suggested for a rapid UN force,[10] because the UDL must be able to address three crises or humanitarian emergencies at once. However, it is hardly an unprecedented number. In 1992, Senator David Boren (D-Oklahoma) called for a UN "rapid deployment force of 100,000 volunteers," and Boutros-Ghali's 1992 report, *An Agenda for Peace*, arguably implied a similar number.[11]

As illustrated in Bosnia, Rwanda, and Somalia, casualties among soldiers on humanitarian missions are liable to produce public reactions that can undermine the whole mission. These reactions have weakened western resolve and given forces behind mass atrocities great incentives to inflict highly sensational deaths on intervening troops. US military commanders often oppose humanitarian missions to prevent such casualties—as Colin Powell's ignominious opposition to even small uses of US forces in Bosnia and Rwanda illustrated.[12] Such attitudes badly hamstring coalitions and UN peacekeeping missions: retreating from a fight with bullies to avoid a bloody nose emboldens the bullies, as we have seen repeatedly in Bosnia, Rwanda, Darfur, Ukraine, Syria, and many other theaters of war.

To solve this democratic cowardice dilemma, I suggest that the UDL's "Humanitarian Guard" be *an all-volunteer elite*, drawn from members of regular national militaries who have specifically asked to be loaned for fixed terms to the UDL. No soldier on dangerous rapid deployment missions would be ordered by their national government into this role; they would choose this distinctive and honorable service. Moreover, unlike rapid forces proposed for the UN,[13] the UDL's Humanitarian Guard volunteers would be deployed by a unified executive with approval by a democratic legislature. Without a doubt, national governments would not pledge the needed number of troops, naval vessels, and aircraft to the league military command without strong conditions on deployments: they would be placing great trust in the DC and chancellor. But as we have seen, this is the only way to solve the CAPs that dog any system that gives nations vetoes or makes executive control indirect.

Unlike the UN, a democratic league could also enforce a fair division of the burdens both in military combat and rehabilitation stages. This overcomes the free rider problems that so badly affect coalitions of willing nations and even NATO. For example, when ISIS started taking large areas of Syria and Iraq in 2014, Turkey was not willing to be the main (let alone sole) provider of ground forces to stop ISIS: Turkey wanted a larger coalition, but the United States and EU were unwilling. Thus the ground war was left to unmotivated Iraqi Shia forces, which ISIS quickly scattered before capturing Mosul. America eventually reconstituted Iraqi forces, and organized courageous Kurdish forces and a few Sunni militias to combat ISIS in Syria, but without trying to reconcile the Turkish government with Kurdish parties. Instead, during spring 2018, the Trump administration abandoned our Kurdish helpers to massive Turkish attacks in northwest Syria. The Kurds expected something in return for their sacrifices, but we are letting Turkey spoil their reward. This series of debacles illustrates the price of discoordination between democracies.

Europeans and Sunni-majority nations in the Middle East won this chicken game by waiting for US commanders, Iraqis, and Kurds to act. A democratic league would have avoided this inequity by binding all members of the league to contribute a fair share to stop ISIS, and its rapid reaction forces could have surrounded ISIS fighters advancing towards Mosul. The UDL would also be able to offer incentives to other nations in the affected regions that either share responsibility for the problem or benefit from its remedy. For example, in this case, a UDL could have imposed sanctions on Saudi Arabia, Jordan, Kuwait, Qatar, and Egypt if they refused to make major contributions to the joint war against ISIS.

As noted, democratic states are also presently deterred from military cooperation to solve crises by fear of being stuck with most of the necessary postwar security and redevelopment. Just war theorists rightly stress these duties on intervening nations; but that only increases the incentive not to get involved when intervention is most needed. Like preventative efforts to strengthen failing states, *jus post bellum* rehabilitation often demands larger and longer deployments of troops, as well as civilian experts and major financial inputs (chapter four). For these cases, the UDL would need a better system for drawing on larger numbers of troops from its member states, and possibly partnership with UN peace enforcement missions. Thus the UDL should stand up a larger force distinct from its Humanitarian Guard, closer in style to UN peacekeepers (i.e., more lightly armed), trained in cooperation with humanitarian aid organizations and in winning hearts/minds, and recruited again on an *all-volunteer basis*. Despite the risks, the chance to prevent mass atrocities before they happen or prevent relapse into chaos after a civil conflict would motivate some of the best soldiers in democratic nations to volunteer.

Such a "Humanitarian Reserve" force could be drawn from the regular militaries of member nations, along with able retirees and reservists, and potentially citizens with police or security experience—who would be provided with full conflict prevention and resolution training. Given the history of UN peacekeeping missions, with more demands likely if all components of the R2P doctrine were taken seriously, I suggest a Humanitarian Reserve of no less than 80,000 personnel. Like UN peacekeeping missions, this force would include civilians who offer expertise of many kinds in medicine, infrastructure, and domestic civil services. At this level, one could imagine all sorts of partnerships with NGOs and programs of regional IGOs.

Together, the Humanitarian Guard and Reserve forces would quickly end global opportunities for absolute despotism in smaller states. Knowledge that their atrocities will motivate volunteers across democratic nations can help deter such crimes by tyrannical regimes and terrorist groups. As the UDL proved its worth, recruitment would become easier: serving in either humanitarian force would come to be seen, rightly, as a noble calling. We would beat terrorist groups by showing young people a far better alternative. Indeed, service in the Humanitarian Guard would quickly attain a status like that of elite commando units in the United States or British armed forces. For both the Guard and Reserve, the most likely problem is that, within a few years, eager volunteers will outnumber available slots by 10 to 1.

Member nations could also offer qualified young persons a chance for fixed terms of service in the larger UDL Reserve as an alternative to regular national service, or for a robust package of benefits—possibly even including immigration into UDL nations. A broad representation is crucial to show people on the receiving end that they are not being colonized by some small set of nations seeking to expand their power or corporate investments, and that the mission has wide support across the world. National diversity within the UDL forces also ensures that long-term solutions implemented in a war-torn nation can be sustained with buy-in from many nations.

Thus a strong and diverse UDL should be able to assure us that any humanitarian interventions undertaken to stop mass atrocities are followed up with sufficient postwar support, reconstruction and demilitarization. It would also prevent more crises from ever reaching that point (as the R2P doctrine intended). This is the solution to the dilemmas of Libya and Syria posed at this book's outset. Winning the peace is more than half the battle for a nation's long-term stability and capacity to protect rights; but single western nations or small coalitions are increasingly unlikely to justify the costs of such missions to their citizens. Thus we need an alternative system guaranteeing that particular nations will not be punished by unsustainable burdens if they are willing to participate when only military intervention can prevent mass atrocities.

Mutual protection and global financial oversight

The proposed UDL system has another advantage that the UN and even NATO do not: once the UDL proved effective in military operations, its member nations could reduce spending on their own domestic militaries quite significantly, relying on the *pooled strength* of the league to protect them. In particular, the need for US missions would be cut at least in half. Beyond the tasks envisioned for the Humanitarian Guard and Reserve, the league's charter would contain a provision analogous to Article 5 of the North Atlantic Treaty, providing that an armed attack on any one member constitutes an attack on all, assuring mutual protection, and extending these terms to cover massive cyberattacks. Obviously a large ground invasion would require the regular forces of the UDL's members to counter it; but as we have seen, air assaults, attacks by satellites, or cyber-hacking are more likely.

The UDL Charter's enforceable limits on unilateral military action would also make massive national militaries less useful. By solving the problems at the heart of the UN's design, the democratic league would ensure that wars can be waged *only for just purposes, approved by a just multinational process.* Because the UDL would be a more legitimate authority to declare and wage such wars, all just nations could rely on it. But this great goal becomes achievable only if the UDL is not limited to acting solely when the UNSC fails to act, as Buchanan and Keohane proposed.[14] An effective UDL cannot play second fiddle.

The UDL would also exercise significant *jus ad vim* powers (less than wartime military force). For example, it would protect league member nations and prospective democracies by taking on the tasks that Pogge proposed for a "Democracy Panel under the auspices of the UN." Pogge suggested creating a judicial body to approve military interventions if a young democratic nation is overthrown or threatened by a military coup (with preauthorization for such intervention in that nation's constitution); to deny international loans and financing to brutal dictators (especially those ousting a democratic regime); and to manage a "Democracy Fund" to help pay sovereign debts of developing democracies.[15] Pogge also suggests that the panel enforce provisions in national constitutions that prohibit coup leaders from selling national assets,[16] and I would extend this to any case (including long-running dictatorships) where rampant corruption is robbing an impoverished nation. These ideas are all on the right track, except that a panel operating under the UN would be far too weak to enforce them. By contrast, a wide league of democracies could perform all these tasks and more, instituting a much more robust version of Pogge's imagined anti-dictatorial world financial regime.

Enumerated powers of the United Democratic League

At this stage, we can restate the central functions envisioned for the democratic league, expanding the earlier summary (see the Introduction) with the range of GPGs in mind. Yet this list of functions for the UDL is intentionally narrow in order to facilitate initial agreement, with the idea that a successful UDL could then take on other functions when it earns the trust to do so. For example, the idea of making the ICC part of the UDL framework would remain aspirational until most ICC members could agree to it as an amendment to the Rome Statute; likewise protection of global environmental resources and general poverty relief efforts would await amendments of the initial UDL Charter.

List 5.1 Enumerated powers of a United Democratic League

1 The United Democratic League will authorize and organize sanctions and military means to prevent and turn back aggressive wars, and to protect national boundaries against forcible change from outside. This includes the direct common defense of all democratic member nations and, on appeal, defense of prospective members from incursion or attacks, including likely imminent attacks, *irrespective of prior UNSC approval.*

2 The league will authorize various forms of force, including financial restrictions, trade embargos, travel bans, cyber-controls, and, as a last resort, military intervention to prevent attacks by terrorist groups. To defeat terrorists and prevent new arms races, the league must enforce new systems to control WMDs, weapons of moderate destructiveness, cyber-weapons, robotic weapons, microwave weapons, and space-based weaponry.

3 To the extent possible, the league will protect the most central and morally urgent human rights of all peoples in all nations. It will assume the responsibility to protect civilians from the war crimes and crimes against humanity listed in the statute of the ICC, from other mass atrocities listed in the ICISS report of 2001, and from protracted tyranny and extreme kleptocracy. This requires the power to levy sanctions, to restrict nations' sales of natural resources and banking privileges, to deploy armed forces in humanitarian emergencies, and to partner with international networks for reconstruction after the removal of tyrannical regimes.

4 For the three paramount ends listed above, the UDL would maintain (a) standing armed forces with rapidly deployable and experienced personnel, naval vessels, and aircraft, raised from all member states proportionate to their population and wealth, under direct UDL command; and (b) a larger reserve including experts in conflict prevention, nation-building, and post-conflict

List 5.1 (Continued)

> disarmament and rebuilding (working with UN peacekeeping missions when appropriate)—both to be deployed only on approval of the Democratic Council and the high Chancellor of the UDL.
>
> 5 In dealing with entrenched dictatorships that are a long-term threat to the progress of democratic ideals (such as China), the UDL would have the power to create uniform sanctions regimes binding on all member nations, and when warranted, secondary sanctions on third-party non member nations who seek to profit from primary sanctions.
>
> 6 The UDL would also have the power to requisition financing from its member nations proportional to their economic means, measured by national average per-capita income and the wealth of the richest 2 percent of their citizens. It might also collect revenue directly from global taxes on international capital transactions or natural resources sales between league members.
>
> 7 The UDL would seek to provide a new, firmer foundation for international law through its BDR, its Court of Review, referral of cases to the ICC, and enforcement of ICC indictments. In the long run, ICC could become part of the UDL framework. The UDL would also create a standing body to promote national truth and reconciliation commissions for post-conflict resolution.
>
> 8 The UDL would aim to regulate global capital markets and banking systems to ensure stability in the world economy and to promote the paramount goals listed above, including making it impossible for tyrannies, kleptocracies, and other rogue regimes (harboring terrorists, people traffickers, and drug lords) to use sovereign debt and natural resource sales for financing. It would also use sanctions to force reform in any state operating as a tax haven or promoting money-laundering.
>
> 9 For weak or failing states, the UDL would undertake nation-building activities necessary to promote respect for basic human rights, a working independent legal system, a civil service free from corruption, an objective educational system free from fundamentalist indoctrination, and a decent standard of living in whatever economic system a people chooses to develop in accordance with their values.
>
> 10 The UDL would admit new member states according to collectively accepted criteria. This could include admitting them (a) as full and thus permanent member states or (b) as associate members on the way to full membership. The UDL would also (c) recognize friendly partner states that are not yet prospective members.

This last topic of membership needs further explanation to allay concerns about the breadth of the envisioned league and the intended forms of access to the privileges and protections it would provide.

Membership and founding of the United Democratic League

Critics have suggested that devising a fair process for membership in a democratic league might be impossible. For example, Daniele Archibugi responds to McCain, Ikenberry, and Slaughter by asking "Which countries deserve membership [in] a League of Democracies?" and he argues that this has been a difficult problem for the EU. He adds (against Robert Kagan) that if "the EU criteria were applied the United States would not be admitted" because the United States retains the death penalty.[17] But Kagan remains correct that it is not "too hard to decide" which nations are sufficiently democratic for a UDL.[18] In this section, I will argue that such objections about membership are not so difficult to answer.

Membership criteria

Archibugi's objection is exaggerated; obviously a democratic league would have to compromise on some controversial issues on which human rights are not clearly settled, such as capital punishment, abortion, affirmative action, entitlement of minority groups to special protections via group rights, animal rights, a basic income and non-basic health care, gay marriage, and perhaps even on church-state separation and equal treatment of all religions. The UDL could never get off the ground if prospective founding nations insisted on making litmus tests of such issues. The point of the UDL is to unite democracies for mutual protection, to stop the most horrendous mass atrocities, to block the rise of terrorist groups and weapons trafficking, and resist the spread of Chinese and Russian soft despotism—not to foster bickering on questions of bioethics, animal ethics, and other social issues closely related to family life, which are the source of almost all the deepest disagreements between cultures about human rights.[19] Focusing on such divisive issues at the start would be like shooting oneself in both feet, and the UDL founders should resist being co-opted by any special interest group that could alienate potential allies.

Of course, lines have to be drawn, because democratic rights are linked to other basic human rights: in particular, as Joshua Cohen notes, equal political rights for men and women are now a *sine qua non* for democracy,[20] as are basic free speech rights, objective education for all children, and protections from gender-based violence and discrimination. But all such lines must be drawn in pragmatic fashion in order to ensure that the UDL can be broadly inclusive, without which it cannot serve its fundamental purposes. According to the linkage approach to human rights, the relevant political institution—in this case, the founding members of the league—would have to articulate the rights-standards in their charter that would govern admission of future applicant nations. But in doing so, they must obviously focus on standards that many nations can meet (perhaps with modest reforms).

When the lines are drawn at the most settled basic rights and requirements for deliberative democratic processes, the fear that there are not enough truly democratic nations proves to be exaggerated. In arguing persuasively against the idea that a just global government should have the consent of all national regimes, however corrupt, Daalder and Lindsay concede that most nations are not sufficiently democratic in the sense of representing

> the interests or perspectives of [most of] the people they rule.... Real legitimacy, like real sovereignty, resides in the people rather than the states, which is why state decisions to confer international legitimacy must rest in democratically chosen representatives of the people, not in the personal whims of autocrats or oligarchs.[21]

This problem entails that admitted nations must hold "regular, free and fair elections," which the government does not "stage-manage or heavily circumscribe," e.g., by handpicking the candidates, as China does for Hong Kong. For this reason, Daalder and Lindsay would not invite some of the nations invited into the CDem in 2000, such as Qatar, Azerbaijan, Bahrain, and Jordan, "none of which can be called democracies under any reasonable criteria." I agree with this assessment. The minimal criteria include "both fundamental political rights (not just to vote, but also to organize and participate in government) and basic civil rights (to speak, assemble, and freely practice [one's] religion)—and those rights must be guaranteed by law."[22] They argue that even if the admission criteria demand that these rights are "so rooted in society that the chances of reversion to autocratic rule" are negligible, more than 60 nations would qualify—more than enough for a UDL to function well.[23]

The number jumps by 20–30 nations if, as I would recommend, a member nation's transition to democracy can be more recent and uncertain: for UDL membership would help stabilize such democratic regimes and strongly deter potential coup-plotters. This would be one of the major benefits of the UDL for developing democracies: it would encourage political leaders who are considering democratic reforms that this step would win them a nearly invincible support network. As Lindsay and Daalder note, "as the Concert [of democracies] becomes more established and effective," its very existence would serve as a powerful incentive to democratize—just as the EU and NATO have done in eastern Europe.[24]

Together, these points suggest a fairly clear set of minimal conditions for membership in the UDL. Following Daalder and Lindsay, the EU criteria, Cohen, and other recent democratic theorists, I suggest the following preliminary list. These criteria are based both on the common core of political rights in long-standing democracies and on lessons of experience concerning the civil society supports that functioning democracy requires:

List 5.2 Democratic membership criteria

1 Equal rights of political participation, including universal equal suffrage (with allowances for federal arrangements); freedom of association and party-formation; freedom to run for and hold political office; as well as rights of free political expression limited only by substantial public interests (such as limits on campaign spending and political advertising, or limits on ultrafundamentalist and hate groups).
2 While the nation may run a parliamentary system or a separate legislature and executive, it must have a representative legislature with regular or sufficiently frequent elections. Supermajority requirements for changing constitutional law are highly desirable.
3 There must be judicial review and a sufficiently independent judiciary upholding due process of law in criminal proceedings, including the right to a trial by a jury of sufficiently impartial peers, and equal protection of the law for all, including members of minority groups (no discrimination by race, gender, or ethnic background, unless for temporary remedial purposes).
4 In criminal justice and foreign policy, there must be a modality constraint prohibiting use of torture, and other cruel or unusual modes of combat, interrogation, or punishment (as per the Geneva Conventions).
5 The offices of government must be sufficiently free from corruption, which implies effective limits on the extent to which political positions can be used to extract bribes or control business decisions in the private sector.

List 5.2 (Continued)

6 Freedom of the press must be preserved, especially regarding coverage of political issues and candidates. If there are government-funded media, they must be sufficiently independent of control by any administration in power (i.e., run by an independent civil service).

7 Because democracy should be understood as a deliberative process, all children must enjoy an equal right to basic education based on sufficiently objective and impartial sources not only building basic skills but introducing them to science, history, art, literature, and the comparative study of cultures, along with basic civics.

8 Hiring in the business and nonprofit sectors must be largely on meritocratic bases, with equal opportunity for people of all backgrounds (which implies equal opportunity for admission into higher education programs).

9 Rights to emergency medical care and subsistence must be recognized and secured.

10 Rights to privacy, bodily integrity, and personal property must be recognized and secured. It is assumed that member nations will allow some form of free market, albeit limited by regulation to secure public goods.

11 If the nation has an established religion or allows government funding of religious institutions, it must protect free exercise for all religious groups within the bounds of safety, strictly limit any preferential treatment for service in the police or armed forces, and prohibit religious discrimination in business and hiring (excepting only religious institutions themselves).

These protections are the most central or weighty ones within the scheme of human rights held together by the overarching right to popular sovereignty. This list does not attempt to develop in detail all the basic rights that any just democracy worthy of membership in the UDL should recognize and protect, because it is only a partial draft of the rights to be included in the league's BDR. Its limited purpose is simply to show that it is not that difficult to outline highly plausible and familiar conditions on which founding members could agree as a basis for their statement of basic democratic rights.

The UDL Charter would also include other conditions for membership implied by the powers and functions of the league, such as commitment to "peaceful settlement of any … border dispute or other international conflict, minimum defense spending and military preparedness," acceptance of the terms for the UDL Humanitarian Guard and Reserve forces, and promises to collaborate "on a range of multilateral agreements tackling security issues such as international terrorism, money laundering, and arms transfer"[25] through the mechanisms of the league parliament and council. Except in direct self-defense, member nations would commit to deploying armed forces *only* with UDL approval, including for humanitarian interventions.

Note that this list does *not* specify terms of economic union among the UDL member nations, although presumably something close to a free trade zone would be passed by the UDL legislature once the league existed. Close economic cooperation and alignment of central banks would probably be required for the league's financial accountability goals, and to incentivize new members. The UDL Charter would spell out conditions requiring member nations to comply with economic sanctions voted by the whole league to punish a particular member for violations of UDL law or to sanction non member nations for aggressions, massive totalitarian oppressions (e.g., North Korea), kleptocratic practices, facilitating money laundering, acting as tax havens, excessive free riding on the UDL, and so on.

But it is important to stress that the proposed UDL has very different goals than the OECD, which strives for globalized free markets and restricts membership based on economic strength. The UDL should not mandate a capitalist system with private ownership of large amounts of capital, or toleration of massive income and wealth gaps; members may legitimately differ in the values that inform such decisions on economic and tax policy. The UDL is thus clearly not intended to force libertarian policies onto developing nations. On the contrary, in joining the UDL, wealthy nations would agree to some minimal level of league governance over multinational corporations, the international sale of natural resources, and the sale of weapons—as implied by the enumerated power and functions described above. In time, we could expect the UDL to establish minimum anti-corruption, labor, and environmental standards for all companies doing business within the UDL. Eventually the league would help build a unified immigration system and procedures for fairly distributing and aiding refugees to secure the global right to asylum. But these decisions could be left up to the UDL's legislative processes rather than hardwired into its charter.

The admissions process and founding nations

Critics also ask who would decide the thresholds of sufficiency on the eleven conditions listed above for new member states. The obvious lesson of history is that only the *founding members* can collectively apply the criteria to admit new applicants; this privilege is an incentive for getting in as a founder. Like the proverbial chicken-and-egg, any political institution run by law must get going before its own processes can be used to expand its reach or adjudicate conflicts between its parts. The peoples of the founding nations can operate democratically in first forming a league of democracies even if they exceed the bounds of existing positive law in doing so: that is the idea of originary sovereignty. Once the league is created, newly admitted nations could later have a voice in amending the UDL Charter, including the admissions process, if they see fit. The EU has been able to develop this way without being solely controlled in that evolution by its few founding members in 1958 or even its expanded membership of 1973.

The objection then becomes that the founding members cannot legitimately police themselves, because they will tailor the initial conditions to suit their interests. By this logic, though, no government could ever legitimately be founded, because no set of persons or groups can legitimately cooperate for a joint end unless they do so according to established impartial rules—which is manifestly absurd. Internal checks and balances will hold founding members to account, although initially, founding members can only police each other. No doubt some bias is inevitable in the initial membership; no one would expect a real political process to be a perfect product of Kant's Kingdom of Ends. But this should only worry Chomskian skeptics or Schmittian anti-moralists who will automatically interpret any new proposal as another stratagem for US world domination, no matter what its content is. Despite all the evidence to the contrary in the last three decades, such critics are determined to see any event in maximally Foucauldian terms, erasing any possibility of a global order founded on objective rights.

Cosmopolitans must simply reject such dogmatic extremism and accept that the justice of the UDL's initial conditions would be proven in time by its operation. As long as the league's organs are sufficiently robust, the (population-weighted) majority of its members will be able to check particular founding members who try to game the system for unfair national advantage. Moreover, unlike the UN Charter, the league's charter should be practically amendable without vetoes by any particular nations.

The main answer to the worry about initial membership comes from the intended breadth of these founding member nations. A democratic league can only work if it is started by a group of stable democracies spanning the globe, including both wealthier and developing democratic nations. This very inclusiveness will ensure that the UDL cannot *even appear* to be designed to ensure that the United States and

Table 5.1 Potential founding members of a democratic league

In Europe	In the Americas	In Africa, Middle East, & Asia
Austria	Argentina	Australia
Belgium	Brazil	Bangladesh
Denmark	Canada	Ghana
Finland	Chile	India
France	Colombia	Indonesia
Greece	Costa Rica	Iraq
Germany	Dominican Republic	Israel (?)
Iceland	El Salvador	Japan
Ireland	Jamaica	Kenya
Italy	Panama	Liberia
Netherlands	Paraguay	Mongolia
Norway	Peru	Mozambique
Portugal	United States	New Zealand
Serbia	Uruguay	Nigeria
Spain		Philippines
Sweden		South Africa
Ukraine		South Korea
United Kingdom		Taiwan

Europe dominate the new global system. On the contrary, it will be *facially apparent* that this is not the case: together, India, Indonesia, and democracies from the global south would have a majority in both the UDL Council and Parliament. To show that such breadth is feasible, consider all of the nations that could be likely founding parties, even if their national laws and practices are slightly imperfect on some of the eleven measures outlined in list 5.2 earlier.

· Clearly this group of nations listed in table 5.1 looks very different than the OECD, which has hardly any members from the global South, and only a few from Asia. The UDL could also include other smaller nations within Europe that are not listed here for brevity's sake.

My criteria remain slightly stricter than Daalder and Lindsay's, leading to 50 rather than 60 potential founders. Whether particular nations in Latin America, Africa, or Asia should be added or taken off this list is largely irrelevant to my point, which is simply to illustrate the possible breadth of the founding group, extending well beyond the NATO and EU nations. Similarly, I am aware that including Israel and Taiwan each raise special difficulties; perhaps their admission would best be left to the UDL process after its creation. But even if several nations on this prospective list were struck off due to serious objections, we would still have at least 40 likely founders. If merely 30 of these came together, including enough of the largest like Germany,

India, France, Brazil, and the United States, along with sufficient representation in Asia and the global South, a UDL could begin. Daalder and Lindsay explain the resources that such a group would have:

> the world's democracies possess the greatest capacity to shape global politics. They deploy the greatest and most potent militaries; the largest twenty democracies are responsible for three-quarters of the resources spent on defense in the world today. Democracies also account for most of the world's wealth, innovation, and productivity. Twenty-eight of the world's thirty largest economies are democracies. The average annual income of people living in democratic societies is about $16,000, nearly three times greater than the average income of those living in non-democracies. In the main, the people living in democracies are better educated, more prosperous, healthier, and happier than those who live under authoritarian and dictatorial rule. Harnessing the power that comes from this overwhelming military, economic, political, and social advantage would provide the necessary ingredients for effective international action.[26]

In short, we should have organized such a league long before now. Obviously the list would be stronger if Russia were able to throw off the dictatorship descending on it, restore a free press and free elections, protect minority rights, and respect international boundaries under new leadership. The prospect of such a democratic league might catalyze such a Russian return democracy. As I have stressed, the founding members should express their clear desire for Russia to join them at the earliest possible point, rather than aim to alienate Russia. With a reformed Russia, the UDL would be strongly enhanced. Still, the UDL can begin without Russia, and it must do so as long as Putin remains in control. The same goes for China's oligarchy, but a reformed China could have huge weight within the league.

Associate members and friendly nations

Even if it began with as few as 25–30 founding nations, a league of democracies could easily grow to 50 nations within two decades, given the strong incentives it would create for nations on the margin to improve their human rights records. The league's intention to be inclusive could be further signaled by establishing a category of associate member nations that are on the way to meeting the conditions for full membership. Associate members would gain some of the benefits of the UDL—perhaps including a measure of protection and some economic benefits. This category would be analogous to "candidate status" in the EU admission process. There are many nations that might hope to achieve this status through various reforms, from small states such as Liberia, Armenia, Kyrgyzstan, and Lebanon, to larger nations such as Nepal, the Ivory Coast, Pakistan, Ukraine, Poland, Kazakhstan, Malaysia, and Ecuador. With associate nations, the UDL could quickly increase its fold by another 20 nations within a couple decades, giving it vast reach and authority. The largest global problems that have remained intractable, from environmental issues to the most grinding levels of poverty in the least developed nations, could find solutions within such a new order, as the pressure on kleptocratic regimes and malign dictatorships steadily increased.

Moreover, the UDL would also have an easily available method for recognizing the sort of "decent hierarchical" nations that Rawls, Beitz, and Cohen aim to tolerate in their accounts of international human rights, including benevolent monarchies and theocracies whose people have a little immediate need for more than the cultural forms of "consultation" already in place (e.g., perhaps Jordan and Morocco). The UDL could create a category of friendly partner nations with whom it regularly cooperates for mutual benefit, e.g. via trade relations. Such nations would not be under sanctions or major diplomatic pressure from the UDL. This category would make clear to all that the UDL is not set up to pressure the entire world to democratize, even though it claims that the right to popular sovereignty is a basic human right, and insists on this basis that it has greater legitimacy than the UN to stop mass atrocities and support revolutions against the most intractable totalitarian regimes (e.g., North Korea). The UDL could disagree with friendly partner nations on the questions of democratic rights and its own legitimacy in comparison to the UNSC while still working with such nations on many global issues.

In addition, several friendly partner nations could include democratic states such as Switzerland whose people (for whatever reason) judge it best to remain outside the democratic league for the present. One could imagine a democratized Cuba taking this path, for example. As long as nations in the friendly category do not intentionally free ride in substantial ways on the benefits that the UDL delivers, it should have no quarrel with them. This point further underscores my claim that there is nothing in the UDL's design that aims at world hegemony. The right to live outside the UDL's sphere of direct authority would thus be preserved, and everyone would be assured that leaders of the UDL are not trying to build anything like a world empire—which is probably the most common and sophomoric of all objections raised against the idea of a democratic league.

In addition to these categories, the UDL could also name a group of hostile and belligerent nations on which it intends to maintain significant diplomatic, economic, technological, and even military pressure. This warning would be part of the league's efforts to legitimize its uses of force *ad vim*. As noted, target nations could include the most repressive totalitarian regimes even when they are not conducting mass atrocities, and could extend in time to nations operating as havens from banking regulation and as tax shelters. The UDL might expect associate nations and friendly nations not to support hostile and belligerent nations. However, as the effectiveness of the league's tools increased over time, the number and range of nations in the rogue category would shrink considerably.

This would leave a remainder category of nations classified neither as friendly or hostile, which would therefore not benefit from friendly partner status nor suffer from classification as hostile despotisms. These neutral nations would be affected by incentives not to become hostile and on the contrary to enter into friendly relations with UDL nations, but they could remain indefinitely on neutral terms with the UDL if they so wished.

The relations of the UDL to other transnational organizations and groups

The United Nations

These clarifications lead naturally to the issue of how the democratic league should relate to other global and regional institutions. I have emphasized that the UDL should insist on the right to take forceful action of several kinds without UN Security Council approval against entrenched totalitarian governments and tyrannical regimes. Thus the league would communicate its conviction that the UNSC has neither the democratic legitimacy nor the coordinative power to act as first-decider on crimes against peace, terrorist threats, mass atrocities, or totalitarian repression. Dictators would soon grasp that they could no longer hide behind UNSC inaction. The league's firm stance should be that the UNSC has forfeited its supposedly distinctive security functions; the United States, Britain, and France would continue their presence on the Security Council mainly to prevent it from misdeeds.

However, this emphatically does not entail abandoning the rest of the UN framework. James Lindsay has rightly stressed that a concert of democracies should not seek to end the UN or replace groups like the G8.[27] On my proposal, the UNSC could even continue authorizing and monitoring UN peacekeeping and peace enforcement missions, which would remain necessary while the strength and reach of the league of democracies is growing. Like several other analysts, Stephen Stedman argues that the UN has generally done a good job in peacekeeping, helping to reduce civil wars by 40 percent since 1992: in 2008, it ran "18 peacekeeping missions with over 100,000 peacekeepers deployed," and has helped to end several wars though mediation and negotiation.[28] This trend has continued during the last decade, with almost as many missions and peacekeepers deployed in 2018 (see chapter four). So the UDL need not take over all peacekeeping and peace enforcement functions; it could work with the UNSC and other regional organizations such as ASEAN, the AU, and perhaps even the EU to coordinate nation-building operations and post-conflict resolution.

Yet what if other nations try to free ride on the UDL's nation-building capacity by pulling back their contributions to UN efforts? First, several nations that contribute UN peacekeepers would be good candidates for UDL founding members. Second, other large contributors such as Pakistan and Nepal would probably aim for associate status within the UDL. Third, several other contributing nations in Africa are mainly concerned about their region. If nations see that the UNSC runs effective peacekeeping missions in cases where it has consensus, contributors would have every incentive to continue. Given the UN's proven capacity in this area, the UDL might only need its Reserve forces for conflict-prevention and reconstruction efforts in cases where the UNSC would not approve intervention. In the worst cases, where a major nation reaps large benefits from a UDL reconstruction mission in its neighborhood but refuses to contribute, the UDL would have sanctions available.

Many other agencies and institutions within the UN organization play extremely useful roles that the UDL should support. These include the good programs and works of UNESCO, WHO, the Food and Agriculture Organization (FAO), the UNDP, the UN High Commission for Refugees (UNHCR), the International Maritime organization, and the Postal Union—although the UDL bloc could pressure the UN to ensure that impartial experts measures progress toward the SDGs and similar UN targets (as Pogge has suggested). The UDL could support the work of UN-related agencies and IGOs such as the Telecommunications Union, the World Food Programme, World Bank, and IMF, and support coordination among IGO-based development and poverty-relief efforts. Weiss notes that the Bretton Woods international financial institutions (IFIs) have received far more financial support than UN agencies trying to run projects to help the least developed nations meet SDGs.[29] But this is because funding the IFIs is an assurance dynamic, while UN agencies often face a chicken game instead: they must beg donors and conduct funding drives as if they were mere charities. A democratic league would be able to take votes binding all members to meet financial obligations to such programs, balancing IFI requests with development priorities. Although I have emphasized that poverty relief cannot be the UDL's primary mission, especially at the outset, it would have direct interests in development programs for its nation-building and conflict-prevention efforts.

Thus several UN agencies might be better funded and more effectively coordinated with other IGOs as a result of UDL initiatives supporting them. For example, while the UN Peacebuilding Commission can offer significant financial assets, it completely lacks the tools that a UDL would have for rooting out the corruption that wastes so much donor funding to underdeveloped nations. With UDL carrots and sticks supporting it, the Peacebuilding Commission might be able to achieve ten times more than it presently can. Similarly, IGOs focused on preventing terrorism and the spread of WMDs (such as the IAEA) would be directly supported by UDL actions, even while they continue operating formally under UN auspices.

The UN General Assembly could also continue meeting every fall, so that there remains a venue in which leaders and ambassadors from virtually all of the world's nations come together at least once per year. The General Assembly could continue its longstanding efforts to broker treaties that would reach beyond the scope of UDL nations. But naturally, with a working UDL, many such treaties might build on resolutions that are already binding on all UDL nations. Thus the UDL might make this central work of the UN much easier by taking many global treaty initiatives halfway toward their goal, after which the UN could encourage ratifying nations beyond the UDL members.

In sum, the UDL and UN could have a productive working relationship on many fronts. Most parts of the UN would work better with the UDL in place than they do now, and none need do worse. The democratic league would only reject the Security Council's monopoly on authorizing interventions under R2P and Chapter VII of the UN Charter.[30] In this, it would have many just war theorists on its side, arguably along with precedents in the Nuremberg Charter and the Genocide Convention.[31]

Of course it is possible that several decades after the UDL's found-ing, if half the world's nations were UDL members and another quarter were associate members, with most of the remaining quar-ter holding friendly nation status, it might make sense to move most remaining UN functions under the UDL. But that is hard to foresee, and replacing the whole UN this way should not be part of the UDL's founding aims.

NATO and the EU

Things are different with NATO: what happens with this Cold War institution involves much trickier prudential assessments. It might help foster broad acceptance of the democratic league if NATO were to be disbanded with the UDL's founding. This would especially make sense if most NATO nations had become UDL members (and right now, Turkey is the only NATO member that definitely could not join the UDL, although Hungary is problematic). Democracies from Asia and the global South would take this as further confirmation that western democracies were committed to working with them as equal partners. Perhaps promising in writing to disband NATO within ten years of the UDL treaty taking effect would persuade Russia to make the democratic reforms necessary to be approved as a UDL founding member: Russians would thus have a golden opportunity to replace NATO with an organization that they could help to shape.

On the other hand, some critics would doubtless argue that the league of democracies is simply NATO 2.0. This would be a specious criticism if half the UDL's founders were not NATO nations. However, it might help appearances if western nations planned to continue NATO for some time, but with a return to its narrower mutual secu-rity mission and a guarantee to respect the UDL's higher authority in all cases beyond direct defense of NATO members. For if the UDL works, NATO would no longer need to undertake missions of the sort it undertook in Kosovo, Afghanistan, and Libya. This would assure non-NATO nations that western democracies would never try to use NATO to bypass the new authority of the democratic league.

Either way, it must be clear that the league of democracies is not simply a new NATO with the United States still in a dominant role. This much is essential for the legitimacy of the new organization, and for acceptance of the UDL throughout Asia and the developing world. It may be useful in selling the UDL proposal to European and North American nations to argue that it will build on NATO's suc-cesses within a fundamentally new framework involving a larger set of purposes and more consolidated powers to match them. But the distinctive identity of the UDL will help make it politically possible for a reformed Russia to join, and perhaps eventually a reformed China as well. Their eventual inclusion is the threshold for the UDL's ultimate success. For if China democratizes and joins, it would be obvious that Russia gains much more inside the UDL than outside of it.

Finally, I have already suggested that regional organizations like the EU, AU, OAS, and ASEAN could continue largely as they have been, though they would have to decide how much to cooperate with the league of democracies. For the UDL to succeed, presumably most EU nations would have to join as founding members or fairly soon after its start. Obviously, without Germany, Britain, France, Spain, and Italy, there could be no UDL. This means that if a worthwhile democratic league came into existence, it would include most of the EU, just as it would include most NATO nations. But unlike NATO, there would be no reason for the EU to disband; it serves economic functions that would not be on the UDL's agenda, at least in its initial decades. However, the EU's intended foreign policy and security functions have never been robust. These functions could be largely handed off to the UDL; indeed the EU might work better with these divisive issues off its agenda. The EU could also rely on the democratic league to stop Mediterranean people smugglers, rectify the disorder in Libya, and give Turkey a motive to restore civil rights and free medias.

In other areas, such as tax harmonization and financial stability, the EU could greatly aid the UDL's work. The EU Court of Justice could work as before; its functions differ from those proposed for the UDL Court of Review. Similarly, the European Court of Human Rights (which is independent of the EU) would continue its vital work; European human rights standards will be more demanding than those in the UDL's list of basic democratic rights. Similarly, European commitment to the ICC will still be very important. In sum, it is possible that the advent of a UDL would eventually require amendments to the EU's constitutive treaties, but there should be no immediate conflict. Indeed, creation of the UDL might go a long way to repairing the disastrous rift opened by the folly and offense of Brexit.

Appealing to increasingly isolationist parts of Europe alienated by the EU might still be difficult. Leading proponents would have to make clear that the UDL will not be another bloated Brussels-style bureaucracy aiming to micromanage business regulations and product safety standards. To avoid fatigue with proliferating levels of governance, it would help to pare down the Brussels legislature and assure Europeans (as well as skeptical Americans) that the rise of an effective

UDL would allow some reductions in staff and programs at both the EU and UN. The phasing out of NATO might also help in this regard. Still, Europeans would be faced with electing a third set of legislators, in addition to those representing them in their national governments and in the EU Parliament. Right now, there is no way to avoid this result, given that its legitimacy rests on making both the UDL's legislative houses and chief executive directly elected. Direct election is also crucial for the UDL's greater coordinative power and consolidated authority, which will transcend those vested in the EU Council and Commission on some matters. But for efficiency, EU treaties might be revised to allow some representatives in Brussels also to represent their nations in within the UDL's Council or Parliament—a double duty that would also raise the status of the European Parliament as well, making it partly a European caucus of the UDL.

Conclusion

This chapter has explained how a league of democracies could be structured to be effective in performing a limited set of functions that are essential to securing crucial GPGs—especially those related to security and protection from mass atrocities, but also resistance to totalitarianism and anti-corruption efforts that are essential to promoting basic human capabilities in the poorest places on Earth. With the plausible criteria for membership laid out here, such a democratic league could include up to 50 founding nations, and offer other nations different types of attractive relationships with the league. These details, together with the case made for reciprocally beneficial relations between the UDL and the UN, NATO, the EU, and other regional authorities, should answer many nascent doubts and criticisms.

This institutional outline should also go a long way toward assuring us that a UDL could be founded without negative consequences that would outweigh its intended benefits. But large issues remain concerning perceived western domination of the current world order and whether UN reform is a better option. The last chapter addresses these concerns and compares the UDL with relevant alternatives, before tying all the strands of the global consolidation argument together.

Notes

1. Allan Buchanan, *Justice, Legitimacy, and Self-Determination* (New York: Oxford University Press, 2007), 8.
2. Ibid., 450–53.

3. For this proposal, see Ash Jain, "Like-Minded and Capable Democracies," Council on Foreign Relations Working Paper (January 2013), www.cfr.org/international-organizations-and-alliances/like-minded-capable-democracies-new-framework-advancing-liberal-world-order/p29484.

4. See Daniele Archibugi, "The Hope for Global Democracy," in the Global Democracy Symposium, ed. Archibugi, *New Political Science* 32 (March 2010): 84–91, 87. But Archibugi's own alternative is a version of a "world parliamentary assembly" that would have no actual power beyond making recommendations to the UN (91); see related comments on Singer in chapter six.

5. James Yunker, *Political Globalization* (Lanham, MD: University Press of America, 2007): 63.

6. Ibid., 64.

7. Compare Yunker's point that, unlike old empire, the union of democracies would be "democratically accountable to the entire population" of its members (ibid., 66).

8. Thus for example, Indonesia might get 17 votes, Brazil 15, Mexico 8, South Africa 5, Ukraine 4, Taiwan 3, and the Dominican Republic 2. Nations with less than 1 million people would have to share their vote with other small nations totaling at least 1 million. Such a weighted vote is logistically easier than a system assigning between one and thirty actual councilors to every nation except the smallest.

9. Such a regional veto primary system helps avoid overly divisive candidates becoming chancellor.

10. See Robert Johansen, ed. *A United Nations Emergency Peace Service to Prevent Genocide and Crimes Against Humanity* (New York: World Federalist Society, 2006), cited in Thomas G. Weiss, *What's Wrong with the United Nations and How to Fix It* (Malden, Mass: Polity Press, 2016), 189.

11. See Jeffrey Gerlach, "A U.N. Army for the New World Order?," *Orbis* 37 (spring 1993), 223-38, 224, citing David Boren, "The World Needs an Army on Call," *New York Times*, 26 August, 1992. Gerlach opposed such a UN force for fear of excessive entanglements, but burden-sharing within a wide UDL would avoid this problem.

12. Samantha Power, *A Problem from Hell* (New York: Basic Books, 2002), 262 and 350-53, noting Powell's insistence on evacuating UN peacekeepers rather than bolstering Dallaire's forces in Rwanda.

13. For example, see C.A.J. Coady, "The Ethics of Armed Humanitarian Intervention," *Peaceworks* 45 (Washington, DC: United States Institute for Peace, 2002), 34; Robert Johansen, "Put Teeth in 'Never Again' Vow with Fast, Full-Scale UN Response Force," *Christian Science Monitor*, 7 September 2004; and Malloch-Brown, *The Unfinished Global Revolution*: "what is really needed is a NATO-like capacity to lift the [UN] blue helmets quickly into trouble spots to contain trouble or police the peace…" (198).

14. Allan Buchanan and Robert Keohane, "The Preventative Use of Force," *Ethics and International Affairs* 18 (March 2004): 405–38, 406.

15. See Thomas Pogge, "Achieving Democracy," *Ethics and International Affairs* 15, no. 1 (2001): 3–23.

16. Ibid., 169–70.
17. Daniele Archibugi, "A League of Democracies or a Democratic United Nations?" *Harvard International Review* 30 (November 2008), 6, hir. harvard.edu/archives/1758.
18. Robert Kagan, "A Case for a League of Democracies," *Financial Times*, 3 May 2008.
19. See Christina M. Cerna, "Universality of Human Rights and Cultural Diversity," *Human Rights Quarterly*, 16 (1994): 740–52, 746.
20. Joshua Cohen, "Is There a Human Right to Democracy," in *The Egalitarian Conscience*, ed. Christine Syponowich (Oxford, UK: Oxford University Press, 2006): 226–48.
21. Daalder and Lindsay, "Democracies of the World, Unite," *The American Interest* 3, no. 1 (2007), 6.
22. Ibid.
23. Ibid., 7.
24. Ibid.
25. Didier Jacobs, "From a League of Democracies to Cosmopolitan Democracy," in the *Global Democracy* Symposium, ed. Daniele Archibugi, *New Political Science* 32, no. 1 (2010): 116–21, 119.
26. Daalder and Lindsay, "Democracies of the World Unite," 4–5.
27. James Lindsay, "The Case for a Concert of Democracies," *Ethics and International Affairs* 23, no. 1 (Spring 2009): Roundtable section, www.carnegiecouncil.org/publications/journal/23_1/roundtable/002.
28. Stephen Stedman, "America and International Cooperation: What Role for a League of Democracies?" *Policy Analysis Brief* (The Stanley Foundation, November 2008), 4, col. 2.
29. Weiss, *What's Wrong with the United Nations and How to Fix It*, 3rd ed., 194–95.
30. See Alex Bellamy, *The Responsibility to Protect* (Oxford, UK: Oxford University Press, 2015), 14–16.
31. For example, see Jürgen Habermas on NATO's defense of Kosovo, in "Bestiality and Humanity," *Constellations* 6, no. 3 (1999): 263–72. The Nuremberg Charter should be distinguished from the "Principles of the Nuremberg Tribunal" document adopted by the UN that attempted, in Westphalian fashion, to limit "crimes against humanity" to contexts of international war.

6 Standard objections, alternatives, and replies to critics

- Confusions about universal inclusion
- Western domination, American hegemony, or colonialism?
- A new Cold War?
- Democratic insincerity and Darfur
- Lack of cohesion among democracies?
- Instead, reform the UN to uphold basic human rights?
- Conclusion: The completed global consolidation argument, and the future

The previous chapter addressed common questions concerning how a league of democracies could be formed and the criteria for its founding nations, as well as its possible relations with the UN, IGOs, and other regional organizations like NATO and the EU. These are largely answered by the proposed institutional structure, list of functions, and membership conditions for the United Democratic League (UDL).

This chapter responds to published objections concerning likely consequences of forming a democratic league, and considers arguments for other options, such as trying to make fundamental reforms to the UN. I will argue in each case that the proposed UDL remains indispensable and fears about its likely effects can be allayed. In contrast, comparable reforms to the UN are impossible. In conclusion, I review how all the pieces of the argument for the league of democracies fit together, and consider its momentous implications.

Confusions about universal inclusion

The most common normative objection to a league of democracies concerns the UN's decision to accept every national government, no matter what their record (see chapter four). As Daalder and Lindsay note, this complaint assumes that "the legitimacy of an action increases with the number of countries supporting it, with the universalism of the UN imprimatur being the gold standard."[1] This assumption is so common that it is needs a name: I will call it *statist universalism*. For example, Stephen Schlesinger suggests that other democracies will "question the legitimacy of a body that restricts membership to 'free' states" and excludes Russia and China; by contrast, in his view, the UN derives unique authority from inviting "all nations into its ranks."[2] Similarly, Charles Kupchan argues that Europeans will oppose a democratic league because they rightly see UN Security Council approval as essential to the legitimacy of any military intervention:

> If democracies are legitimate because they represent the will of their citizens, could a global body that spoke for less than half of the world's population and represented less than a third of the world's nations ever be considered legitimate? Should China's 1.3 billion citizens be doubly disenfranchised—no voice abroad as well as no democracy at home?[3]

These statements typify the ethical confusions behind statist universalism: they conflate a conclave of ambassadors from all nations (or from 15 nations in the UNSC) with a "universal membership" of all human persons.[4] It is absurd to imply that the average person in China is "enfranchised" within the UN; the consultative hierarchy in Beijing does not extend beyond an oligarchic elite—the upper echelons of the Communist Party, including much less than 0.1 percent of China's population. As explained in chapter four, the UN Charter employs an associative conception of collective "self-determination" that does not require internal democracy; but this fiction cannot survive critical scrutiny either in democratic theory or practice. It is outrageous to imply that the UN ambassadors from China, Syria, Bahrain, or Sudan "represent" their peoples in any meaningful sense. Their aspirations might be better represented by a UDL in which leaders of resistance movements in these countries could have a voice. Similarly, as we saw, the current Russian authority directs and manipulates Russian people by totally controlling most of their media, and threatening or killing anyone prominent who dares to raise objections.

Thus Daalder and Lindsay are too kind when they say that the statist view has "a deeply flawed conception of legitimacy"—both because the moral grounds of collective action matter to a government's legitimacy, and because procedurally, the endorsement of nondemocratic states justifies nothing:[5] their will is mere power without right. In fact, the UN is *less* morally legitimate, not more, because it includes the governments of China, Syria, Sudan, North Korea, Iran, the DRC, Eritrea, Venezuela, and Putin's Russia. The UDL would gain greater legitimacy by excluding such dictatorships. Moreover, no one is *directly* represented in the UN's General Assembly or Security Council, whereas at least the peoples of democratic nations would be directly represented in the UDL. *Direct representation* is the authentic gold standard, as the US Federalists' conception of rightful primary sovereignty indicates. We should understand such representatives as trustees who are free to deliberate about public goods and to educate their publics rather than as mere aggregators of people's preferences, but direct accountability is still necessary.

Thus statist universalism is really an offense to the basic dignity of persons, which has only gained popularity because the UN became associated in many minds with liberal-progressive credentials. It became "politically correct" to speak as if the UN is more "inclusive" because the cronies of military dictatorships, theocracies, and kleptocracies visit New York and Geneva to enjoy the freedoms and wealth they deny to their own people. When stripped bare, the confusion and insult involved in this way of speaking should be clear.

This statist anathema should be distinguished from legitimate concerns about "transnational exclusion" that keeps developing nations out of dominant great-power groups like the G7, which make decisions that can dramatically affect their lives. Raffaele Marchetti argues cogently on this basis for "a cosmopolitan system in which all world citizens are included within a scheme of direct representative participation under an overarching authority that governs the democratization of world affairs" through a "world federalist system."[6] Marchetti is right about the need for direct representation, but there is no immediate way to include people living in nondemocratic nations whose government will not allow them to vote in a free election for league representatives (see chapter four). The proposed democratic league would try to protect such people by (a) pre-empting any credible danger of mass atrocities; (b) putting serious economic pressures on entrenched totalitarian regimes and anti-corruption controls on international finance; and (c) by offering clear and robust incentives to democratize. Maybe the UDL could also (d) include regular consultation with diaspora groups and NGOs that can indirectly represent the interests of people living under dictatorships, giving their concerns a voice within league forums.

There is a related last-ditch legal objection against a UDL based on how traditions in international law have evolved since the founding of the UN. Schlesinger insists that "when the league [of democracies] tries to act against non-members, its edicts will essentially be null, because they have no standing in international law."[7] He adds that its "all-inclusive membership is what gives the force of law to the UN."[8] These are question-begging claims, which simply declare that international law depends on the Westphalian inter-state order. On the contrary, the historical record shows that Westphalian statism was a temporary compromise, not an ultimate principle (see chapter four). While international law has adapted to the UN's existence, its customary and moral sources are hardly limited to the UN's framework. In particular, the history of just war theory shows that customary international law predated modern nation-states; and even in the seventeenth and eighteenth centuries, it retained the right of legitimate sovereigns to fight tyranny anywhere.[9] The development of standards concerning crimes against humanity, from Nuremberg to the ICC, provides another strand in international law that is not dependent on UN ratification. Pace Schlesinger, international law is squarely founded on the Enlightenment principle, and we have reached the point where humanity can progress beyond Westphalia to an international order more in accord with this foundation.

Moreover, it is ironic to worry that a democratic league would weaken the hold of international law on *non-democratic* regimes that have always ignored such customary standards and treaties whenever it suited them. On the contrary, a working UDL would give teeth to international humanitarian law by backing the verdicts of transnational courts with enforcement. No doubt tyrannical regimes would hypocritically protest that decisions of the UDL have no legal legitimacy. But such complaints must appeal to the EP distinction between right and might that these regimes flagrantly violate every day. The pragmatic contradiction is obvious: if the totalitarian regimes had a sound complaint based on a just legal standard grounded on EP, then they would necessarily be illegitimate regimes with no standing to lodge the complaint. What critics really fear, correctly, is that the worldwide respect quickly garnered by an effective democratic league would expose the nakedness of statist emperors.

Western domination, American hegemony, or colonialism?

Issues concerning initial membership in a UDL (see chapter five) are sometimes linked with a normative claim that definitions of "democracy" are arbitrary and assessments of democratic credentials merely strategic. For instance, Schlesinger poses a string of queries about a UDL's structure and procedures (which descend to the level of asking where its headquarters would be located). He asks, "After all, what constitutes a democracy?" as if not much work had been done on this, or as if no clear principles had emerged from experience beyond the minimalist requirement that there be some kind of elections—which would require us to admit "such illiberal democracies as Zimbabwe and Thailand."[10]

This kind of complaint ignores recent work in political philosophy on democratic conditions, as noted in the prior chapter. While there are different conceptions of collective self-determination, the criteria I outlined for member nations are implied by virtually any conception more robust than brute voluntarism (a.k.a. pure majoritarianism)—which is well-known to be riddled with antinomies. These standards, moreover, are rooted in conceptual and pragmatic relations between rights to popular sovereignty and other basic human rights that the former help secure and define.[11] According to the linkage approach, democratic conditions are ultimately justified by the need for people collectively to articulate how their human rights are secured through positive law and informal social practices (chapter one). Far from being a sign of arbitrariness, this articulation by dialogue among persons is a necessary result of the reflexivity built into human rights and their relation to the social and legal realms.

A more extreme version of the arbitrariness objection charges that a democratic league would always be a front for domination of the world by western powers, led of course by a bellicose United States bent on recolonizing non-western peoples. In much recent "postcolonial" thought,[12] this attitude is absurdly extended to any form of power aiming to defend people from atrocities in the name of universal rights. Dictators across the world would gladly invoke such postmodern rhetoric against proposals for a democratic league, because they know that a UDL would pressure them to stop killing and robbing their people blind. Nothing better defends the world's dictators, from Putin to Maduro, than the hatred that they and others have cultivated toward perceived US domination—a simplistic Chomskian narrative that many US tactics from the Cold War to 2003 have made easy to sell.

Yet this excessive fear is also stoked by mainstream western critics like Kupchan who simply assume that proposals for a league of democracies could only be a strategy to impose American priorities: "the United States cannot win back its good standing abroad with grand schemes foisted on an unwilling world."[13] Similarly, Thomas Carothers argues that "many democratic societies harbor deep skepticism about the expansive global role in which many U.S. foreign policy experts—including the proponents of a League of Democracies—sincerely believe." Latin American, African, and Southeast Asian peoples will object to "U.S.-led military interventions" in the future; similarly, "US policies toward the Muslim world" have angered a high percentage of citizens not just in Arab states but also in Indonesia and Turkey.[14] That is correct, but irrelevant: Carothers is assuming a version of the league with America at its helm, which is not what I intend. His critique is simply damnation by association with McCain's support for the 2003 US war to overthrow Hussein in Iraq. A democratic league linked with American war hawk attitudes is a straw man. In fact, the multilateral UDL decision process that I proposed would probably have prevented the 2003 Iraq invasion.

Thus this worry is avoided once we grasp that the United States and Europe will be balanced by democracies from Asia and the southern hemisphere within a UDL. For a democratic league to succeed, it would have to be clear to the nations Carothers lists that this league could restrain any US adventurism (which will not be difficult, given rising US isolationism), and provide developing nations a way to achieve the equal respect they have sought from America. That India and Indonesia, along with Brazil, Argentina, and South Africa would have so much weight within the UDL Parliament and Council, given their combined populations, should assure them of benign US intentions. The main point of the UDL is to make possible a truly multilateral process that provides security for democracies and protection from mass atrocities without domination by NATO or OECD nations. In this process, devotion to basic human rights, rather than western economic interests, would drive policy. This is the only moral foundation that can provide a strong consensual basis for a new organization capable of securing more GPGs.

As noted in chapter one, this implies a grand compromise: just as Europeans and non-western democracies will have to give up their insistence on working through the paralyzed UNSC, Americans will have to abide by the common will of the democratic league on steps to promote international security and human rights. Thereby all sides gain the huge advantages offered by a perpetual alliance among so many democratic nations, including a united front against rising Russian and Chinese despotism. In this bargain, European, Asian, African and South American partners would get the collective decision-making they want, with more attention to economic development, fairness in trade relations, and environmental issues. In return, Americans would no longer be asked to carry most of the human and financial costs of responding to security crises and humanitarian emergencies, or leave the world rudderless when they balk. As Ikenberry and Slaughter have argued, free riding on the United States would be minimized as European and other democratic nations would have to do their fair share.

Moreover, I have explained how the UDL would lower the costs and risks of intervention to any given nation by spreading those costs so widely. In technical terms, the UDL provides the needed levels of assurance with distributive equity. No one or two of the most powerful nations, like the United States or United Kingdom together, could block UDL action, as arguably they did when the Security Council considered Rwanda: if most of the rest of the democratic world saw a dire need to act, western powers could be overruled, but the risks of intervention and costs of reconstruction would remain small for any one nation.

Finally, all the impediments that have blocked deployment of ground troops when they were most needed decrease under my proposal: for over half the soldiers would come from non-western nations, and they all would have specifically *requested* this kind of humanitarian mission. Within militaries around the world, volunteers would compete for the *special distinction* of serving the democratic league in its highest purpose of preventing mass atrocity crimes. If the UDL acted properly, these men and women would be honored everywhere for doing what UN peacekeepers in Bosnia and Rwanda were not allowed to do. These multicultural brigades of humanitarian soldiers would bring to the world's most beleaguered victims the message that the world's free peoples stand in solidarity with them—the exact opposite of the message we sent to Assad's victims. Their partners in the UDL's Reserve Corps would constitute a globalized version of the Peace Corps, helping to prevent conflict and end corruption everywhere they work.

Thus, far from promoting "American imperialism," the UDL would be the absolute end of it. It would also deflate the self-righteous pretenses that have made it easy for intellectual pacifists to oppose all humanitarian interventions in the name of preventing "western hegemony." Once a democratic league was in operation, it would no longer be even remotely plausible to justify inaction in the face of genocide by irresponsible postmodern convolutions. If non-western democracies united with western allies, scholars still trying construe all forceful opposition to tyranny as mere "colonialism" would simply look foolish.

A new Cold War?

A different objection is likely to come from Kissingerian realists who suspect that anything like the proposed UDL would re-divide the world, pushing China further away from cooperation with democratic nations and reducing cooperation between democratic and nondemocratic nations across the world. For example, Gideon Rachman responded to McCain's proposal by objecting that it would "exacerbate tensions with Russia and China."[15] Yet ten more years of reaching out to China and Russia and deepening trade ties have gained us nothing but enormous data theft, currency manipulation, repression of Hong Kong, seizure of Crimea, and a massive cyber-campaign to sabotage our elections.

This frequent objection makes several related errors. First, it fails to recognize that the Cold War never really ended: Russian and Chinese dictators simply developed more subtle tactics. Both have used the time granted by our repeated, futile efforts to befriend them in order to remake their expansionist strategies; by supporting regimes like Assad in Syria and the Kims in North Korea, they have caused grave new threats to democratic nations. While we cling to the hopes of 1989 and chastise ourselves for upsetting them, Russia and China have doubled down on repression at home and done everything they could to stymie the progress of human rights ideals around the world. For example, China threatens its neighbors all across the Pacific rim and steals massive amounts of western technology. It is hard to see how a democratic league could make their behavior any worse.

Second, this objection pursues the mirage of appeasement. For example, Kupchan says that "If a new global order is to emerge, Washington and Brussels will have to adjust to the preferences of rising autocracies, just as Beijing and Moscow have had to adjust to the West."[16] This is a counsel of total defeatism: it says that the best we can do is to tweak a *modus vivendi* that is turning ever more against the collective interests and principles of democratic peoples; if we try instead to get to the root of the problems, rather than letting autocracies have their way, the sky will fall. The illusory safety of appeasement will only embolden dictators bent on crushing democratic movements and ideals at all costs.

In short, the Kupchan approach will only lead to a world dominated by soft despotism. By contrast, with a strong league of democracies, it is Russia and China that would have to "adjust" to democratic control of the global economy on which they depend. If the UDL responded to Putin's aggressions by making Europe entirely independent of Russian natural gas, Putin would have few options. Similarly, if China became increasingly aggressive, the UDL could impose tough trade reductions (see chapter one). Thus if Russia and China responded to a UDL by starting a new Cold War, it would be a lot shorter this time around. On the other hand, once either Russia or China becomes a member of the UDL, the other would have to seek friendly nation status or risk total isolation.

Third, the objector sometimes argues a democratic league would *unite* the enemies of democracy into something like a new but more powerful Warsaw Pact. Kupchan implies this in his response to Robert Kagan, saying that if we create "an alliance of democracies," then illiberal states will balance it with a league of their own.[17] This is even more implausible: there is little chance that China will join ranks with the Taliban or other Islamic theocracies. China's leaders hate fundamentalist religion and face their own Islamic terror threats; nor does their soft-despotist strategy mesh well with Assad-style absolute tyranny, either. China is open to allying with African dictators but these face increasing internal opposition that a wide league of democracies could quickly strengthen. Similarly, while Putin has unstable alliances with Assad and the hardliners in Iran, his regime has thereby alienated average Sunnis throughout the Middle East.

The bigger danger, as I have argued, lies in the BRICS coalition, which Russia and China already created to drive a wedge through the democratic world. They were not pushed by a democratic league into this effort to persuade non-western democracies that they are better off putting trade deals with dictatorships ahead of human rights. The UDL would put an end to this sophistical effort to corrupt developing democracies on the pretense that this helps them stand up to hegemonic western aspirations (see chapter one). Without the UDL, this trajectory may continue, with Russia also controlling more satellite states around its borders and making pacts of convenience with Islamic dictators where it can.

With the UDL, the world may divide temporarily into three groups: a growing league of democracies; an increasingly pressured "Greater Russia" aligned with an increasingly stymied China; and a string of dictatorships and theocracies from parts of north Africa to Afghanistan. This third group will be more focused on its internal struggles (including Sunni versus Shia). However, a UDL might strengthen moderate reformists in many of these nations, and encourage Turkey to return to full civil rights and make a final peace settlement with Kurdish groups. The UDL also stands more chance of brokering a final two-state peace deal between Israel and Palestinians, in part by insisting on this as a condition for Israel's entry into the league.

On all these measures, then, prospects are much better with a democratic league than in our current status quo. Any new divisions arising from its creation would be very different from the NATO versus USSR standoff, and more open to negotiated settlements. The difference is that united democracies would be negotiating from a position of far more strength. Making the division between democracies and their anti-democratic rivals more salient would provide invigorating moral clarity, cutting through the miasma of ideological rhetoric that dictatorships peddle to disguise oppression of their people as cultural solidarity. Once more people see through such efforts to promote primitive nationalism, dictators may face more opposition at home, and democratic nations may recognize that through our cooperation, we can forge a much better world for generations to come. That is the scenario that really terrifies the politburos in Beijing and Moscow.

Democratic insincerity and Darfur

Critics of a democratic league argue, on the contrary, that democracies are not likely to work well together, especially to stop mass atrocities in the making. For example, Archibugi argues that democratic nations have often been at odds since 1989, especially over 2003 Iraq invasion. He also thinks that democracies have rarely been a united group that was stymied by Russia and China; in his view, this has happened only when democracies were pressing for UN action in Kosovo (though maybe now he would add Syria). In particular, regarding the 2004–2006 decisions about the genocidal violence in the Darfur region of Sudan, Archibugi insists that

> [t]he Security Council would gladly have approved intervention by a "coalition of the willing" if only someone had been willing to provide the required resources and run the necessary risks. And so, it is false to claim that the United Nations cannot act because of an alleged divergence between the democratic countries and the despotic ones.[18]

Kupchan instead admits that European nations have been happy to hide behind Russian and Chinese vetoes in the UNSC, for example when Russia took the heat for resisting even stiffer sanctions against Iran. But he agrees that "the main impediment to Western military action in Darfur" was not China's refusal and consequent UNSC stalemate, but rather "the reluctance of the United States and its democratic allies to assume the costs and risks of intervention."[19] A similar point applies to the Rwandan genocide. Thus an effort to organize a UDL might only expose how hollow our pretenses are.

This objection involves several serious errors. First, it conflates what democracies would do within an institution enforcing collective decisions and efforts, on the one hand, with their uncoordinated, voluntary moves in chicken and Rambo games, on the other. Kupchan, Luban, and other critics are correct that democratic nations have often shown reluctance to put their troops in harm's way for the sake of foreigners. But decisive UDL action would not depend on consensus among all the major powers; given the UDL's standing forces and the necessary super-majority support, a few holdouts could not spoil collective action.

Moreover a league of democracies could demand that nations in the region help a UDL effort to prevent or stop mass atrocities—for example, Arab League nations should have supplied half the troops and costs for a ground mission in Libya, and for a coalition in Syria. If they refused urgent requests from the democratic league in such cases, it should impose huge reprisals for free riding. Compelling significant contribution from capable nations in the region (especially when they share cultural ties with the nation in crisis) would make UDL action more feasible: for then citizens in UDL nations would not feel unfairly used, as many did when facing prospective intervention in Rwanda or Darfur. Kupchan and Archibugi ignore this trilemma with which we began.

If disagreement among league members still blocked interventions to stop a genocide in progress, democratic peoples would have to blame themselves for the allowing hundreds of thousands of persons to be murdered and millions driven into exile, and for all the knock-on effects of this. The excuses for inaction that currently rule us would be gone. Given assurance of sufficiently wide cost-sharing for intervention and reconstruction, UDL nations would not have refused to join African forces to stop the murderous rampages of Omar Bashir's Janjaweed militias in Darfur.

Third, Archibugi's and Kupchan's accounts grossly misrepresent what happened with Darfur. In fact, Russia and especially China *were* the main obstacles to any military intervention strong enough to stop that regime's systemic efforts to radicalize Arab tribes against non-Arab ("black") Africans in Darfur.[20] During 2003 and 2004, Sudanese helicopters and jets, followed by Arab militias, razed between 700–2000 non-Arab villages (destroying hundreds of mosques). "The attacks this time were far more systematic…including the looting of animal herds, burning of fields, mass rape of women, abduction of children, and destruction of infrastructure."[21] Almost 2 million displaced persons were herded into camps where starvation and disease raged (while the regime stalled aid charities).[22] Thus the regime and its militias killed over 200,000 people. *Human Rights Watch* reported in January 2005 that the initial UNSC Res. 1556 was far too weak:

> By July 2004, stronger measures directed at the government were justified and necessary, but they weren't adopted because at least one permanent member—China—and possibly another—Russia …

would have vetoed any resolution that included sanctions against the government or authorized direct U.N. intervention. ... Thus even in the shadow of Rwanda, the Security Council in 2004 failed to muster the collective will necessary to act quickly and decisively to end the humanitarian catastrophe in Darfur....[23]

This came immediately after twenty years of on-off civil wars in southern Sudan and Darfur that killed "over 2 million black, non-Muslim civilians," leading even a reluctant G.W. Bush administration to pass the Sudan Peace Act (2002).[24] As a leading US expert on Darfur, Eric Reeves, wrote in August 2005, "China in particular has paralyzed the UN Security Council, ensuring that no effective action is taken against a regime that has allowed Chinese oil companies to become dominant in Sudan's burgeoning petroleum industry."[25]

Reeves shown in meticulous detail that China, which also supplies Khartoum much of its weapons, worked to ensure that Bashir could continue bombing Darfuris and attacking them with Janjaweed militias.[26] After the UNSC in 2004 authorized a woefully inadequate AU force that could not even protect NGO aid workers, let alone Darfuris, UNSC Resolution 1706 (August 2006) finally authorized a stronger force, but with "a critical caveat: deployment would occur only if Khartoum accepted the Security Council 'invitation' to allow the [international] force in Darfur."[27] Of course, Bashir's government did *not* accept; instead they began a new offensive, forcing months of further negotiation to arrive at a hybrid UN/AU Mission in Darfur (UNAMID). Sudan insisted that it be limited to African forces because they knew that the fledgling AU could only deploy inadequately trained, poorly equipped, and uncoordinated troops.[28] Weiss comments that "[t]he collective waffling, reflecting unadulterated respect for Khartoum's sovereign prerogatives," was "baffling even by UN standards."[29]

But the explanation is straightforward: China gutted out the heart of R2P to protect its oil interests and statist ideology. The extreme Westphalian caveat in Resolution 1706 was China's price for any UN action. As Reeves explained,

the UN DPKO [Department of Peacekeeping] made plans for a large UN "'peace support'" operation, one that could have made a real difference if rapidly deployed. The UN resolution passed on August 31, 2006, with China abstaining. But China had also insisted [on the "invitation" caveat]... Khartoum of course refused and the UN...simply acquiesced.[30]

Thus the lack of highly skilled and powerful forces in UNAMID was largely a result of China's machinations in concert with Sudan's genocidal regime. China did not stop blocking more direct action until mid-2007, after which less than 10,000 UNAMID forces deployed in 2008 only *under restrictions* preventing them from going wherever the Janjaweed were roving or Bashir's bombs were falling.[31] After five years of ethnic cleansing and genocide, we got a UN mission that was dependent on the Bashir regime to avoid casualties (the reverse thinking problem we noted in the Bosnian and Rwandan cases). Because of China, the Security Council tolerated Khartoum's constant obstruction of UNAMID movements.[32]

As a result, by late 2012, more than 1.2 million people were displaced in Darfur, and "well over 2 million Darfuris" were forced into "squalid and dangerous camps" either within Sudan or neighboring Chad. The regime was also able to bomb these camps with impunity. On the most conservative count, between 2007 and 2012, the government carried out "more than 1000 confirmed aerial attacks on civilian and humanitarian targets ... throughout Darfur, the Nuba Mountains, Blue Nile, and South Sudan,"[33] where its proxy militias have prevented peace. The actual number of bombing runs, as Reeves notes, is far larger. Indeed these systematic efforts, mixing ethnic cleansing and genocide, have continued to this day, although western nations have long since forgotten, and UN officials and western governments have gone to scandalous lengths to cover up the true depths of UNAMID's failure.

However, Kupchan and Archibugi were correct that western nations refused even to offer the helicopters and other heavy transport equipment and logistical aid that UNAMID desperately needed. As Stedman also argues, there were "few takers for robust military action, and this is as true of democracies as non-democracies."[34] This is partly because the Darfur crisis came during the years right after the US invasion of Iraq and the NATO intervention in Afghanistan; but that is no excuse. As Reeves says, western leaders knew in 2005 that the AU required such equipment, along with more expert leadership and coordination among its woefully undersized forces, to give UNAMID any chance of even partial success.[35]

But rather than being evidence against the likely effectiveness of a democratic league, this example is a compelling illustration of why the league is needed. The main problem in 2004–2007 was the absence of a political process that could assure sufficient contribution from all responsible parties when a majority (or supermajority) determines that military intervention is indispensable. If elite divisions of multiethnic UDL Humanitarian Guard from all continents had been available for quick deployment on the best air and sea transports, African leaders would have had assurance from non-western democracies on the UDL Council about the goals and terms of their deployment. China would have had no veto and the Darfur genocide would have been averted.

Lack of cohesion among democracies?

It is now clear that the Archibugi-Stedman objection interpreted the proposed democratic league as merely a concert of democratic nations making decisions by consensus—like a larger NATO. In this form, the proposal is easy to critique as too optimistic about democratic "cohesion." But this is to confuse what legitimates a league of democracies (its meeting the demands of DP) with what gives it coordinative power (as required by CP): democracies do not have to stand in *prior* consensus on all the difficult policy questions if a democratic league precommits them to binding decisions by majority rule. No proponent of a democratic league ever said that CAPs vanish just because all the parties are democracies. The CAPs are solved by consolidation of authority enabling strong majorities to steer the collective action of all members. As James Lindsay put it, "by constructing a common identity among liberal democracies," a league "will *change* how democracies interact and thereby further facilitate their cooperation."[36]

Instead, Stedman recommends replacing the G8 or G7 "with a new G16 that would include Brazil, China, India, South Africa, Mexico (the 'Outreach 5') and Indonesia, Turkey, and Egypt, key Muslim majority states." Such a G16, he contends, could help negotiate solutions "to major global challenges, and strategies for their implementation." Thus it could "be a force for making the UN and other multilateral and regional bodies more effective."[37] But this proposal seeks greater legitimacy without giving the organization sufficient coordinative power: functioning by consensus, such a G16 would remain unable to solve the relevant CAPs. It also lacks the clearer standards set by UDL membership criteria: why these nations, but not Argentina, South Korea, and Nigeria? Power is the wrong criterion for membership, given that together, under the UDL, democracies could speak as one within any larger transnational working groups or treaty frameworks. Imagine a G30 group with 15 democratic and 15 nondemocratic nations: the first half would have much greater leverage with the UDL behind them. So there is much to gain and little to lose from a UDL for the purposes of forging new working groups of nations.

Jain looks instead for a democratic group because Russia and China have "sought to frustrate U.S. attempts to expand democracy, particularly in countries ruled by anti-western regimes." They have also undermined R2P; despite allowing UN approval for the NATO mission to save Benghazi, "Russia and China handily condemned NATO's military actions" when they resulted in Qaddafi's fall, and Russia and China vetoed "successive UN Security Council resolutions that sought to condemn and impose sanctions against the Bashir-al-Assad regime for atrocities against its own people." Similarly, they have "continued to supply arms" to Sudan, Zimbabwe, Venezuela, and Syria while working to water down sanctions against Iran and North Korea.[38] Jain's analysis is confirmed by Russia's air campaign in Syria, which bombed tens of thousands of rebel targets *not aligned with ISIS* or Al Nusra in effort to help Assad's persecution strategy succeed.

Yet Jain's alternative is a D10 group, including the G7 nations (without Russia, which "rendered the G8 ineffective"), along with Australia, South Korea, and the EU. Jain argues that a larger group makes proceedings more formal and thus more difficult,[39] but that holds only if decision is by consensus. Jain is assuming that the best we can attain is a "consultative forum" without "mutually binding commitments," and that D10 nations could leave at will.[40] By contrast, the more robust procedures of UDL policymaking can avoid the problem that Jain notes of India, Brazil, and South Africa "free riding on the contributions" of older democracies that support democratic ideals and human rights around the world.[41] Jain believes that India, Brazil, and South Africa will continue resisting efforts to enforce R2P by military intervention: understandably, because of "their colonial legacies, rising democracies are deeply skeptical of international intervention, and often privilege national dignity, sovereign equality, and non-discrimination over other concerns."[42] Hence Jain's preference for a group that leaves out these nations until they change their priorities.

While I agree with Jain's concerns, I hold that a UDL requires India, Brazil, and South Africa among its founders to be sufficiently legitimate. Leaving them out also abandons them to Russia's and China's efforts to buy them into the BRICS coalition and thus deepen their beliefs in the Westphalian ideology that has become so invaluable to dictatorial regimes. Instead, we must move proactively to persuade rising democracies to see through such Westphalian illusions before it is too late. Here's why this can work.

The policy patterns of India, Brazil, South Africa and other major developing democracies (such as Argentina, Nigeria, and Indonesia) suggest *three* main motives for resisting greater cooperation with established democracies in the name of universal human rights and the prevention of mass atrocities: (1) the popular idea that state sovereignty assures them equal recognition and protects them from "neo-colonial" manipulations; (2) the sheer economic wealth flowing to their elites from trade with China, Russia, and other autocratic states; and (3) the belief that fully developed democracies will do the work for them if humanitarian war really needs to be waged.

The UDL design solves the first problem by assuring these rising democracies that they will have a proportional voice in all parts of the UDL framework. If Brazil, India, Indonesia, and South Africa join, then, especially with other nations in Latin America, they could have controlling majorities in the league's legislature. The UDL's majority procedures and enforcement powers solve problem (3) by *assuring compliance* from all members. By contrast, any decision to use force by Jain's D10 would have to rely on NATO or another "separately formed coalition of the willing,"[43] thus reintroducing chicken CAPs. Finally, the UDL solves problem (2) by offering rising democracies much greater economic incentives than Russia and China can, even together.

Thus the grand bargain is feasible. Once inside the UDL framework, India, Brazil, South Africa, Indonesia, and other rising democracies would have no weighty incentive to act as spoilers: for their fortunes would then be tied to the fortunes of the entire democratic group. With their help, the democratic league would quickly prove that fears of western domination are misplaced.

'All roads lead to Rome:' every alternative we consider and compare with the UDL only further clarifies why a diverse, directly elected league of democracies acting by majority decisions with direct enforcement powers is the best among feasible possibilities. We have to 'think big' enough to really get our arms around our most challenging problems in the twenty-first century world, and reach deep enough to get to their roots. As Didier Jacobs indicates, a democratic league would specify minimum contributions from all members proportional to population and means, thus making possible the follow-through needed to reconstruct nations after intervention, and to shore up failing states to prevent civil war and chaos.[44] While such mechanisms would give the league powers greater than the UN or any other treaty organization, the democratic credentials of its members along with their global diversity would *justify* these greater powers. When force is really necessary, developing democracies would see that it is not controlled by American preferences. Through this league, a new kind of global solidarity can grow.

Instead, reform the UN to uphold basic human rights?

Among ethicists and philosophical theorists, the most popular argument against a democratic league asserts that it would be (a) morally better, or (b) more politically effective (or both) to improve on the UN structure, which has the great advantage of already existing. Before getting to the details, however, we should remind ourselves that among the UN's founders, the democratically oriented never saw it as the final answer to the main problems of global governance (see chapter four). It was only a large step in the right direction, compromised by accommodations to geopolitical realities, to be improved on when such circumstances permitted—as they have since the mid-1990s. Thus we should never take for granted that reforming the UN must be morally superior to replacing it with something new, as if the UN were sacrosanct. Global stability hardly depends on the UNSC retaining a supreme authority that it can almost never use, and thoughtful proposals to replace it should never be wantonly demonized as attacks on multicultural tolerance, intercultural respect, or peace. Such kneejerk reactions and crude "straw man" misrepresentations must be set aside before considering serious UN reform proposals.

Amend the UN Charter? Gareth Evans's Argument

Evans plays to UN cultism just a bit in his very brief critique of the league proposal. After naming only Republican proponents of a democratic league (Kagan and McCain), he lists three problems. First, "it would be institutionally unworkable because there are profound differences of outlook with the democratic camp on most of the relevant issues," especially along the North-South divide. This is the objection addressed with Archibugi, Stedman, and Jain in the previous section. Second, a democratic league "would be deeply counterproductive to the cause of finding solutions" not only to problems of terrorism but also "to other challenges that can only be resolved by common and cooperative strategies, including nuclear nonproliferation and disarmament, climate change, and mass atrocity crimes" (a claim similar to Kupchan's, also refuted earlier). Evans here severely underestimates what a well-crafted league could accomplish. Third, a league of democracies would fatally undermine the UN, not merely supplement it:

> the institutionalization of competing ideological alliances would simply be very dangerous, directly undermining the whole premise on which world order has been founded since the catastrophes

of 1914 to 1945. ... For all its problems, the UN system—with the Security Council at its heart on issues of war and peace and civilian protection—is the only credible international institution we have, or are ever likely to have, with the necessary combination of *legitimacy and authority* [or power]. The task as always is not to replace or bypass what we have but to make it work better.[45]

On the contrary, I have argued that the UN is *not* sufficiently legitimate for today's world, and that its powers are hopelessly hobbled by fundamental flaws in its design. Certainly the kind of democratic league I have proposed would undermine the remnants of authority left in the UNSC; replacing a UNSC now fatally corrupted by Russia and China is the UDL's main point. However, I have argued that this can be done while keeping most other organs of the UN operating as usual, or working even more effectively with UDL support. If we delay, China and Russia will increasingly focus cyber-attacks on critics across the whole world.

Evans's worry about "competing ideological alliances" sounds like the alleged danger a new Cold War addressed above. Unfortunately the leaders of Russia and China never moved toward the West after 1989; despite our overtures, they simply changed tactics, becoming ambidextrous. With their left hand, they use the Security Council even more effectively to make human rights standards such as R2P meaningless; while with their right, they conduct ever more vicious repressions and propaganda campaigns to manipulate other nations. Attitudes like Evans's play right into their hands. Given this reality, we can hardly portray the Security Council as too precious to lose; on the contrary, dictators have turned it into a shield behind which they could put their campaign to spread soft despotism into overdrive.

In fact, creating a broad and robust league of democracies would change little in the strategic situation except to strengthen the hand of nations that believe in defending human rights. It could hardly undermine a *nonexistent* mutual respect between democratic governments and tyrannical regimes, kleptocratic military dictatorships, or fundamentalist theocracies. The small extant types of cooperation between such governments and democracies for some GPGs depends on treaty organizations and international civil society networks rather than on the UN, and could continue with a UDL in place. Evans cannot believe that Russia and China would no longer participate in international postal systems, or global satellite communications, or the International Space Station, unless they were allowed to protect genocidal regimes with UNSC vetoes and continue their cyber-propaganda wars?

Evans's third worry is a version of the conservative adage proffered since time immemorial that we are better off tinkering with the current system, even with its potentially fatal flaws, than to risk replacing it with an untried new system. But if this conservative adage always ruled our decisions, there would never be anything but the slowest incremental progress in human institutions, for which many of our biggest global problems leave insufficient time. In the Continental Congress during 1776, John Dickinson made a similar argument against the risks of independence, and he was proven wrong.

The American Federalists faced similar arguments that to "abandon" the Articles of Confederation would be to court total disaster. We know the Articles are imperfect, the antifederalists said, but it is better to work (through decades) for tiny changes to them than to try a radically new "experiment." Every current argument against a league of democracies had its mistaken analog among the antifederalists of the 1780s: the 13 states are too different to work together; our union will unite European powers against us; the new federal government will become a tyranny; we will lose the only federal council we are ever likely to have ("for all its imperfections") and end up with nothing! All these counsels of despair were refuted by experience. The conservative adage is useless when the status-quo institution clearly *cannot* be made to "work better" in its most fundamental respects—as was obviously the case in 1776 and 1787, and with the UN Security Council now. In such a predicament, we should remember not only Hamilton's innovative spirit, but also Martin Luther King's courage and wisdom when he asked: "If not now, when?"

However, some still maintain that the UN can be fundamentally reformed. Evans is realistic, noting that the P5 have shown "rock-like resistance" to any initiative to weaken their veto rights, or to extend vetoes to new permanent members. Similarly, the need for basic reforms "to the whole UN administrative system—everything from setting and administering budget priorities to sanctions monitoring" and hiring of personnel—has been repeatedly documented, yet foundered on resistance from particular states and "groups like the G77 representing the global South," who fear "that their voice or influence will be weakened."[46] This should remind us of the behavior of smaller states in the early US Confederation who feared that any change would weaken their *de facto* veto powers: they had little incentive to accept a new deal until larger states made it clear that they would otherwise abandon the whole system of mutual protection that gave these small states such lopsided advantages. Similarly, too many nations (or rather their elites) prefer the privileges they have within the current UN framework; they have no incentive to concede any of them *unless the core of that system is threatened.* This is the reason that revolutionary institutional change is now indispensible.

Evans, like other commentators, adds his own insightful suggestions for improving the capacities of the UNSC and several regional organizations to implement the R2P doctrine. He is right, for example, that missions headed by "special representatives" of the Secretary-General could be far more proactive in working to pre-empt conflicts. But imagine how much more effective their missions would be if power-brokers and special interests in the offending nation knew that, should the UN mission fail and mass violence break out, a powerful UDL will punish their inexcusable obstructionism and perhaps remove their regime.[47] Yet as we saw, even pleas for a small rapid-deployment force of 5000 soldiers under direct UNSC control have been constantly blocked by Westphalian pretensions.[48] It seems clear now that too many UN member nations will never trust the Security Council with even a tiny armed force of its own—which brings us to the issue of R2P.

Like Bellamy, Evans notes the wide international support for R2P that developed from 2005 to 2009; but he can only point to one occasion in which R2P was partially implemented: namely, the UNSC authorization for "all necessary measures" to stop Qaddafi's advance on Benghazi.[49] But as we have seen, the reliance on a small coalition only willing to fight from the air meant in this case that none of the later steps necessary to rehabilitate Libya were funded or undertaken (the UNSC resolution on Libya also banned any foreign ground troops, so this also is partly Russia and China's fault). Weiss notes that in 2012, "a record number of states took to the floor" in the General Assembly to support Secretary-General Ban Ki-moon's report about "R2P's coercive dimension," with "only Venezuela speaking against the policy."[50] Still, Evans and Weiss admit that this did nothing to alter the "impasse" over Syria, with its dramatic effects on Iraq, Turkey, Lebanon, Jordan, and Europe.

Thus it should now be clear that R2P—the single most important change in UN doctrine in since its founding, requiring more than a decade of tremendous effort—has been rendered *merely symbolic.* Russia and China decided almost immediately, during the Darfur crisis, to prevent its full implementation, and later seized on regime change in Libya as an excuse for this.[51] Weiss also admits that Ban Ki-moon's "timid report" in 2012 tried to deemphasize coercive enforcement in favor of other nations merely assisting a state in helping itself,[52] which is exactly how China intentionally misconstrued R2P during the Darfur debates.[53] Thus at least a million more victims have been murdered by genocidal regimes since the adoption of R2P, and Russia and China have removed its central innovation limiting state sovereignty. I regard this infinite offense as the final decisive proof that the Security Council cannot be fixed. Instead of continuing to play Russia and China's rhetorical games in the UN, it is time to cut bait and try a more confrontational approach.

Held and Weiss

Like Evans, David Held also argues that the UN "delivers significant international public goods" and remains essential to global networks that operate "below, above, and alongside the nation-state."[54] With Archibugi, Held follows Habermas in arguing for a "cosmopolitan democracy" that delinks citizenship rights from territory-based nations;[55] and he calls for "new, more extensive institutions" to deliberate and make decisions necessary to secure GPGs, with "effective, accountable international security forces for last resort use of coercive power in defense of cosmopolitan law."[56] Held rightly starts from the ideals of "deliberative democracy" and aims to solve CAPs via institutional innovation.[57] Yet I have argued that only a UDL can achieve his goals of combining sufficient power with the accountability required by justice. Instead, Held looks to reform the UNSC "to improve the legitimacy of armed intervention, with credible threshold tests," to represent "all regions on a fair and equal footing," and to include economic and social concerns within the UNSC's charge.[58]

Tragically, however, such deep UN reforms are not feasible. As Weiss argues, when the High-Level Panel on the UNSC prepared for the 2005 World Summit, its suggestions for Security Council restructuring proved useless: adding more permanent seats to the UNSC would simply alienate major nations that are not included, and do nothing to "improve the chances for reaching consensus regarding the use of force."[59] Indeed, giving more nations a veto would reduce the UNSC's small coordinative power even further. The only effective way to represent all regions sufficiently is to invite qualified nations to join a new institution supporting the cosmopolitan moral principles that Held sets out.

Similarly, the UN will never get the powers Held suggests to tax carbon emissions, sales of natural resources, cross-border capital movement, or nations' GNP to relieve the worst poverty and to secure environmental goods.[60] Wealthy nations will never give this kind of power to a global body without the strongest assurances that increased aid will be combined with rooting out corruption and security problems in the least developed nations. Democratic nations would also rightly say "no taxation without representation." Thus the main agents of an institution with such global taxing powers must be directly chosen in free and fair elections.[61] Obviously the UNSC will never meet this standard.

Held also puts some faith in the network approach, for example disaggregated decision-making through intergovernmental ties, business and expert groups establishing "transnational regulatory mechanisms," "NGOs and transnational advocacy networks;" "the opening up of IGOs to key stakeholders and participants; "multilayered governance" and authority "diffused" through "a network of democratic fora from the local to global."[62] This is the idea that through hundreds of different entry points, concerns coming directly from the people (and NGOs helping them) will percolate up to policy-makers, or impact global policies and practices by changing habits and perceptions.

But as we saw in chapter three, this network approach is no substitute for direct electoral power. This indirect, disaggregated way of trying to satisfy the DP requirement also ensures that we will not meet the demands of CP. It may work to an extent when moral suasion, mass changes in consumer preferences, and assurance about common standards are enough. Yet these methods are *not* enough to stop terrorism, new arms races, or mass atrocities (chapter four); and the same could be added for many global environmental problems, threats to financial systems, and discoordination in immigration and refugee policies across nations. These problems require too many changes in national laws for NGOs to manage, even if they can leverage fair trade movements to alter some business practices.

Although Weiss also emphasizes the importance of such networks, he is refreshingly frank about their limits. He argues that the current enthusiasm for "global governance through nonstate actors" reflects not only their "sheer growth in numbers and importance" but also an unduly pessimistic *adaptation* to the assumption that actual global government is not feasible:

> By abandoning a utopian vision of world government, ... [maybe we] are throwing out the baby with the bathwater. At minimum, without such a vision, we risk accepting and strengthening the contours of the current unacceptable international system. By not imagining a fundamentally different system, we make the continuation of the current lackluster one all the more inevitable.[63]

This is exactly the trap into which Evans, Archibugi, and others have fallen. Weiss is right; like Hamilton he sees that we should dream bigger. We need new ideas beyond simply improving the "decentralized system of states and a pooling of corporate and civil society efforts"[64] to see us through the twenty-first century (with peak population).

The league of democracies described in chapter five fits this bill. It grapples directly with the sad fact that more responsive transnational networks will never be sufficient by themselves.[65] As I emphasized in the Introduction, the UDL proposal avoids the common false trichotomy which assumes that our only options are the current neo-Westphalian order, increasing networked global governance, or a totalizing world government encompassing all nations. Instead, the UDL would be global in the sense of including many nations in all regions, and yet could serve its main purposes even if quite a few nations remained outside it. The UDL would also enhance what transnational networks and IGOs can do to help secure essential GPGs.

Malloch-Brown and Singer

Reflecting on decades of experience, Mark Malloch-Brown acknowledges that the UN lacks the power to secure many vital GPGs: "no global policy-making arrangement exists to address them, no individual and no institution to take charge, no parliament or executive."[66] Like Annan, Weiss, and Held, he had hoped that the 2005 World Summit could produce a "real meeting of minds around how the world might cooperate better to govern itself." But there was too much paranoia about any UN Charter change in response to the High-Level Panel proposals.[67] He recommends adding India, Brazil, and South Africa to the UNSC, perhaps with Britain and France sharing their veto power with Germany and the rest of Europe. But the new UNSC members should be on "long-term renewable terms" rather than holding permanent seats. And perhaps (following Kemal Dervis's suggestion), vetoes should be replaced with a "weighted voting system ... similar to that of the World Bank. A country's vote share could be determined by its relative GDP, population, UN financial contributions, and peacekeeping and aid levels."[68]

These are interesting ideas, despite the fact that at least three of the P5 will never give up their veto power. Malloch-Brown is certainly right that long-term membership in the UNSC should require responsibilities to go along with membership privileges;[69] his proposal would also increase incentives to contribute to the UN's main budget and aid programs along with peacekeeping operations. But giving greater voting weight to the richest nations with higher GDPs that can contribute more would upset developing nations. Some nations are also especially at risk from certain global public harms such as aspects of climate change, but there is no obvious way to add such considerations to the weighting of UNSC votes. Most problematically, Malloch-Brown's proposed criteria do not reward nations for *improving the moral legitimacy of their governments*, or better promoting human rights. China might even be willing under such a weighted scheme to contribute a lot more money and/or peacekeepers to the UN: with its rising GDP and huge population, it might thereby secure a third of all voting power in Malloch-Brown's expanded UNSC. Yet the Scandinavian nations would not gain anything from their generally exemplary human rights record.

By contrast, the proposed league of democracies puts conditions the other way around: nations must reach a level of democratic legitimacy first, with population then influencing voting weight, and contributions proportional to means required as part of the deal. The UDL's upper house, the DC, would include Brazil, South Africa, and India, but also Japan, South Korea, and other democracies from the southern hemisphere. My proposed UDL Council gives no nation a veto and treats all according to the same criteria, so there is no need to pick particular nations via backroom bargaining. In comparison with this coherent and principled UDL system, even the best imaginable fixes to the UNSC's state-centric model could not do half as well. They are like adding *ad hoc* epicycles to Ptolemy's geocentric model of the solar system.

Peter Singer has also promoted UN reform for at least two decades. He was quick to appreciate the significance of the ICISS report and to support its main criteria for intervention, suggesting in 2002 that the UN could "develop an authoritative procedure for specifying when intervention is justifiable," e.g. thresholds.[70] He also considered the possibility of refusing UN membership to tyrannical governments,[71] which would make it more of a treaty-organization among democracies and benevolent autocracies. This interesting Rawlsian alternative would be more inclusive and weaker than the UDL, but still fundamentally different than the current UN. In the name of making the UN more representative, Singer also recommends expanding the Security Council and replacing the P5 vetoes with a requirement that decisions be made by a two-thirds or three-quarters supermajority.[72] This is more likely than Malloch-Brown's suggestion because it retains a supermajority threshold, but it does not include his incentives to contribute to the UN's budget and peace enforcement forces. The UDL proposal combines both these reforms with stronger powers to enforce DC decisions.

To address the problems of the General Assembly, Singer also recommends a directly elected world parliament, like the EU Parliament, with representatives proportional to populations. There have been versions of this idea at least since UK Foreign Secretary Ernest Bevin's 1945 proposal, as Singer notes. For example, some cosmopolitans have proposed a world parliament of peoples meeting *alongside* the UN General Assembly. But Singer's proposal is more radical; unlike Archibugi, Falk, Held and other world parliamentarians, he suggests that a directly elected world parliament *replace* the current General Assembly. He recognizes that this would only work for democratic nations, however, which brings his reform closer to the proposed UDL Parliament. But Singer also suggests that nations refusing to allow a UN-supervised free election would only get one voting representative. This system "would provide experience in democracy for the citizens of most countries, but would retain the inclusiveness that is an important feature of the United Nations."[73]

This is an intriguing idea, but how workable would it be for UN officials, for example, to conduct an election of world parliament representatives in China? For such an election to meet the minimal democratic norms outlined earlier in this chapter, it would have to allow candidates full freedom of speech to talk about the issues they would address at the world body—without fear of reprisals against them or their family members by the ruling party apparatus. Newspapers, websites, Twitter and Instagram accounts, etc. would have to be free to report on the candidates' positions and points made in their debates. Given the large number who might wish to run, multiple political parties would also need to be allowed to make a system of primary elections possible.

UN officials could not remake the systems of Chinese politics in these ways to allow an election of world parliament members in China without effectively providing Chinese people a way to democratize their *national* government. For candidates could run on platforms that demanded changes in the way their own nation worked (or would the UN officials somehow try to forbid any reference to domestic politics?). With a free press covering the election online, what would the UN election superintendents do when a candidate (perhaps with no living relatives) decided on a live TV broadcast to call for everyone who can to turn up in Tiananmen Square tomorrow at noon, and simultaneously in squares in Shanghai and other major cities—thus providing the key element of coordination that might well spell the end of one-party rule? There is a clear dilemma here: if the UN's procedures for election of its delegates did not include liberties that would make this possible, these world parliament elections would not really be democratic at all. But if they did, then entrenched dictatorships would never allow such a free election.

Singer's intention is still similar to part of mine—namely, a lower house directly elected by people in each member nation, who choose representatives with votes roughly proportional to their populations. Singer's world parliament differs mainly in giving non-democratic governments some presence. This is possible: directly elected and appointed representatives can be combined in one house. However, it could add over 120 ambassadors from nondemocratic governments—operatives whose main goal would probably be to prevent this parliament from working at all, if possible. How much difference this makes would depend on the total number of representatives (or votes) from democratic nations. But nondemocratic regimes would never consent to an acceptably small share like 5 percent of the whole.

This potentially fatal unintended consequence suggests that a global parliament should find a different way of giving some voice to nondemocratic nations. My proposal for associate members and a friendly nation status, which should be more formally defined than OECD offers of "partnership" with nonmembers, opens up some options. The league could allow representatives of friendly nations to attend and speak in the UDL Parliament, but without voting rights; this would give friendly nations a presence at UDL, like major NGOs that spoke at hearings of UDL committees. Meanwhile, associate members with some democratic credentials might be offered one voting representative with low voting weight in the UDL Parliament—a version of Singer's idea.

Thus parts of Singer's proposal are advisable roughly insofar as they tend in the direction of a league of democracies that works to include perspectives from decent nondemocratic regimes as much as possible. That is what my proposal does. But Singer envisions all this as a reform of the UN structure. In fact, the world's powerful autocratic regimes, such as the Chinese party elite or the family owning Saudi Arabia, would never allow the UN Charter to be altered in these ways. The crucial changes needed in the Security Council would be blocked by some of the P5 nations, which *all* have to approve any UN Charter amendment.[74] Singer's proposal for the General Assembly also could not garner a two-thirds vote of the current General Assembly in support of such an amendment, since more than one-third of the world's regimes are strongly opposed to democratic reforms that threaten their rulers' abilities to sell their nation's resources for private gain while letting their poorest die of easily treated diseases.

This is the ultimate problem for UN reformers: the UN's amendment clause is very similar to the requirements for amendment within the old US Articles of Confederation, which required the consent of *every* state. This is exactly why the 1787 convention had to take the revolutionary step of violating that clause and exceeding its original mandate. However, the proponent of UN reform could try to follow this precedent more literally: why not have democratic nations call for a new world conference to write a new UN Charter from scratch, proposing that it come into force when adopted by (say) 130 nations— roughly two-thirds of UN members? Unfortunately, nondemocratic nations could attend such a conference in order to make it fail. But more to the point: if democratic nations were willing to go that far, why would they not *form a democratic league instead*? For, having pooled their strength to try to force changes to the UN despite Putin's and Xi's implacable opposition, they would already be more than halfway toward forming a UDL, but nowhere close to gaining 130 nations' votes for a radically altered UN Charter.

Moreover, by going the UDL route, democratic nations would leave the current UN structure in place, thus achieving revolutionary change without the unprecedented furor and circus involved in trying to rewrite the UN Charter outside of its legal amendment process. Gathering a convention to write a UDL Charter would certainly occasion large global controversy and much screaming from dictators. But it would be less disturbing to moderate nondemocratic regimes and less legally disruptive than trying to force revolutionary change onto the UN itself. Better to leave a house of rotting timber to the intransigents who insist on staying in it, and move into a brand new dwelling with a much stronger frame. Those living in the new house of steel can always visit their deadbeat relatives in the moldering old house when needed.

Thus it turns out to be politically easier to create the needed kind of democratic league than to fix the central problems that prevent the UN from coordinating the most essential GPGs. In fact, there is probably only one way that China, Russia, and nations aligned with them could be brought to accept the sort of radical reforms needed to make the UN even half as effective and legitimate as the proposed UDL. That would be *to bring the project of creating a league of democracies near to success.* If the present Russian and Chinese governments saw that such a league was a real prospect, in panic, they might try to undermine it with last-ditch compromises on UNSC reform. But it would be crazy to accept such half-measures at that late stage, when a much better institutional solution was within reach. Bullies who run a corrupt club may grudgingly offer concessions when a third of their members are about to desert them and form a much better club capable of ending bullying. But at that point, why would the latter stay and continue to take abuse? Like Lot, they should depart without looking back.

Conclusion: The completed consolidation argument, and the future

The analyses in this chapter have shown that none of the main objections to a league of democracies are compelling. The UDL would not be a concert of great powers, but rather a union based on principle and right. In particular, arguments that it would be better to reform the United Nations generally fail to grasp why the UN amendment procedure prevents the kind of deep reforms that are needed to fix its structural problems. Most of the P5 nations will never give up their veto unless all the others do. Critics also overstate the difficulties of starting a democratic league or getting democracies to cooperate within such a framework.

Among the other objections considered, many can also be answered simply by refining the institutional proposal for the league along the lines I have suggested. Some worries, such as those foreseeing a league of dictators or grimly forecasting a new world war, massively exaggerate likely harms or costs from forming a UDL. Others are largely scare tactics based on straw-man versions of the league proposal. There is no evidence that the entire UN system, including all its peacekeeping operations, subordinate agencies, and related IGOs will collapse if many democratic nations no longer treat the Security Council as the sole or primary agent for countering aggressive invasions, preventing terrorism, promoting arms control, implementing R2P, and enforcing at least minimal human rights standards throughout the world. The proposal is only for the UDL to replace a few of the UN's main functions today, namely the ones that it performs least well.

Thus the final step in the global consolidation argument for the democratic league is complete: we have supported the last premise, namely that the UDL can be created without disproportionate costs or harms. The argument as a whole goes through: as long as it is conceived roughly along the institutional lines sketched in chapter five, a league of democracies is justified by a logic analogous to Hamilton's case in the *Federalist Papers*. The full argument can now be summarized as follows.

List 6.1 The global consolidation argument for a league of democracies

1 There are several vital public goods that cannot be reliably secured without coordination through law and enforceable policy at the global level. {empirical premise supported by the arguments in chapters 3 and 4}

2 The Consolidation principle, as part of instrumental reason. {premise: see chapter 2}

3 There is strong prima facie reason to establish government at the global level as a means to the public goods at issue (i.e., the government-apt GPGs). {from 1 and 2 by *modus ponens*}

4 The Democratic principle of legitimacy, with its practical conditions. {premise: see chapters 2 and 5}

5 There is strong prima facie reason to make the global government democratically answerable to all the residents of the nations that consolidate power in this new global institution—i.e., to make it a league of democracies. {from 3 and 4 by *modus ponens*}

6 When the institutional structure and effects of the proposed league of democracies are spelled out, no convincing objections emerge to show that it would have unjust effects or untoward costs (in comparison with other relevant alternatives). {premise: chapters 5 and 6}.

7 Conclusion: therefore, a league of democracies ought to be established. {from 5 and 6 by *modus ponens*}

This is the result of applying Hamilton's logic to our global challenges and the CAPs that prevent their resolution through our current institutions. Of course, we should also try to improve global governance networks, the UN, and the IGOs that help nations work together, but this will not be enough by itself.

Although I have argued against defeatist thinking, promoting the sort of democratic league described in this book would clearly be a monumental task. The proposal would have to be circulated among leaders in north Atlantic, Asian, South American, and African democracies; it would require wide support from essayists, talk show hosts, and VIPs with large social media followings. A conference to discuss the idea would be a serious endeavor only if convened by foreign secretaries (or equivalent) among many of the proposed founding nations. They would have to move quickly, because in our systems, critics and lobbyists with vested interests pile on to stop any major new initiative, and make leading politicians pay heavy prices for venturing to support any departure from the familiar. The Russian cyber-sabotage machine would also kick into high gear to oppose a serious UDL proposal. But it makes no sense to assume that developing democracies are locked into national interests that align with autocracies, or that they are married to the UNSC as a way to keep internal state sovereignty absolute.[75] For the point of the UDL proposal is to *change* their calculus: it offers a global order in which more of their deeper interests would be better protected in the long run.

Although we do not have forever, as I argued in the Introduction, an education process would be necessary to make sure people understand what is proposed and all that is at stake. Many people will like this proposal once they understand it: there is deep frustration with the status quo and hunger for a better option that gets to the roots of global problems and shares the burdens of viable solutions more fairly. But it takes mental effort to overcome the inherent human bias against fundamental change. It is always easier to raise objections, envision roadblocks, and imagine disastrous consequences than it is to frame any genuinely new institution that can secure progress toward justice in this world. That is why it has happened so rarely in human history.

The American federalists were similarly faced with shrill campaigns to prevent the US federal government from being created; but they overcame the shortsighted (and often self-serving) doomsayers by a combination of persistence and reason. To create a democratic league will take even greater leadership, requiring heroic politicians across the world to join forces in starting the process; but we have a moral duty to try before it is too late.

That duty is both to the future and to the past. Over 70 years ago, people in democratic lands responded to the Holocaust by promising that "never again" would we let mass atrocities happen. As Václav Havel and Desmond Tutu note, we have broken that promise again and again,[76] despite renewing it under the Genocide Convention, and backing R2P in 2005. Long after the world's democracies collectively had far more than enough power to stop mass atrocities with relatively little sacrifice of blood and treasure, we have let millions be slaughtered and driven into exile. If our way of life is ever to have the inner moral strength needed to survive, we must finally live up to this sacred promise and protect all peoples from such systemic crimes against humanity. For the sake of our children and their children to come, democratic peoples should unite to put an end to tyranny on Earth.

Notes

1. Daalder and Lindsay, "Democracies of the World, Unite," *The American Interest* 2 (1 January 2007): 1–17, 5.
2. Stephen Schlesinger, "Why a League of Democracies Will Not Work," *Ethics & International Affairs* 23, no. 1 (2009): 14.

3. Charles Kupchan, "Minor League, Major Problems: The Case Against a League of Democracies," *Foreign Affair* 87 (November–December, 2008): 96–109, 103.

4. See Schlesinger, "Why a League of Democracies Will Not Work," 18.

5. Daalder and Lindsay, "Democracies of the World, Unite," 6.

6. Raffaele Marchetti, "Fighting Transnational Exclusion: From Cosmopolitanism to Global Democracy," in the *Global Democracy* Symposium, ed. Daniele Archibugi, *New Political Science* 32 no. 1 (2010): 103–10, 105–6.

7. Schlesinger, "Why a League of Democracies Will Not Work," 14.

8. Ibid., 18.

9. John Davenport, "Just War Theory, Humanitarian Intervention, and the Need for a Democratic Federation," *Journal of Religious Ethics* 39, no. 3 (2011): 493–555.

10. Schlesinger, "Why a League of Democracies Will Not Work," 16.

11. These points will be clarified in my planned book on *A Universal Human Right to Democracy*, which includes two chapters on democratic rights that could not be published in the present book for reasons of space.

12. For more on this topic, see my critique of Amy Allen's postcolonial rejections of "progress" in the *Notre Dame Philosophical Reviews* (October 2016), https://ndpr.nd.edu/news/the-end-of-progress-decolonizing-the-normative-foundations-of-critical-theory/.

13. Kupchan, "Minor League, Major Problems," 107.

14. Thomas Carothers, "Is a League of Democracies a Good Idea?" *Foreign Policy Brief* (Carnegie Endowment for International Peace, May 2008), 3.

15. Gideon Rachman, "Why McCain's Big Idea Is a Bad Idea," *Financial Times*, 5 May 2008.

16. Kupchan, "Minor League, Major Problems," 107.

17. Ibid., 100. By a rising "league of dictators," Kagan was simply referring to the strategic alliances of Russia and China with illiberal leaders in Belarus, Uzbekistan, Zimbabwe, and Myanmar. He also noted that Russia and China are determined to prevent the UN from using effective sanctions against the worst human rights violators: see Kagan, "A League of Dictators?" *Washington Post*, 30 April 2006, www.washingtonpost.com/wp-dyn/content/article/2006/04/28/AR2006042801987.html.

18. Archibugi, "A League of Democracies or a Democratic United Nations?" *Harvard International Review*, 19 Nov. 2008: 1–5, 4–5, http://hir.harvard.edu/article/?a=1758.

19. Kupchan, "Minor League, Major Problems," 104.

20. See the history recounted in Julie Flint and Alex de Waal, *Darfur*, rev. ed (London: Zed Books, 2008), chs. 5–6., e.g. concerning regime efforts to arm and brainwash Arab clans (122-31). These clans had also been influenced by Qaddafi's Arab Supremacist movement to radicalize Bedouins since the 1970s, and by civil wars sparked by the regime's seizures of lands from non-Arab tribes: see Andrew Natsios and Zachary Scott, "Darfur, Sudan," in *The Responsibility to Protect*, ed. Jared Gensler and Irwin Cotler (New York: Oxford University Press, 2012): 235–59.

21. Natsios and Scott, "Darfur, Sudan," 241.

22. Flint and de Waal, *Darfur*, 145–46.

23. For example, "The United Nations and Darfur," www.hrw.org/legacy/
    wr2k5/darfur/3.htm. China also repeatedly opposed even economic
    sanctions against Khartoum.
24. Nat Hentoff, "Genocide: Sudan Found Guilty!" *Village Voice*, 6–12
    November 2002, 27.
25. Eric Reeves, "Darfur: Shame and Responsibility," *Dissent* 52, no. 4
    (Fall 2005): 5–10, esp. 5, col. 2.
26. Eric Reeves, *Partners in Genocide: A Comprehensive Guide to China's
    Role in Darfur* (2007), at http://sudanreeves.org/2007/12/19/partners-in-
    genocide-a-comprehensive-guide-to-chinas-role-in-darfur/.
27. Eric Reeves, *Compromising with Evil: An Archival History of Greater
    Sudan*, 2007–2012, Section I, 29, www.compromisingwithevil.org/
28. Ibid., Introduction, 6.
29. Thomas G. Weiss. *What's Wrong with the United Nations?* 3rd ed.
    (Malden, Mass: Polity Press, 2016), 146.
30. Reeves, personal correspondence, August 2015 (quoted by permission).
31. Experts like General Dalliare had called for 44,000 or more in a hostile
    environment with government proxies actively fighting the interveners.
32. Reeves, *Compromising with Evil*, section IA, "Darfur and 'Genocide by
    Attrition.'" Also see the details under "Annex IV: Darfur Humanitarian
    Updates, 2009–2012."
33. Ibid., Introduction, 3.
34. Stedman, "America and International Cooperation: What Role for a
    League of Democracies?," *Policy Analysis Brief* of the Stanley Founda-
    tion (November 2008), 1–10, 4–5.
35. See Reeves, "Darfur: Shame and Responsibility," 6–7.
36. James Lindsay, "The Case for a Concert of Democracies," *Ethics and Inter-
    national Affairs* 23, no. 1 (Spring 2009): Roundtable section, https://www.
    carnegiecouncil.org/publications/journal/23_1/roundtable/002 (my italics).
37. Stedman, "America and International Cooperation," 8–9.
38. Ash Jain, "Like-Minded and Capable Democracies," Council on
    Foreign Relations Working Paper (January 2013), www.cfr.org/
    international-organizations-and-alliances/like-minded-capable-
    democracies-new-framework-advancing-liberal-world-order/
    p294843-4.
39. Jain, "Like-Minded and Capable Democracies," 10.
40. Ibid., 16.
41. Ibid., citing Stewart Patrick, "Irresponsible Stakeholders? The Dif-
    ficulty of Integrating Rising Powers," *Foreign Affairs* 89 (November–
    December, 2010): 44–53.
42. Ibid., 11 and 16.
43. Ibid., 11.
44. Didier Jacobs, "From a League of Democracies to Cosmopolitan
    Democracy," in the *Global Democracy* Symposium, ed. Archibugi,
    New Political Science 32, no. 1 (2010): 120–21.
45. Gareth Evans, *The Responsibility to Protect* (Washington, DC: Brook-
    ings Institution Press, 2008), 180 (my italics).
46. Evans, *The Responsibility to Protect*, 179. Weiss largely concurs in
    What's Wrong with the United Nations, chs. 2–4.

47. Ibid., 201–2. Evans offers great suggestions on UN management (203–4). The development of reserve corps of professionals is an especially good idea (209–10).

48. Ibid., 215-18. Compare Thomas G. Weiss, *Global Governance* (Malden, Mass: Polity Press, 2013), 107–8.

49. Ibid., 115. The 2011 French intervention in the Ivory Coast is a later case that prevented thousands of deaths by rocket and burning: see Marco Chown Oved, "In Côte d'Ivoire, a Model of Successful Intervention," *The Atlantic*, 9 June 2011; www.theatlantic.com/international/archive/2011/06/in-c-te-divoire-a-model-of-successful-intervention/240164/

50. Weiss, *Global Governance*, 116.

51. Coming from Russia and China, the complaint that NATO exceeded its mandate in Libya was totally disingenuous. Even if NATO continued bombing too long, R2P cannot require intervention so narrowly tailored that it always manages to leave the regime committing atrocities in place. Regime change can be a side effect of necessary protection measures without being a mission aim.

52. Weiss, *Global Governance*, 116. Given its other failures, R2P had been the 2005 World's Summit's main accomplishment.

53. As Jennifer Welsh notes, China and Russia always intended to hold that R2P only allows international "assistance in ways that do not undermine [state] sovereignty." Efforts in UN reports to deemphasize the forcible intervention component of R2P played into their hands. See Welsh, *Implementing the Responsibility to Protect* (Oxford, UK: Oxford Institute for Ethics, Law, and Armed Conflict, 2009), 5, www.elac.ox.ac.uk/downloads/R2P_policybrief_180209.pdf

54. David Held, *Cosmopolitanism* (Malden, Mass: Polity Press, 2010), 99–101, 113.

55. Ibid., 178–79.

56. Ibid., 106–7.

57. Ibid., 218–19; compare 233.

58. Ibid., 170.

59. Weiss, *What's Wrong with the United Nations*, 57–60.

60. Held, *Cosmopolitanism*, 109; compare 169.

61. As Held's own principles imply (ibid., 72).

62. Ibid., 32–35, 107, 240.

63. Weiss, *What's Wrong with the United Nations?*, 228, 232.

64. Ibid., 234.

65. Ibid., 236. Compare Weiss' remarks in *Governing the World?*, 91 and 101.

66. Mark Malloch-Brown, *The Unfinished Global Revolution* (New York: Penguin Books, 2012), 188.

67. Ibid., 181–83.

68. Ibid., 192–93.

69. Ibid., 194–95.

70. Singer, *One World*, 2nd ed. (New Haven, Conn: Yale University Press, 2004), 126–27. In *One World Now* (New Haven, Conn: Yale University Press, 2016), Singer cites the ICC definitions of genocide and crimes against humanity, along with Walzer and Annan, as a basis for his own standard (140–44).

71. Ibid., 134–35; compare Singer, *One World Now*, 171.

72. Ibid., 145; compare Singer, *One World Now*, 169.
73. Ibid., 147–48; compare Singer, *One World Now*, 170–72.
74. I have been asked why the United States, Britain, and France would agree to give up their vetoes in a league of democracies if they would not do so for UNSC reform. But it is surely obvious that within the UNSC, they constantly need to counter threats from non-democratic regimes, which also control the General Assembly.
75. Morton Halperin and Ted Piccone make this naive assumption in "A League of Democracies: Doomed to Fail?" Brookings (June 2008): 47–48, www.brookings.edu/opinions/a-league-of-democracies-doomed-to-fail/. In this editorial, they raise most of the objections to which I have replied in this chapter.
76. Václav Havel and Desmond M. Tutu, "Introduction," *The Responsibility to Protect*, ed. Gensler and Cotler, xxv–xxvi.

Select bibliography

Buchanan, Allan. *Justice, Legitimacy, and Self-Determination: Moral Foundations for International Law* (Oxford, UK: Oxford University Press, 2004). While there are several excellent philosophical works on global justice in recent years, few address conceptual fundamentals so deeply and apply them so well to issues like secession and the limits of national sovereignty. This book is comparable in depth and range to Richard Falk's work but philosophically more rigorous.

Caney, Simon. *Justice Beyond Borders: A Global Political Theory* (Oxford, UK: Oxford University Press, 2006). This work offers a rigorous yet accessible philosophical framework for global justice issues that incisively defends universal human rights and their implications for humanitarian intervention. Like some of Cécile Fabre's work, it offers a potent defense of the moral cosmopolitanism on which my own argument relies.

Carothers, Thomas. "Is a League of Democracies a Good Idea?" *Foreign Policy Brief* (Washington, DC: Carnegie Endowment for International Peace, 2008), http://carnegieendowment.org/files/pb59_carothers_league_final.pdf. An excellent example of principled skepticism by a leading scholar of contemporary international affairs.

Daalder, Ivo, and James Lindsay. "Democracies of the World, Unite," *The American Interest* 2 (1 January 1 2007): 1–17. This is probably the best essay-length argument for a democratic league written for contemporary policy experts and politicians. Daalder later served Barack Obama as the US Ambassador to NATO.

Davenport, John. "Just War Theory Requires a New Federation of Democratic Nations," *Fordham International Law Journal* 28, no. 3 (2005): 763–85. This essay offers a template for the argument in this book, but starting instead from sources in just war theory that support the responsibility to protect.

Ellis, Joseph J. *The Quartet: Orchestrating the Second American Revolution, 1783–1789* (New York: Vintage/Penguin Random House, 2015). While there are several excellent works on the *Federalist Papers*, this gripping historical account of the road to the Constitutional Convention clarifies the knotty problems that motivated Hamilton and his fellow federalists.

Habermas, Jürgen. *Between Facts and Norms: Contributions to a Discourse Theory of Law and Democracy*, tr. William Rehg (Cambridge, Mass: MIT Press, 1998). While most philosophers writing on the topic agree with John Rawls that democracy is not a fundamental human right, Habermas offers a normative framework that effectively links democracy to the very possibility of human rights. This book is the foundation of a whole genre of work combining cosmopolitan themes with democratic theory.

Hale, Thomas, David Held, and Kevin Young. *Gridlock: Why Global Cooperation Is Failing When We Need It Most* (Malden, Mass: Polity Press, 2013). A comprehensive and clear overview of three areas of global problems—environment, security, financial instability and inequalities—with insightful analysis of the inadequacies in current global institutions.

Holzinger, Katharina. *Transnational Common Goods: Strategic Constellations, Collective Action Problems, and Multi-Level Provision* (New York: Palgrave Macmillan, 2008). This work, like Sandler's, offers especially clear explanations of collective action problems between nations. It also includes an analysis of the basic dimensions of CAPs that yields something analogous to a periodic table for social interactions—the best single graphic in this genre.

Ikenberry, G. John, and Anne-Marie Slaughter. *Forging a World of Liberty Under Law* (Princeton, NJ: Princeton University Press, 2006), https://www.peacepalacelibrary.nl/ebooks/files/373430078.pdf. This is the final report of a three-year "bipartisan initiative to develop a sustainable and effective national security strategy for the United States of America," hosted by the Wilson School at Princeton University. While there have been several expert panel reports on such topics, this one is distinctive for its recommendations concerning a concert of democracies to backstop the UNSC.

Jacobs, Didier. *Global Democracy: The Struggle for Political and Civil Rights in the 21st Century* (Nashville, Tenn: Vanderbilt University Press, 2007). This book, by a scholar of international affairs with practical experience in the international aid NGO sphere, offers a distinctive argument for developing a league of democracies out of NATO.

Kasparov, Garry. *Winter Is Coming: Why Vladimir Putin and the Enemies of the Free World Must Be Stopped* (Philadelphia: Public Affairs/Perseus Group, 2015). A well-argued account of what went wrong in Russia after 1990 from the perspective of an insider who witnessed it. While Kasparov is best known for his genius in chess, he brings hard-edged, refreshing moral clarity to issues about which many westerners have grown complacent. His diagnoses, like those of Douglas Schoen, have been amply vindicated since 2015.

Kaul, Inge, Pedro Conceição, Katell le Goulven, and Ronald Mendoza, eds. *Providing Global Public Goods: Managing Globalization* (New York: Oxford University Press, 2003). This is the second of two invaluable UNDP collections that helped define the study of global public goods among economists and political scientists focusing on international relations.

Malloch-Brown, Mark. *The Unfinished Global Revolution: The Road to International Cooperation* (New York: Penguin Books, 2012). This work explains the challenges that the United Nations faces from the point of view of a statesman who worked directly with Secretary-Generals and saw repeated attempts at basic UN structural reforms fail.

Power, Samantha. *"A Problem from Hell:" America and the Age of Genocide* (New York: Basic Books, 2002). Inspired by the making of the Genocide Convention, this journalistic *tour de force* is one of the most comprehensive accounts of the reasons that western governments frequently refused to intervene during genocides, from the Armenian genocide and Saddam Hussein's atrocities to the horrors of Bosnia, Rwanda, and Kosovo. It can be supplemented with Eric Reeves's hard-hitting work on Darfur and Christiane Amanpour's *Scream Bloody Murder* series on CNN.

Sandler, Todd. *Global Collective Action* (Cambridge, UK: Cambridge University Press, 2004). This work remains one of the most accessible introductions to collective action problems in international relations, along with the foundational game theory involved. While Holzinger stresses distributive equity issues, Sandler is especially helpful on aggregation supply issues and his many tables are invaluable.

Schlesinger, Stephen. "Why a League of Democracies Will Not Work," *Ethics & International Affairs* 23 no. 1 (2009), https://www.carnegiecouncil.org/publications/journal/23_1/roundtable/003. Perhaps the best-argued criticism of Senator McCain's proposal, which was widely discussed in 2008; also see my response to Schlesinger in the same online roundtable.

Singer, Peter. *One World Now* (New Haven, Conn: Yale University Press, 2016). This is the newest version of a widely taught book that clearly addresses global justice issues, including economic inequalities and the need to prevent mass atrocities; it is quite frank in addressing needs for fundamental institutional changes.

Weiss, Thomas G. *Global Governance: Why? What? Whither?* (Malden, Mass: Polity Press, 2013). While there are several excellent textbooks on global governance issues today, this work remains one of the clearest regarding the global problems that are insufficiently addressed by today's global institutions; it ranges from normative fundamentals to technical problems.

Index

accountability, diffused, 125
adverse selection problems, 98.
    See also principal-agent problems
Afghanistan, 19; NATO mission
    in, 193; U.S. in, 161; war in, 146
Africa: Chinese influence in, 23;
    democracy in, 16; following
    decolonization, 13; Russian
    influence in, 23
Africa, sub-Saharan, 118. *See also*
    the Sahel
African slaves, forcible importing
    of, 84
African Union (AU),144: in design
    of UDL, 194; and humanitarian
    catastrophe in Darfur, 209;
    in Somalia, 161
African Union - United Nations
    Mission in Darfur (UNAMID):
    failure of, 210
AIDs, spread of, 119
Albright, Sec. Madeleine, 33
Al Qaeda, 159
al-Sisi, Abdel Fattah, 17
Amazon.com Inc., market share of, 97
America, European partners of, 37,
    37. See also United States
Amnesty International, 81
Annan, Sec. Gen. Kofi, 60, 80,
    159, 220
anti-associationism, 49. *See also*
    Cosmopolitanism
anti-egalitarian tendencies, of
    network systems, 127
Apartheid, in South Africa, 21

appeasement, illusory safety of, 205
Arab-Israeli war, 145
Arab League nations, 208
Arab Spring, 16, 37
Arab Supremacist movement,
    Qaddafi's, 228n20
arbitrariness objection, to UDL, 202
Archibugi, Daniele, 181, 207, 208,
    210, 211, 214, 218, 220, 222
Argentina, 11, 23; influence in UDL
    of, 203; policy pattern of, 212
Aristotle, 46
armed forces: proposed for UN, 143;
    standing, 179; of UDL, 10, 174–7
armed intervention, legitimacy
    of, 218. *See also* humanitarian
    interventions
arms control, treaties for, 144,
    148–52, 156, 157
arms exports, 151, 152
arms race, 63, 149; prevention of,
    163; in space and robotics, 155, 156
Arms Trade Treaty (2013), 151
"Articles of Association," of First
    Continental Congress, 67
Articles of Confederation, 135; and
    American federalists, 216; under
    confederal law, 71; of Continental
    Congress, 68
Asian financial crisis, of 1997-1998,
    107
Assad, Bashar Hafez al-: chemical
    attacks of, 149; and intervention
    of western nations, 2; opposition
    to forceful action against, 12;

criminal justice, and UDL
  membership criteria, 183 list
Cruz, Sen. Ted, 1
Cuba, democratized, 189
Cuban Missile Crisis, 143
culture: disintegration of, 8;
  distortions of, 162
cyberattacks, 18, 25, 215; deterring,
  152–5
cyberbots, 155
cybercrime, systemic, 154
cyber-mercenaries, Russian, 155
cyber-propaganda, 1, 25, 85, 104,
  114, 155, 160, 162, 215
cyber-sabotage, 154
cyber-shields, 155
cyber-trolls, 25; and democracy, 21
cyberwar, 155; preparation for, 153
cyber-weapons, 154

Daalder, Ivo, 9, 23, 33, 36, 37, 39,
  142, 182, 183, 188, 189, 199
Dagestan, 14, 15
Dallmayr, Fred, 138
Darfur, 210; genocidal violence
  in, 207–11; humanitarian
  catastrophe in, 207–9; Janjaweed
  militias in, 208; mass murder in,
  3; war in, 175
data, weaponization of, 18
decision-making: multilateral, 119;
  "publicness" in, 126
Declaration of Independence,
  passing, 67
defense companies, 151
deficit, annual US, 147
de Klerk, F.W., 21
democracies: from Asia and
  southern hemisphere, 203;
  colonial legacies of, 212; in crisis,
  17, 18; emerging African, 25, 26;
  enumerated powers of, 179;
  illiberal, 202; lack of cohesion
  among, 211–13; non-western, 11,
  36; people living in, 188; proposals
  for uniting, 32; protecting and
  promoting, 18; rights-respecting,
  16; rise of, 13; and soft despotism,
  17–25; transnational harms to, 12;
  well-established, 18, 19

democracies, developing, 22; global
  order for, 227; joining UDL, 38
democracies, league of: enumerated
  powers of, 179; global
  consolidation argument for, 4;
  justification of, 225, 226 list; need
  for, 5. *See also* United Democratic
  League
democracy: definitions of, 201;
  deliberative, 218
"Democracy Fund," for UDL, 178
Democracy Index, 17
Democratic Council (DC), of UDL,
  9, 10
"Democratic 10" (D10), 169, 213
democratic governments, statistics
  for, 17
democratic nations: and founding
  of UDL, 12; ideas for associations
  of, 32; passivity of, 21; threats to,
  5, 19–25, 31
democratic principle (DP), 73,
  76, 86, 126, 157, 170–2, 211;
  and consolidation argument,
  77, 78; and networks, 219; and
  rights-based sovereignty, 139
Democratic Republic of Congo
  (DRC), 98; and public harm,
  104; on UN Human Rights
  Council, 141
democratic rights, linked to human
  rights, 181, 182
democratic systems, cyberattacks
  on, 155
Dervis, Kemal, 220
despotism: new kind of, 5; soft,
  17, 20, 22, 25, 31, 115, 181, 205,
  206, 215
deterrence, 139, 143–5, 149, 160;
  and cyberattacks, 152–4; and
  terrorism, 162
developing nations, 103, 105, 108,
  110 list; average income in, 42;
  exclusion of, 200; high costs of
  corruption in, 105, 118; and IMF,
  41, 118; in UDL, 22, 23, 32, 35
"development before democracy"
  approach, 115
Diamond, Larry, 15, 18
Diana Spencer, Princess, 150

European Union (EU)
Commission, 86
European Union (EU) Council,
"qualified majority" of, 86
European Union (EU) Court of
Justice, 194
Evans, Gareth, 134, 141, 214–18, 220.
See also Responsibility to Protect
evidence, universally acceptable
bases of, 52
expectations, 54; and basic structure
of society, 54, 55; customary/
informal, 64, 80, 99; and human
rights, 54
exploitation, preventing, 96. *See also*
free riding
externalities: for all public goods,
103, 104; major causes of, 97; and
market failures, 95; negative, 96,
107; "network," 127; size-based, 97
extinctions, mass, 13

Facebook, propaganda pages on, 155
facial recognition systems, 19
fairness, management of global
economy for, 112 list, 113 list. *See
also* distributive equity problems
fair trade movements, 219
fake news campaigns, 115
Falk, Richard, 58n64, 57n23, 222, 234
famine, 31, 32
fanatics, ideological, 6. *See also*
terrorism
federal government: compared
with confederation, 72; issues
controlled by, 86; principles of, 73;
sovereign authority of, 71, 72
federalism: and consolidation
argument, 76–87; world, 57n23
Federalist Papers, 4; central
argument of, 87; and
Confederation Congress, 70; and
consolidation argument, 76, 77,
92; pamphlets, 70
federalists: American, 61, 62, 78, 170,
227; classical, 87; conception of
sovereignty of, 73; Cosmopolitan,
61, 62; and individual liberties, 75
federalist tradition, 55
federal unification, 83

Federal Union of Democratic
Nations (FUDN), 38, 39, 171
Ferguson, Niall, 126
Fichte, J. G., 137
financial crisis of 2008-2009, 37
financial markets, corruption in,
159. *See also* money laundering
Financial Services Agreement, of
WTO, 41
Fine, Robert, 50, 55, 56
firearms, profits from, 151. *See also*
arms control
fisheries, loss of, 26
food: reserve, 121; rights to, 116;
supply, 111 list
food aid, short-term emergency, 121
Food and Agriculture Organization
(FAO), US, 191
force, UDL approval of, 7. *See also*
humanitarian interventions; military
foreign invasion, security from, 109
list; UDL and, 7, 185, 205; UN
and, 136–45, 163
foreign policy: and EU, 86, 194; and
UDL membership criteria, 183
list; and US confederation, 68, 70
fossil fuels, heavy dependence on,
105. *See also* corruption
founding members, of proposed
UDL, 186–8, 187 table
"Fourteen Points" speech,
Wilson's, 46
Fox News, 41
Freedom House, 17
free markets: central economic
argument for, 63; globalized,
40; limitations on, 100, 101;
nonexcludability in, 94; process,
94; WMDs in global, 148
free press, 184 list, 188; and election
in China, 222, 223
free rider problems, 2, 3, 103, 126;
and coalitions of willing nations,
175; and market failure, 96;
reprisals for, 208; and UDL's
nation-building capacity, 191;
on U.S., 204. *See also* collective
action problems
free trade, 12, 23, 32, 41, 60, 67,
83–6, 103, 112 list, 185–9; and